MODELLING BETWEEN DIGITAL AND HUMANITIES

Modelling Between Digital and Humanities

and Humanities

Thinking in Practice

Arianna Ciula, Øyvind Eide, Cristina Marras, and Patrick Sahle

OpenBook Publishers

https://www.openbookpublishers.com

©2023 Arianna Ciula, Øyvind Eide, Cristina Marras, and Patrick Sahle

Any digital material and resources associated with this volume will be available at https://doi.org/10.11647/OBP.0369#resources

ISBN Paperback: 978-1-80511-098-9
ISBN Hardback: 978-1-80064-811-1
ISBN Digital (PDF): 978-1-80064-846-3
ISBN Digital ebook (EPUB): 978-1-80064-895-1
ISBN XML: 978-1-80064-949-1
ISBN HTML: 978-1-80064-970-5

DOI: 10.11647/OBP.0369

Cover photo by Jason Leung, 'White, pink, green and yellow pained wall, https://unsplash.com/photos/xnFOY9SfcgI.
Cover design by Jeevanjot Kaur Nagpal

Table of Contents

0. Introduction

0.1 Aims and Context

This book describes the results of the authors' combined efforts over the last years to clarify and better understand the use and role of models in humanities research supported by computational methods – part of the field currently known as "digital humanities". Digital Humanities (DH) is an area of research engaged in exploring how humanities scholarship is transformed and extended by the digital and vice versa. This mutual transformation and extension concern tools (technology) as well as epistemologies (how we come to know). One of the core practices of DH research is indeed modelling (McCarty 2005, pp. 20-72; Buzzetti 2002; Flanders and Jannidis 2015, 2018), which implies the translation of objects of study and concepts into models to be manipulated (processed) computationally. The context of the research presented here was the project "Modelling Between Digital and Humanities: Thinking in Practice", which was funded by the Volkswagen Foundation from 2016 to 2018,[1] with the authors of this book as principal investigators.

The project idea grew out of a combination of design, computer-assisted research, and theoretical studies. Integration and connections of these activities and associated domains has been a long-term interest and aspiration of the authors, as seen for example in the effort to compare schemas for encoded texts produced in scholarly editing with abstract representations of database structures created for cultural

---

[1] The project was funded as Application A115838 to the funding programme "'Original - isn't it?' New Options for the Humanities and Cultural Studies", Funding Line 2 "Constellations" (2016–2017).

      https://doi.org/10.11647/OBP.0369.06

heritage documentation systems in ontology development (Ciula and Eide 2014).[2]

Identifying that overlap was the first step in recognising that an exchange exists across those modelling efforts and the resulting models which required further investigation. In line with critical approaches in the DH tradition, our aim is to build on the productive tension between digital methods and humanities research opened by modelling activities. Our research looks beyond the distinction between digital and humanities towards integrated methods and findings. This book, and the project it emerged from, are about modelling in the integrated space of digital and the humanities.

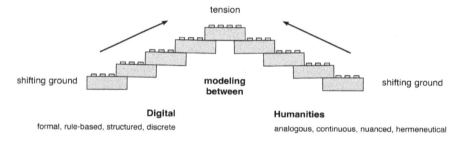

Fig. 0.1 Metaphorical illustration of one of the aspects of modelling between digital and humanities: the tension across modes and methods of research presented as a LEGO bridge.[3]

2	In Ciula and Eide (2014) we explored the conceptual and historical connections as well as the divergences between documents encoded based on the Text Encoding Initiative (TEI) standard and factual/hypothetical information in CIDOC-CRM based databases. Both types of data are relevant for humanities research and are digital – they belong to the digital as well as to the humanities, but emerged from different contexts, have different technical characteristics and fulfil different purposes.

3	An overview of the project and its outcomes, including a bibliography, is still accessible on a static site at http://modellingdh.eu/. A description of the implementation, including rationale and some main accomplishments, can be found in Ciula et al. (2018, pp. 11–16). A key milestone of the project was the interdisciplinary workshop "Thinking in practice", held at Wahn Manor House in Cologne on January 19–20, 2017. The proceedings were published in Historical Social Research Supplement, 31 (Ciula et al. 2018) and offer the basis for further reflections thematised also in this book (see for example Chapter 1, Section 1.3). The project proposal is available from this web page: http://modellingdh.eu/index.php/resources-2/material/. Research associates in the project were: Christopher Pak (King's Digital Lab, King's College London, UK, October 2017–April 2018), Zoe Schubert (University of Passau and University of Cologne, DE, November 2016–December 2017), and Michela Tardella (CNR-ILIESI, IT, July 2016–July 2017).

The project was based on the assumption that DH modelling is a creative process of reasoning, in which meaning is made and negotiated through the creation and manipulation of external representations. The ambition of model-based research in DH is making scholarly arguments practical via the creation and manipulation of digital models. Making external representations to reason has been part of the scholarly Western tradition at least since the Enlightenment; DH extends this practice by actively creating digital artefacts in different media. Through the lenses of critical humanities traditions and interdisciplinary takes on making and using models, the project had the ambition to reflect on the novelty of DH research: making explicit and integrating existing diverse models of cultural phenomena (e.g. texts; events). DH research was therefore a playfield for the authors and project team to: (i) explore possibilities for a new interdisciplinary language of modelling spanning the humanities, cultural studies, and sciences; (ii) analyse modelling in scholarship as a process of signification; (iii) develop connections between modelling as research and learning strategies.

An additional premise to further clarify the aims and context of this book is that what we would call "models" can be experienced in a number of quite different settings (Sahle 2018). As the title itself indicates, this book favours a specific view on modelling, emerging from the authors' work on modelling in a scholarly context. The explorative project has been an opportunity to develop this view further as a research group, negotiating and integrating different perspectives and experiences. This book is also about "thinking in practice" as it investigates modelling intended in a practical sense: creating, using, manipulating, deforming, and playing with models. This practical modelling is also a form of thinking: the practice of thinking-while-doing, or even thinking-in-doing. The theory of modelling foregrounded in this book is based on practical modelling work, yet the practical modelling work is in turn influenced by theoretical considerations in a constant movement between the practical and the theoretical, i.e., of thinking and doing jointly.

Research assistants in the project were: Nils Geißler (University of Cologne, DE, April 2016–July 2018), Elli Reuhl (University of Cologne, DE, November 2016–July 2018), and Julia Sorouri (University of Cologne, DE, January 2017–July 2018).

"Modelling between Digital and Humanities" presupposes a certain tension. When the digital is discussed in the context of the humanities, formalisation and operationalisation, and sometimes "algorithmic thinking", are concepts used to understand and explain what takes place. The ability to abstract is considered a common aspect across these concepts, which pushes modelling into a primary position in the development of scientific and scholarly thinking and practice. Even within this specific perspective on modelling, formalisation can be used for two different yet connected purposes. First, formalisation is needed in order to make computers operate on the sources or objects of study for the humanities. This is known as data and process modelling, necessary for building computer systems and for the population of such systems with data. And second, when this formalisation takes place, new objects (models) are created and the objects or processes being formalised themselves change.

The change is complex but it follows certain patterns in relation to context, reduction of variation, and structural simplifications. In these processes of modelling for operationalisation, the change of the sources (loss of variation, gain of processability) thus enables formal processing and at the same time highlights what cannot (within the limitations of specific processing methods) be formalised and thus is left behind. This affordance of digital to humanities thinking, with its risks and limitations, is the topic of this book.

0.2 Building on the State of the Art

In the twentieth century, modelling as an explicit term grew in significance in the sciences, not the least in empirical work. Moreover, the introduction of computing machinery enabled simulation to grow in importance as an alternative path to exploring relationships and patterns in observational settings, complementing experiments and theoretical speculation. At the same time, modelling as an explicit methodology became an inherent part of computer science as the field gained momentum. Much of the early work in the then so called "humanities computing" used modelling in similarly development-oriented contexts. After 2000, a growing interest in modelling, beyond application in the techno-sciences, became visible, most noteworthy in McCarty's seminar chapter on modelling in his 2005 book *Humanities Computing*. Here the concept of modelling, found in multiple areas of scholarship, supplemented the practice-based use of the concept imported from computer science. McCarty's argument included a link back to the period in which modelling was a central topic of discussion in social and cultural anthropology, roughly from the 1950s to the 1970s, recalling for example Geertz's[4] distinction between *model of* and *model for*.

The expansion of the concept of modelling in anthropology was also connected to the development of models in economics.[5] This link to economic modelling, rational actors, and game theory is also central to Stachowiak's seminal *Allgemeine Modelltheorie* from 1973.

The critical view on modelling developing in DH in the early 2000s reached out beyond the traditions from computer science into the humanities at large, as well as to the sciences. With the "new spring" of research into the history of the humanities[6] an important foundation to connect modelling in DH to the history of the humanities was laid. The first chapters of this book point further towards the terminological exploration of the concept of modelling in the longer history of human thinking.

---

4   This specific example is taken from McCarty (2005, p. 27) and refers to Geertz (1973, pp. 93–94).

5   Frederic Barth, who was central to the development of modelling in anthropology in the 1950s and '60s, was influential in several disciplines including economics (Barth 2007) and wrote two books based on research and lecture series at the London School of Economics (Barth 1953, 1966).

6   See publications and activities of the Society for the History of the Humanities: https://www.historyofhumanities.org/.

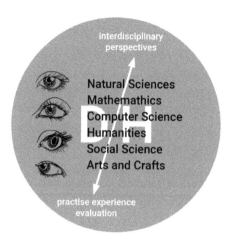

Fig. 0.2 The Digital Humanities not only benefit from interdisciplinary perspectives to conceptualise modelling but also employ them to create models that work.

The project and this book also present a further perspective on modelling in DH grounded in the concept of iconicity as it is known in Peircean semiotics, building on more general proposals by Knuuttilla (2010) and Kralemann and Lattman (2013), and connected to the specific view on models as media products. Examples in the book emphasise how modelling and visual thinking can be used as explicit tools to capture the complexity of typical targets of modelling for the humanities, for example: what a text really is. Chapter 5, in particular, engages with this question by re-presenting (quoting) and sometimes representing (by remediating) diagrams or other visuals associated with the definition and modelling of texts offering an anthology that includes a heterogenous range of glosses about what (a) text is, e.g.:

- Pre-theoretic category denoting a verbal expression; an act of communication; a sequence of language signs, a type or mode of media;

- (Re-)presentational layers in the scale of textual representation mostly given as media products, but sometimes codified as data that may be considered ontologically different from the documents the data is derived from and from those media products that are generated from the data;

- Operator object that connects a sender to receivers on many levels;
- Dynamic cultural object/s (material documents as well as conceptual objects) contingent on the contexts of their production and reading or fruition, expressed in a wide range of manifestations from linear to discontinuous narrative, from manuscripts to printed editions, from analogue codes to digital re-coding, encompassing hybrid modalities;
- Texts are constructed through models of text and perceived through models of understanding;
- Texts represent knowledge and can be the basis for knowledge processing (e.g. in DH); in stylistic terms, texts can be described by their similarity to each other; they are meant to convey information which can be extracted and represented as a set of assertions (like in RDF triples) or values (like in key-value pairs in an entity relationship model).

0.3 Terminology

The research behind the book dedicated particular attention to the terminology around modelling, starting from a discussion of possible definitions of the term 'model' and the verb 'to model', and continued with the unpacking of the use of some key terms attempting a sort of re-semantisation of the concept, building on other work in the project (Geißler and Tardella 2018).

Indeed, models and modelling could be referred to as what in mathematics are called "undefined terms", i.e. things that "can't be explained using more fundamental concepts, but have explicable uses and meanings" (Elkins and Fiorentini 2021, p. 5). To add to this challenge, as will be discussed in Chapter 1, any discussion on modelling – given the breadth of its possible applications and its porosity in relation to many fields of scholarship – has to tackle the problem of interdisciplinarity and the opportunities and weaknesses of polysemy which has developed over the history of use of the terms.

What follows below (Subsection 0.3.1) is a list of key terms extracted from the book chapters. The entries, in alphabetical order, offer the readers some reference to the intended scope of the terms while still including their polysemy.

The selection of terms was guided by the claim made in Chapter 1 that a language can be developed around modelling in DH via mapping of relevant uses in the humanities and cognate disciplines. This process also aims at establishing the language anew, taking inspiration from the history of the concept and its intrinsic polysemy. Needless to say, many terms and concepts that would be relevant to enrich this landscape are not dealt with in this book. Examples include the study and approaches around mental modelling, and prototyping and meta-modelling. When relevant, references to the literature on modelling in areas such as the philosophy and history of science were used to encourage comparisons and reflections.

This list of keywords acts as a conceptual map, a sort of terminological guide to the book. The proposed definitions are borrowed from other fields but related to DH when appropriate. Ontological and epistemological aspects of the concepts in the list of terms are mixed. This interrelation is central to the discussion of what modelling means and is thus a basis for the book as a whole. The aim is to illustrate how the building blocks of the ontology of models and modelling are mainly analytical devices with an epistemological and pragmatic function. It will be up to the readers to find their ways across these terms while juggling the complexity of the conceptual field under examination.

0.3.1 Key Terms

Affordance/s: 1. Fundamental properties of a thing that determine how it could be used. 2. Aspects of the models (in particular its modalities and modes) that can support or restrict how models are actionable.

Digital Humanities (**DH**): 1. Field of research engaged in exploring how humanities scholarship is transformed and extended by the digital and *vice versa*. 2. Applied computer science in humanities research; development and practical application of computational tools for supporting research and teaching in the humanities.

Iconicity: Resemblance, similarity or analogy between the form of a sign (*representamen*, source) and its object (target).

Icon/s: Signs whereby the dominant relation with the objects they represent is one of similarity; the relation of similarity is enacted (1) via simple qualities of their own in case of images; (2) via analogous relations between parts and whole and among parts in the case of diagrams; (3) via parallelism of qualities with something else in the case of metaphors.

Language, Metaphoric: Recurring conceptual scheme in structuring knowledge.

Media product: Mediated expressions working as cognitive transport device used in communication between producing and perceiving human minds.

Media representation: 1. A media transformation that takes place when one media product is represented in another medium. 2. Expression of something with a media product that has been conceptual before (like a mental model); also called "mediation".

Meta-modelling: 1. Combination and integration of different models or perspectives of analysis of models, contingent on the modeller's languages and theories. 2. Accounts for the integration of practices of 'analogue' modelling with practices of modelling oriented towards a digital implementation. 3. In computer science, meta-models refer to abstract formalisms which include rules to generate other modelling languages. They are often referred to as schema languages or meta-languages.

Metaphor/s: 1. Carriers and creators of meaning; they define their own semantic fields, which have the potential to expand across related domains. 2. Cognitive tools which help their users and creators understand, interpret and express their world, theories, knowledge and findings; they enable them to grasp the unknown via what is known, both by making implicit knowledge explicit and by leveraging unexpected connections with other semantic domains. 3. Models of knowledge; they define what knowledge is as well as the scheme within which knowledge, conceptual systems and specific concepts operate; they play a fundamental role in structuring and modelling our conceptual systems; they lead narratives (e.g. around a project language) and reshape their contexts of production and use. 4. Meta-models generate other models. 5. → **Metaphor, Conceptual.** 6. → **7. Language, Metaphoric.**

Metaphor, Conceptual: 1. Meaning from one knowledge domain to another; they perform conceptual integration by mapping a source domain onto a target domain. 2. Condensation of complex ideas in simple terms; frequently used to understand how scholarly theories, models, objects, and knowledge emerge as a result of embodied physical and social experiences.

Modality/ies (media modalities): 1. Building blocks of media products (mediated expressions). 2. A set of four analytical categories (material, sensorial, spatiotemporal and semiotic) used to understand media products. 3. Include a number of possible modes.

Mode/s: 1. A way to be or to do things. 2. Building blocks of media products (mediated expressions) and their modalities (e.g. important modes characterising material modality are 'demarcated materiality' such as human bodies, and 'not demarcated' materiality such as smell).

Model/s: 1. Object/s aiming at channelling knowledge of something else by means of different forms of representation (i.e. notes, diagrams, images, tridimensional objects). 2. Key role player in reasoning processes (both formal modes of reasoning and representation, pertaining to deductive scientific methods, and less formal ones, mostly attributable to *analytical* research approaches) and knowledge development and sharing; model-based reasoning is a social problem-solving strategy grounded in everyday signification. 3. A heuristic tool (*lens*) by means of which an object is re-described as a result of a modelling process; provides a shareable language to talk about and understand (hence communicate) existing or possible realities. 4. An artefact, a concrete (visual, perceptible), shareable representation or expression embedding an element of theory, abstraction, a framework, or a sign; a media product used in modelling activity. 5. Objects mediated by the conditions and constraints of their perception and their language/s of expression; contingent, created in actual scholarly situations of production and use; partially arbitrary in that the same inferences drawn by manipulating one model could have been reached in other ways, for instance using a different model. 5a. **Factuality** of models refers to their form, their morphology and topology as well as their rule-based formality; the size, production process, language of expressions, materials, modalities, context of use of a model are part of its factuality. 5b. **Fictionality** of models refers to their subjectively determined dependency on prior knowledge and theory, on interpretative visual and verbal languages, on the rules of the technical systems following which they are created and used. 5c. Factuality and fictionality of models are entangled and concur to determine their affordances. 6. Sign-functions initiate a sign-relation (**model-relation**) in the form of icons; the iconic relationship between the model and the objects or processes being modelled (target) is partly externally determined (it relies on the similarity between the model and the objects or processes) and partly internally determined (it depends on theory, languages, conventions, scholarly tradition, etc.); they are a type of sign mediating between the impressions of experience and freedom of association: 6a. **Image**-like models rely on and enable morphing reasoning, for example, real-life sketches where single qualities such as forms and shapes enable them to act as signs of the original objects they represent in given circumstances. 6b. **Relational or structural** models rely on and enable corresponding reasoning, for example, diagrams such as the relation exhibited in the graph of a mathematical equation. 6c. **Metaphor**-like models represent attributes of the original by a non-standard kind of parallelism with something else which generates further models; they rely on and enable metaphorical reasoning. 7. **Metaphoric model** 7a. An adaptable model working transversally at the experimental, theoretical and practical level. 7b. In → **Digital Humanities** (**DH**) a guiding metaphor that structures the digital artefact it originates at—at least—the three levels of data acquisition, data storage, and data presentation.

Modeller/s: 1. Modelling agent/s, subject/observer, those (e.g., researcher/s, designer/s) who create and use models. 2. In the semiotic perspective on modelling, the interpreter. 3. Machines/systems made by humans in the case of deep learning models and cycles of modelling activities where the human-machine interaction is highly entangled and where interpretability of all modelling steps might become secondary.

Modelling: 1. A process of signification and reasoning in action, a heuristic strategy of coming to know spanning multiple scientific cultures and epistemic traditions, where meaning is negotiated through the creation and manipulation of external representations combined with an imaginative use of languages with different levels of formalisation and modes of expression; a creative and highly pragmatic process in which metaphors assume a central role. 2. Context-dependent and object-oriented dynamic process (the act of modelling) of selection of features (or salient qualities), motivated by the aims and the purposes of the modeller, to establish a partial mapping between the model and the object being modelled. 3. An activity where one or more modellers (human beings using various tools) use a media product (the model) as a means to: a) understand the targets of the modelling better (model of), and/or b) create new modelling targets, e.g. (model for): modelling = (modeller+, model (media product+), target+). 4. A process of *formalisation* in the sense of giving form, analysis, translation and interpretation, e.g. correlating (via models) facts and data or enacting a media transformation (as in the case in *critical stepwise formalisation*, where a media expression is studied through the process of adapting it into a new expression in another medium through a number of sequential steps). 5. A communicative act where models are shared and critiqued. 6. From a semiotic perspective, an open-ended process of signification (or meaning-making) enacting a triadic cooperation among object, *representamen* (form of a sign) and *interpreter* (significate outcome of a sign); a signification function which defines the relationships in the sign triple, where the object is the target, the representamen is the model or media product, and the interpreter is the modeller. 7. From an intermedia studies perspective, when the target of the model (a media product) is also a media product or a technical or qualified medium, modelling is a media transformation process, an act of translation between two media products or between a qualified medium and a media product, a process of establishing one media product based on aspects taken from either another media product or from a qualified medium. 8. In science and scholarship, modelling is a special case of modelling strategies humans adopt in everyday life; in this sense modelling is a research strategy intended as a process by which researchers make and manipulate external representations to make sense of objects and phenomena; this process is constrained and enhanced by the idiosyncratic contexts and purposes of research endeavours. [9]. One of the core practices of research in → **DH** and its earlier incarnation as humanities computing; translation of complex systems of knowledge into models to be manipulated (processed) computationally; translations and negotiations of meaning occur both in modelling processes engaged with abstraction of complex phenomena into rule-based procedures and in modelling directed at the re-integration of the results of that abstraction or reduction into interpretative frameworks such as explanatory diagrams and data visualisations; a pragmatic activity framed within the complex cognitive, social, and cultural functioning of → **DH** practices affected by cross-linguistic and interdisciplinary dimensions.

Modelling, Pragmatic: 1. A process of thinking in practice anchored to theory but also rooted in the language in use, combining formal and experimental modelling techniques with a constructive use of verbal and visual languages; it unfolds in relational and dynamic cycles which are elicited via negotiations over the use of modelling languages (e.g. by narrowing and broadening categories of analysis, or borrowing categories from other disciplines); its pivot lies in the manipulability, negotiability and flexibility of models. [2]. A conceptual device to position the study of modelling in critical scholarship by privileging the specificity of the modellers, objects and the contexts of use, by recognising that modelling acts operate within relational and dynamic cycles which are elicited via negotiations over the use of modelling languages (e.g. by renaming categories of analysis or adopting neologisms); it strives to make the perspectives of study of modelling objects explicit, both in interpretative and technical terms; research and learning strategy that takes into account the complex intellectual, social, and cultural dimensions within which → **DH** operates.

Operationalisation: Process via which concepts of humanistic inquiry are operationalised, that is, made observable, measurable, formalised into rules (from algorithms to software systems and applications) hence creating empirical objects of study which bear theoretical consequences for the discipline to which they are applied.

Source domain: Conceptual domain from which metaphorical expressions are drawn to understand a target domain.

Target/s: Object/s or system/s being modelled; the objects being modelled in the humanities are usually, but not exclusively, cultural constructs (whether artefacts or concepts) made by humans; in → **DH** research, the privileged objects of modelling activities have been texts but they can include single objects of art or literature as well as large historical and cultural frameworks or concepts.

Target domain: Conceptual domain that we try to understand via the source domain.

Transmediation: 1. The result of a media transformation process. 2. A media transformation that denotes the creation of an impression in one media expression, the *target*, based on another expression in another medium, the *source*.[7]

0.4 Summary of Chapters

In the first chapter ("Towards a new language for modelling"), a selection of lexical ramifications and a semantic excursus on the terms model/modelling is proposed. Some etymological reflections on the terms and selected occurrences in the Western history of thought are mapped out. In addition, the concept of "pragmatic modelling" as it has evolved in our research project is introduced and contextualised.

In the second chapter ("Modelling and metaphoric reasoning"), the act of modelling is discussed. In particular, its representative and descriptive functions and how it operates within a context which includes a metaphorical language are considered. Metaphors adapt to, and at the same time transform, this language. The concept of pragmatic modelling is discussed further and is connected to how metaphorical language operates in DH as well as other (mainly interdisciplinary) modelling contexts. Furthermore, the chapter exemplifies how metaphors themselves are models of knowledge, as they define the schemes within which specific concepts operate and knowledge is established and expressed. In particular, in a DH context, the use of metaphors can have practical outcomes for how affordances influence data processing, storage, and design, and for how data are presented and interfaces are built. It is proposed to consider modelling as a creative and usually highly pragmatic process of thinking and reasoning in which metaphors assume a central role and where meaning is negotiated through the creation and manipulation of external representations combined with an imaginative use of formal and informal languages.

---

7   Sahle (2010) has developed a different concept of 'transmediation', where the representation of a media object through model-based encoded information is considered to transcend the media qualities of particular media objects. Recoding towards a model-oriented abstraction in data that is not used as a communication medium but to generate media expressions is therefore called 'transmediation'. However, this notion of transmediation is not used in this book.

In contrast with the common theorisation of the practice of modelling in DH informed by the techno-sciences and computer science in particular, Chapter 3 ("Modelling as semiotic process") refers to model-making, theorised within a semiotic framework. Modelling is framed as a process of signification (semiotic process or meaning-making). This semiotic framework allows us to see modelling primarily as a strategy to make sense (signification) via practical thinking (creating and manipulating models). It enables us to stress the dynamic nature of models and modelling, and to reinstate in renewed terms the understanding of modelling as an open process of signification enacting a triadic cooperation (among object, *representamen* and interpreter). Referring to Charles Sanders Peirce's classification of hypoicons, we reflect on some DH examples of modelling in the form of images, diagrams and metaphors, claiming that a semiotic understanding of modelling could ultimately allow us to surpass the rigid duality object vs. model, as well as sign vs. context. In Chapter 4 ("Modelling as media transformation"), we dwell on the tangible physical forms of models as material and mediated media products expressed and shared in human communication. The forms models take are discussed in terms of configurations of media modalities. This intermedia studies approach, whereby modelling is studied as a media transformation process, complements the semiotic perspective of Chapter 3 by revisiting some of the previous examples and integrating them with a variety of heterogeneous models, from archaeology to theatre studies, and media transformation processes, including formalisations undertaken in DH research.

Chapter 5, the last chapter in the book, "Modelling text – A case study", presents a case study examining examples of activities of modelling around the concepts of text and textuality. This is a particularly rich case study as it spans various disciplines and illustrates different modes and functions of making implicit and explicit models, covering a broad range from theoretical descriptions to concrete applications in the realm of text technologies and knowledge representation. The authors' experience in practical modelling and theoretical studies on modelling contributed to a selection of examples. These aim to offer a "graphical" argument for how different models represent conceptualisations of and perspectives on texts in different ways, illustrating key concepts discussed in the previous chapters, and opening up the discussion for readers to engage with the topic further. The argument takes a different form of expression from the other chapters by discussing models and their visualisations with the presentation of topical quotes extracted from the literature alongside their iconic counterparts, either in their original version or as interpreted visually by the authors and the designers. This effort is in itself an example of modelling as a translation process in action. In this chapter, models are exposed primarily as specific and situated visual representations that we experience when studying and modelling texts. They are presented according to a 'What You See is What You Get' approach, without accompanying extensive verbal explanations nor the discursive argument present in the other chapters. The chapter qualifies therefore as an anthology, a gallery, an empirical study, and an experiment on finding a different mode of argumentation to "change the launch pad" into future discussions around modelling.

0.5 Acknowledgements

The writing and completion of this book would not have been possible without the support, contributions and advice of institutions, colleagues and friends. We would therefore like to thank, first of all, the original project team's research associates and assistants: Christopher Pak, Zoe Schubert, Michela Tardella, Nils Geißler, Elisabeth Reuhl, Anna Wibbeke, Julia Sorouri, and Thinette Skicki. The research for this book was part of the project "Modelling between digital and humanities: Thinking in practice", funded by The VolkswagenStiftung.

In addition, we are grateful for the diverse perspectives of all other participants of the project workshop "Thinking in practice" held at Wahn Manor House in Cologne during January 2017 (see proceedings in Ciula et al. 2018): Rens Bod, Nina Bonderup Dohn, Paul A. Fishwick, Giorgio Fotia, Tessa Gengnagel, Günther Görz, Fotis Jannidis, Claas Lattmann, Christina Ljungberg, Willard McCarty, Oliver Nakoinz, Gunnar Olsson, Francesca Tomasi, Barbara Tversky, all played a role in shaping the content of this book.

Special mention is due to the co-organisers and the participants at the interdisciplinary lab "Words and Images: The languages of research",[8] and to other collaborators who contributed to the research, whether as colleagues or students of the authors, namely, Silvestro Caligiuri, Ellen Wiger, Enes Türkoglu, and Torfinn Hørte.

Furthermore, we would like to express our gratitude for the very useful feedback from Open Book Publishers' anonymous peer reviewers and for the editors' patience. Michal Allon (Tel Aviv University) has performed copyediting of the English in this book, which has been invaluable in finalising the manuscript.

Last but not least, whether directly or indirectly, our home institutions and associated dedicated administrators have all supported our work over the years and deserve our acknowledgement here: CNR-ILIESI (Rome, Italy); Department of Humanities, University of Roehampton (London, UK); King's Digital Lab, King's College London (London, UK); Department for Digital Humanities, University of Cologne (Cologne, Germany); Chair for Digital Humanities, University of Passau (Passau, Germany).

We take responsibility for any errors, omissions and flaws that readers may identify, and we welcome feedback to encourage new research.

---

8   The report of the series of events organised within the lab activities is available online (Marras, Caligiuri 2018). On the workshops, see also https://modellingdh. uni-koeln.de/events.

1. Model and Modelling in Digital Humanities: Towards a Renewed Language[9]

1.1 Model, Modelling and Modeller: An Overview of the Metalanguage

In this chapter we turn our attention to the history and the polysemy characterising the terms *model* and *modelling* in order to be able (a) to reflect on their current use, and (b) to bring out the pragmatic elements implied by the concept of model in the modelling practices through language (metalanguage). The underlying assumption is that by analysing the metalanguage, we can acquire a deeper understanding of the practices of modelling and the related processes of conceptualisation, representation, visualisation and communication. The complex scenario we outline is not only in debt to decades of theory about and practices of modelling but it is actually embedded, as we will try to explain, in the roots and history of the terms.

(A) *model* and *modelling* belong to the same lexical family and are polysemic. *Model* is used to identify both formal modes of reasoning and representation, pertaining to *deductive* scientific methods, and less formal ones, mostly attributable to *analytical* research approaches.[10] The first is well explored and theorised by scholars and represents the overall approach adopted in empirical sciences, including some

---

9   This chapter was written in collaboration with Michela Tardella.

10   On the denotative dimension of terms in scientific language vis à vis the presence of pre-theoretical forms, see the examples of "Text: Thought, spoken and written", "Thinking of text", "Text as megaphone" in chapter 5.

     https://doi.org/10.11647/OBP.0369.01

branches of Digital Humanities (DH), while the second has not yet been fully recognised as a form of modelling adequate to DH, nor investigated as such. The analytical approach has been recognised by some epistemologists as *the model of* doing science in which inductive, analogical and metaphorical forms of reasoning acquire a pivotal heuristic function, whereas the deductive one is considered as strictly logical.[11]

Tracing the history of the term *model* back to its etymological roots, it seems to us useful to expand the directions of the research, as we will attempt to explain further below. In fact, despite the tradition of studies,[12] the two approaches mentioned above are complementary rather than separate. This complementarity is implicit in the different meanings of the term, as noted elsewhere:

> Traditionally, prediction and reproduction of results, as well as explanations of observations, have been the main phases of the scientific method in which models in the sciences have been created and evaluated. More recently the creation and use of models to explore rather than measure, predict, or explain have also gained recognition in the philosophy of science. All these functions are associated with what is considered the purpose of models, which is to support analysis and discovery as well as to enhance learning and understanding. Models are indeed considered to be better suited to learn something new about the target systems or objects for several reasons. Their creation and manipulation support surrogative reasoning, where aspects of the system under study are sharpened up in the model and hence made more "observable" than by studying the target systems or objects directly. The novel concept of model-based reasoning captures exactly this. (Ciula, Eide, Marras, Sahle 2018, pp. 8-9).

---

11 See Carlo Cellucci (1988) and Mary Hesse (1966). These categorisations are directly related to an animated debate that took place in the 1990s, in particular in the epistemological domain. The core of the discussion was the dialectic relation between 'real objects' and 'objects of knowledge', where real objects are those objects existing outside of thought, in the real world, which are targets for research, observation, analysis, etc., and objects of knowledge are those objects resulting from the research process; this distinction is well discussed in Silvano Tagliagambe (1995). On the construction of objects in science, see Bruno Latour (1996).

12 For a multidisciplinary approach to the analysis of the term model, see the proceedings of the conference organised at the Accademia dei Lincei in Rome in 1998 entitled *The role of model in science and knowledge; Il ruolo del modello nella scienza e nel sapere* (1999).

The use of models and the process of modelling have a long tradition in the humanities. Going back to early modern Europe, the use of models in what could be called scholarship in 'the Humanities' included modelling in natural philosophy, which later developed into the natural sciences.[13] The long history of modelling is complex due to the only partial overlap between contemporary and current concepts of model and modelling and because often (and in particular in the humanities) models and modelling processes are used implicitly rather than expressed as explicit formal statements. The relationship between models and the objects or systems being modelled (what we call the *targets* of the models) is also complex and hard to define. It varies across research traditions and has developed significantly over time. In the twentieth century, models have been described as representations of their targets; the specific nature of those representations did not attract much attention until the latter part of the century. In the philosophy of science, a pragmatic view on modelling has emerged over the last few decades, such that the relation between a model and its target, traditionally expressed as some kind of representation in the form of formal, structuralist or syntactic morphism (such as isomorphism), is gradually being replaced by an emphasis on a pragmatic relationship, often simply described as a situation where somebody creates a model of something with some purpose (Gelfert 2016, p. 113).

In this chapter, we focus on the use of language in the context in which the object and subject/observer (the researcher who creates and uses models, also called the *modeller* in this book) operate while models are made. This interplay between *model*, *target*, and *modeller* includes an interpretative aspect and can be considered therefore as a process of 'translation'. In this perspective theory and the object being modelled are seen as complementary rather than mechanically related. The relationship between models and their targets is certainly complex and hard to define (Chapter 3 dwells further on this, discussing it in terms of *sign-relation*), as is the nature of the object or target system itself (Gelfert 2016, p. 93; Ciula, Eide, Marras, Sahle 2018). We argued elsewhere that models take a "middle position" (Ciula and Marras 2016) and imply an inductive (bottom-up) method complementary to a deductive (top-down) method (see Key term Model/s 2); epistemologically, they occupy an n-dimensional space defined by multiple axes, they are contingent on

---

13 See Bod (2018).

social practice and on language in use (pragmatics; see Key term Model/s 5).

What follows is firstly an overview of the terminological and etymological references of the terms *model* and *modelling*, which provides some evidence based on a series of occurrences extracted from selected dictionaries, encyclopaedias, etymological vocabularies and philosophical texts. All theoretical issues are deeply connected to their relevant terminology (and the etymology of a term), so that reflecting upon terms and their relationships can help us to piece together the "ontological puzzle" around models (Frigg 2006). In order to show what the roots of the term imply, and to follow its articulated semantic development, we start by mapping the related terms and some of the interlinguistic relations across different terms in a selected set of languages, namely Latin, Greek, English, Italian, French, and German (see Section 1.2).

We are aware of the fact that the semantic dimension of a term is not determined solely by its etymological roots but above all by the users and the contexts in which they are used; however, we cannot but point to a certain evident continuity between the original semantic traces of the terms and the different meanings established over time. It is important to stress that from this terminological overview it emerges that *model* denotes different forms of representation (i.e. notes, diagrams, images, tridimensional objects) that play a key role in the reasoning processes and knowledge development (see Chapter 3).

Beyond it, there is a dynamic process (the act of modelling) that is context-dependent and object-oriented (Section 1.3). Any model is therefore primarily pragmatic because it favours the specificity of the modellers, the objects, and the contexts of use, but also because its pivot lies in their manipulability, in pragmatics terms, their negotiability and flexibility (Verschueren 2012). On the basis of the terminological and etymological evidence we have at hand, we focus on the properties and the elements that make a process of modelling 'pragmatic'. This is to develop a richer and more contextually aware understanding of how representation works in model-based research. We will discuss the concept of pragmatic modelling emerging from the terminological analysis both as it stems from the polysemy of the term and as it has evolved during our research project in a DH context. We will thus highlight the need to adopt a language and a terminology adequate to support, articulate, and capture the complex iterative process of integration and exploration with the repeated loops of testing, feedback, and adjustment that characterise the process of modelling (Section 1.4).

1.2 A Terminological and Lexicographical Discussion

The term *model* derives from Vulgar Latin *modellus*, obtained with the suffix alteration from Classical Latin *modulus*, diminutive of *modus*.[14] Modus mostly refers to "a measured amount", "quantity", "size, extent, length, circumference", "a proper measure, due measure", "the measure of tones, measure, rhythm, melody, harmony, time" and, in poetry, "measure, metre, mode". However, the most revealing meanings are those generated by figurative transfers, like "a measure which is not to be exceeded, a bound, limit, end, restriction", "moderation", "restraint", or "a way, manner, mode, method", namely a criterion, something that controls or regulates an action.[15] In Table 1.1 we sketch an example of these literal and figurative meanings:

MODUS	
General meanings	Figurative meanings
a measured amount	a measure which is not to be exceeded, a bound, limit, end, restriction
size, length, circumference, quantity	a way, manner, mode, method
the measure of tones, measure, rhythm, melody, harmony, time (Music)	a proper measure, due measure
measure, metre, mode (Poetry)	

Table 1.1 General and figurative meanings of Latin *modus*.

---

14   We based our study on the *Oxford English Dictionary*, 21989; *Portail lexical, Etymologie, Centre National de Ressources Textuelles et Lexicales* (CNRTL) http://www.cnrtl.fr/etymologie/; and on the *Dizionario etimologico italiano*, Alessio & Battisti, 1965; *A Latin Dictionary*, Charlton T. Lewis & Charles Short, 1879, online at https://www.perseus.tufts.edu/hopper/text?doc=Perseus%3atext%3a1999.04.0059

15   *A Latin Dictionary, ad vocem.*

Modulus in classical Latin generally means "a small measure, a measure", but was used to express specific technical and diversified accepted uses according to the context; for example, in architecture it was used as "module" (the fifteenth part of a Doric column); in music, "rhythmical measure, rhythm, music, time, metre, mode, melody"; in hydraulic engineering, "a watermeter".[16]

Moreover, the metaphorical uses of *modulus* are particularly insightful; indeed, in some philosophical and literary works, the term acquires the meaning of "prototype" but also of the "measure of intellect" or "measure of ingenium".[17] In these latter cases, the abstract concepts of reasoning, thinking and reflecting are expressed by means of a concrete reference, namely to the measurement of quantifiable substances (columns, sound, water, and so on): some of the features and functionalities (Gensini 2010) of the concrete object and actions implied in its measurement are transferred (*metapherein* means "to transfer" in Greek) to the operations of mind, making them more understandable.

The two terms *modus* and *modulus* therefore do not only convey the general meaning of "measuring" but also that of "method", namely the manner of intellectual measuring (see Table 1.2).

MODULUS		
General meanings	Technical meanings	**Metaphorical meanings**
A small measure	*Module* (Architecture, 15th part of a Doric column)	*Prototype*
A measure	*rhythmical measure, rhythm, music, time, metre, mode, melody* (Music)	*Measure of reason*
	a watermeter (Hydraulics)	

Table 1.2 General, technical and metaphorical meanings of Latin *modulus*.

---

16   *A Latin Dictionary, ad vocem.*
17   In Horace we find a clear example of the latter use: "cur non ponderibus modulisque suis ratio utitur?" [Why does the ratio not use its own weights and measures?] (*Satyrae*, 1, 3, 78).

This semantic nuance, in our opinion, is still present in the transition from Latin to vernacular languages and it is not only related to the substantive *modus*,[18] but also to (its derivative) *modulus/modellus*. The interlinguistic equivalents of this latter term, namely *modelle* (Old French), *modèle* (Modern French), *Model/Modell* (German), *modello* (Italian),[19] bear a wide range of meanings, most of them indicating the result of an activity in which the observer and the object (*observatum*) are integrated.

If we turn from these translational issues to the analysis of the first attested occurrences of the term in the vernacular languages, further complexity emerges. Indeed, the term *model* and its interlinguistic equivalents show a semantic cloud resulting from usage both in ordinary language and in the technical lexicon of different disciplines.

As we learn from the *Oxford English Dictionary*, the term *model* is present in the English language from the second half of the sixteenth century, with the meaning of "an architect's set of designs for a projected building", that is, a *model for* (McCarty 2004), a "representational object" which must be imitated in order to build something else. Other accepted uses, such as "an object of imitation" (i.e. something that is imitated rather than imitates), can be attributed to the same representational concept. In these cases, *model* denotes "an object or figure made in clay, wax, or the like, and intended to be reproduced in a more durable material" (1686); "a mould" (1593); "a person, or a work, that is proposed or adopted for imitation, an exemplar" (1639).

In the same lexicographical sources, we find an alternative meaning, that is, a "set of drawings made to scale and representing the proportions

---

18 One of the most common translations of *modus* is the Italian *modo*, the English *mode*, the German *Mode* and the French *mode*. Notable for example is the use of the German *Mode*, which nowadays is one of the most used German derivatives of the Latin *modus*. However, J. & W. Grimm challenged this notion as early as the seventeenth century; they even doubt a direct relation to (Lat.) *modus*: "dessen unmittelbare ableitung vom lat. masc. modus nicht ohne zweifel steht (man müste denn die geschlechtsänderung durch den einflusz des älteren fem. manière erklären wollen)." See *Deutsches Wörterbuch von Jacob Grimm und Wilhelm Grimm, Mode, ad vo* http://www.woerterbuchnetz.de/DWB/mode.

19 See *Dizionario di filosofia, ad vocem; Oxford English Dictionary, ad vocem; Centre National de Ressources Textuelles et Lexicales, Etymologie, Liste des formes* (CNRTL, http://www.cnrtl.fr/etymologie) *ad vocem; Dizionario etimologico italiano, ad vocem;* Deutsches Wörterbuch von Jacob Grimm und Wilhelm Grimm, digital version 01/23, http://www.woerterbuchnetz.de/DWB/modell and http://www.woerterbuchnetz.de/DWB/model, *ad vocem.*

and arrangement of an existing building". In this sense, *model* denotes a representational object resulting from an imitative practice or activity, namely a *model of*:

> And I shall well my sillie selfe content, To come alone unto my lovely Lorde And unto him... To tel some... reasonable worde of Hollandes state, the which I will present, In Cartes, In Mappes, and eke in Models made.

These verses belong to *Posies* (1575), a book by George Gascoigne, one of the most important poets of the early Elizabethan era.[20] The passage is particularly relevant to our study, because *model* co-occurs with *map* and *chart*,[21] two pivotal concepts in the current discussion of *modelling*. Maps, charts and models are conceived as objects aiming at generating knowledge of something else (a country for example) by means of different forms of representation.

The *Oxford English Dictionary* also attests a "cognitive" role of models (1581):

> The same man, as soone as hee might see those beasts wel painted, or the house wel in moddel, should straight waies grow without need of any description, to a iudicial comprehending of them. (Philip Sidney)

Model as the result of an imitative process is also related to a *working model*, i.e., a tridimensional object built in order to imitate the structure and the movements of the machine that it represents. This representative (imitative) function can also be identified in some figurative meanings, such as "a small portrait" (1622), or "something that accurately represents something else; a person or a thing that is the likeness or 'image' of another", the latter attested in *Richard II* (1593) and *Hamlet* (1602).[22]

Among the most inspiring occurrences of the term, there are some philosophical and technical works, both in Latin and in vernacular languages, dating back to the Renaissance and the early modern period.

---

20 See Hamrick (2005) and Austen (2008).
21 The etymologies of 'map' and 'chart' are outlined in Eide (2012, pp. 29–30).
22 *Model* is also used as a synonym of *modillion*, "an ornate bracket, or a corbel, underneath a cornice and supporting it" (1663) and of *module* (1598) from which it derives, as already said.

A relevant passage, taken from the treatise *Della imitazione* (1560) by the humanist and teacher of rhetoric Giulio Camillo, reads:

Ricordomi già in Bologna, che uno eccellente anatomista chiuse un corpo umano in una cassa tutta pertugiata, e poi la espose ad un corrente d'un fiume, il qual per que' pertugi nello spazio di pochi giorni consumò e portò via tutta la carne di quel corpo, che poi di sé mostrava meravigliosi secreti della natura negli ossi soli, e nei nervi rimasti. Così fatto corpo dalle ossa sostenuto io assomiglio al modello della eloquenzia dalla materia e dal disegno solo sostenuto. E così come quel corpo potrebbe essere stato ripieno di carne d'un giovane o d'un vecchio, così il modello della eloquenzia può essere vestito di parole che nel buon secolo fiorirono o che già nel caduto languide erano (Camillo, 1544, pp. 46-47).

I remember at the time in Bologna an excellent anatomist closed a human body in an all over perforated box to then expose it to a river current, which through those holes consumed and took away all the flesh of that body in the space of a few days. That body showed of itself wonderful secrets of nature, in its only bones and leftover nerves. Similarly, like that body supported by its bones, I look alike the model of the eloquence of matter, sustained only by its design. And just as that body could have been filled with the flesh of a young or an old man, so the model of the eloquence can be filled with words that flourished in the good century or that already were languid in the past one.

Noteworthy here is the comparison between two really different disciplines, Anatomy and Rhetoric, a comparison that implies a *transdisciplinary* understanding of the notion of model. The author argues that these two knowledge domains can be put in relation and compared on the basis of an analogy between their methodologies and practices. Camillo, while trying to develop a good rhetorical method, notices an impressive similarity between the two disciplines. This method implies a retrogradation from the concrete, sensible and compound exemplar (i.e. a particular body/a particular text or discourse) to a set of constitutive elements which can be combined in different ways. In this paradigm, a *model* is conceived as a complex and steady schema, on the basis of which infinite possible contents (textual or anatomical, but the method also fits architectural elements) can be organised (Carlino 2013, p. 85) through a combinatory process. A highly relevant theoretical context, philosophical and epistemological, is the work of the German philosopher G. W. Leibniz. In his *Quid sit idea* (1678) the concept of model (*modulus*) is defined through that of *expressio*:

Exprimere aliquam rem dicitur illud, in quo habentur habitudines, quae habitudinibus rei exprimendae respondent. Sed eae expressiones variae sunt; exempli causa, modulus Machinae exprimít machinam ipsam, scenographica rei in plano delineatio exprimit solidum, oratio exprímit cogitationes et veritates, characteres exprimunt numeros, aequatio Algebraica exprimit circulum aliamve figuram: et quod expressionibus istis commune est, ex sola contemplatione habitudinem exprimentis possumus venire in cognitionem proprietatum respondentium rei exprimendae. Unde patet non esse necessarium, ut id quod exprimit simile sit rei expressae, modo habitudinum quaedam analogia servetur (Leibniz 1678).	That is said to express a thing in which there are relations [habitudines] which correspond to the relations of the thing expressed. But there are various kinds of expression; for example, the model of a machine expresses the machine itself, the projective delineation on a plane expresses a solid, speech expresses thoughts and truths, characters express numbers, and an algebraic equation expresses a circle or some other figure. What is common to all these expressions is that we can pass from a consideration of the relations in the expression to a knowledge of the corresponding properties of the thing expressed. Hence it is clearly not necessary for that which expresses to be similar to the thing expressed, if only a certain analogy is maintained between the relations.[23]

The concept of *expressio* was elaborated by Leibniz in relation to a gnoseological issue: the role of representation in knowledge development and reasoning processes. According to Leibniz it can be defined as a representational connection between two heterogeneous sets of elements, governed by a law of correspondence (Kulstad 1977; Lamarra 1991). As we can understand from the quoted passage, the expressive/representational connection can be established between extremely different domains:

discourses	and	thoughts,
scale models	and	machines,
characters	and	numbers,
algebraic equations	and	geometric figures,
perspective projections	and	solids.

The first set of these pairs belong to the category of *model* as it is understood in the current era, i.e. mathematical models, scale models, notational symbols, and verbal language. The notion of relational

---

23   Loemker 1989, p. 207.

correspondences should be stressed here: something expresses (represents, is a *model of*) something else, when the relations (*habitudines*) between the elements belonging to the first domain match/correspond to the relations between the elements belonging to the second domain. That is one of the most important characteristics of *expressio*: what can be discovered in and said about the *exprimens* (the model), can also be discovered in and said about the *exprimendum* (the target). The heuristic value of the expressive connection lies exactly in a constant and regulated relationship.[24] Furthermore, the representational relation is not rooted in the immediate resemblance between the model and the object, but can be based upon a structural and relational analogy.

If we turn our attention to the complex practice of translation, we can note that the English *model*, the Italian *modello* and the French *modéle* have been chosen by translators to vehiculate some of the meanings of the Greek terms *idea* ('Ιδέα), *paradeigma* (Παράδειγμα), *typos* (Τύπος)[25] (see Table 1.3) and the Latin *exemplar*.[26]

IDEA (eido/orao)	PARADEIGMA	TYPOS
Form - shape (external aspect of an object)	*Copy* (of an existing thing)	*The print or impress of a seal* (associated with "blow" and with "the effect of a blow")
Semblance (appearance vs reality)	*Pattern* (of the thing to be executed)	
Ideal forms – archetypes (Plato' works)	*An architect's plan* (of a building)	

---

24 Namely a constant and regulated relationship between what can be said about one and the other: "un rapport constant et reglé entre ce qui se peut dire de l'une et de l'autre" as Leibniz wrote to Arnauld in 1687 (Leibniz 1978, vol. II, p. 112).
25 The definitions are from Liddell-Scott, 1940. See also the entries in philosophical multilingual dictionaries such as Maso 2010, and also http://www.perseus.tufts.edu/hopper/definitionlookup?q=model.
26 See *A Latin Dictionary, ad vocem.*

Class - kind - principle of classification (Logic)	Example	
	Lesson	

Table 1.3 Meanings of Greek *idea, paradeigma, typos*.

Let us briefly discuss them in turn. *Idea* derives from the verb *eido/orao*, "to see", both as "perceive with the eyes", or "experience", but also, in a metaphorical sense, "see with mind's eyes" or to know something. In its accepted usage, indicating appearances in opposition to the reality of things, an *idea* is connected to the concept of seeing, and not necessarily in conformity to reality. In Platonic philosophy, on the contrary, the "ideal forms, archetypes" are intended as an "intelligible form of things", while tangible reality is just a provisional image.[27] Beside these, there are at least two other meanings of *idea*: one related to Rhetoric ("literary form", "style", "a quality of style"), and another specific to Logic: "class, kind" and thus "principle of classification".

Paradeigma contains among its meanings "the model or copy of an existing thing", "a pattern or model of the thing to be executed",[28] but also "an architect's model (or perhaps plan) of a building", "a sculptor's or painter's model", "example" and "lesson".[29] These uses are clearly related to the more recent categories of *model of*, and *model for*, both of which imply an act of manipulation and representation of certain features of the object/phenomenon under consideration. *Paradeigma* has also been used as "a precedent, an example" and "an argument, a proof from example". These meanings show the *integrative function*[30] of a model, intended as a set of elements and characters unified in an event, a person, a fact, considered as a whole, complete.

Typos, "the print or impress of a seal" (associated with "blowing" and with "the effect of a blow"),[31] introduces an additional semantic

---

27   See Maso 2010, *ad vocem*.
28   *An Intermediate Greek-English Lexicon, ad vocem.*
29   *A Greek-English Lexicon, ad vocem.*
30   This is an interesting suggestion made by the physicist Giorgio Careri (1999, p. 185) in his contribution to the interesting and multidisciplinary discussion on the role of models in the history of thought and knowledge.
31   Here are some other entries taken from *A Greek-English Lexicon*: pl. "marks, letters"; "anything wrought of metal or stone", in pl. "figures worked in relief", then, simply,

element to the present excursus: the relation of similarity. What can be deduced from this term is the mirroring or, more precisely, indexical relation between an amorphous thingness and an object, the seal, that gives a specific form to that thingness defined by its own qualities (a letter, an image, a number, a sketch, etc.).

The complexity pertaining to the theory and practices in modelling, as embedded in the history of the key terms, are summarised and visualised in Figures 1.1 and 1.2.[32] Figure 1.1 illustrates the synchronic and diachronic relations between *model* and the terms belonging to its semantic field via the images of the wheel and its spokes; while Figure 1.2 stresses the historical-diachronic dimension through the metaphor of the tree.[33]

Fig. 1.1 Radial synoptic view of the analysis of the term *model*.

"a figure, image, statue"; "general form or character", "the type or model of a thing"; "an outline, sketch, draught".

32 A first attempt to build a dynamic network graph of terminological connections is the one developed using D3.js by Pak (2018), and slightly reworked by Geißler (2018).

33 For a discussion on visual metaphors and for the use of conceptual metaphors like the tree or wheel, see Chapter 2.

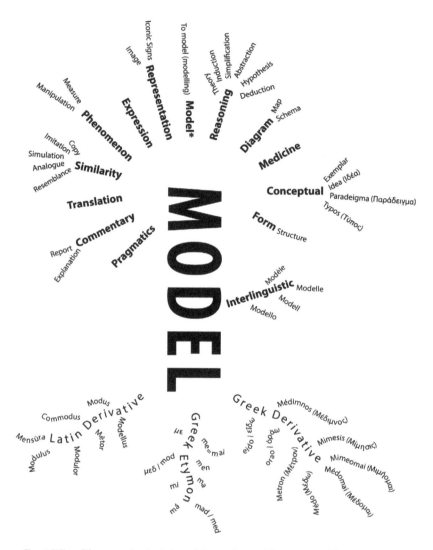

Fig. 1.2 Tree-like synoptic depiction of the analysis of the term *model*. Drawing by Julia Sorouri.

The consequences of polysemy are manifold. The meanings of models and modelling are negotiated within the different disciplines and areas of application. In this respect it is useful to frame DH modelling activities within recent works on model building (i.e. Kralemann and Lattmann 2013; Ciula, Eide, Marras, Sahle 2018). As aforementioned, the complexity pertaining to theory and practices in modelling is embedded in the history of the terms *model* and *modelling*: on the basis of the terminological and etymological evidence we have at hand, we will attempt to develop a richer and more contextually aware understanding of how models operate in reasoning processes. We thus focus on the properties and the elements that make a process of modelling 'pragmatic', namely a process of thinking in practice based on the language in use.

1.3 Toward a Pragmatic Modelling in DH

We want to highlight thus that the current metalanguage used by scholars when reasoning on models and modelling entails both technical and formal languages on the one hand, and metaphorical and analogical ones on the other, but more fundamentally, a complementary use of them. The work done during the project *Modelling between Digital and Humanities: Thinking in Practice*, especially the discussion which took place at the interdisciplinary Workshop "Thinking in Practice" held in Cologne on 19-20 January 2017,[34] are useful to substantiate this interplay between linguistic (and epistemic) variations. Figure 1.2 is a diagram of the words used by the workshop's participants to encircle the concepts of *model* and *modelling*. The terms were gathered not just from the explicit definitions provided by each speaker, but also from the discourse(s) around those concepts with which the participants engaged, both in their own talks and in the discussion that followed. We attempted to represent and freeze the metalinguistic activity around these two terms, by means of which the participants delimited their meanings in their own field of research (Geißler and Tardella 2018, p. 213).

---

34 See http://modellingdh.eu/index.php/events/our-workshop-2017/. On language analysis see, in particular, Geißler and Tardella (2018) and Sahle (2018).

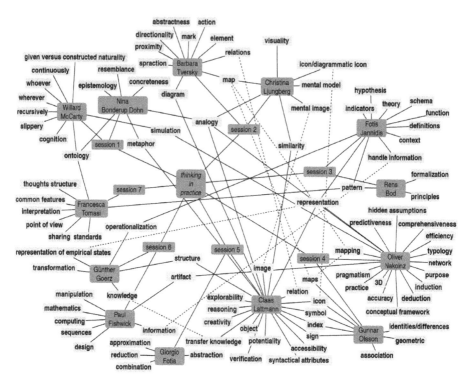

Fig. 1.3 Network Diagram for the terms used in the Workshop "Thinking in Practice" to encircle *model* and *modelling*. Dashed lines indicate similar or related terms (by Nils Geißler).

If we analyse the lexicon used by the participants, we note that they use pragmatic concepts and terms, such as *context, action, directionality, analogy, interpretation, purposes, communicable* (identities/differences), together with some Peircean semiotic categories, such as *metaphor, diagram,* and *icon* (Nina Bonderup Dohn, Claas Lattmann, Christina Ljungberg and Gunnar Olsson). In their metalanguage – that is, the language employed to explicitly define, describe and formalise their statements on modelling – this lexicon coexists with key concepts of formal deductive reasoning in the usage of terms such as *formalisation, deduction,* and *mathematics.*

It is also interesting to note that along with this terminology, instances of some 'frozen metaphors' occur, such as *slippery* (concept), *handle information, explorability, manipulation,* and *transfer knowledge.* These metaphorical expressions are unavoidable even in a technical lexicon;

they are in fact frozen metaphors (based on the conceptual metaphor IDEAS ARE OBJECTS, cf. Chapter 2) in the sense that they belong to ordinary language and by being used extensively, have become an integrated part of the technical metalanguage. It also emerged that the most frequent metaphor employed to explain how the concept of model and the practice of modelling are conceived is the cognitive TO KNOW IS TO SEE. According to this metaphor, modelling is a practice that allows us to look at (to think upon, interpret, represent) an object of knowledge. A model is, at the same time, both a heuristic tool (*lens*) by means of which an object is re-described and a result of a process (Geißler and Tardella 2018, p. 6). In Chapter 2 we will discuss the heuristic and cognitive role undertaken/assumed in structuring knowledge by some selected conceptual metaphorical models belonging to the traditions of Western thought. We concentrate on the creative process of thinking in modelling practices; in particular, we focus on the manipulation of model interfaces with other acts of signification and reasoning when they are facilitated by the use of metaphors.

In analysing the language of the workshop, we also focused our attention on the explicit definition of model and modelling. *Genera*[35] extracted from the definitions can be correlated with some general concepts. Concerning model(s), we found the following *genera*:

- *cognitive instrument* (instrument, thinking tool)
- *icon* (iconic sign, iconic and visual abstraction)
- *representation* (representation, mapping, artefact)
- *method* (ways, guidelines, question, matter, conceptual framework).

With respect to modelling, we can group these dynamic concepts:

- *form* (formalising, form)
- *action* (act, production, actualisation, activity)
- *selection* (choice, identifying, extracting).

---

35 The *genus* is, according to the approach of the "intensional definition", the category the *definiendum* belongs to.

This partial result confirms that the workshop's speakers link the two concepts, model and modelling, both to practical and theoretical dimensions, with an important caveat: modelling is defined by the majority of the participants as an activity, an actualisation, a production, an act; the concept is positioned on the practical side of the theory-praxis axis. In contrast, 'model', although conceived of as an artefact or even a concrete (visual, perceptible) representation, is mainly positioned on the side of theory, for example as an abstraction, a framework, or a sign, even if it is grounded in reality.

Models are contingent on the contexts of their production and use, and contingency is one of the primary aspects of modelling. Therefore, an epistemology of modelling in DH must depart from the specificity of its objects of study.[36] This means that in pragmatic modelling the analytical perspectives of study applied to objects must be made explicit both in interpretative and technical terms (cf. Chapter 3). The pragmatic aspects of modelling should receive in fact further attention in a DH context.[37] A pragmatic approach (Ciula and Eide 2017; Ciula and Marras 2018) allows us to offer a new interdisciplinary perspective on how DH modelling works both in the sense of construction (how models as signs are made, cf. Chapter 3) as well as with respect to its epistemic value, i.e. how something new can be discovered in the process of using models as signs (see Ciula, Eide, Marras, Sahle 2018). Texts, for example, are primary objects in human sciences, and for instance, unpacking a theory of texts as a way of making explicit modelling practices is as important as algorithmic criticism of the use of computers in analysing large corpora of texts.[38] Hence, we can say that somehow all modelling processes,

---

36 The understanding around the nature of objects of experience in science and in the humanities has evolved substantially in the Western tradition from Galileo onward (see Floridi 2011; Bod 2013; Marras 2013). Partially due to this evolution, it can be stated that in DH "[...] the objects that take part in an act of modelling [...] feature both an element of *factuality* (an experienced substance) and one of *fictionality* (they presuppose some rules of artifice). This implies that in a DH modelling activity a process of making explicit both components and their interaction is paramount" (Ciula and Marras 2018).

37 The pragmatics of modelling is also linked to the situatedness of the speaker (Ciula and Marras 2016).

38 "Algorithmic criticism would have to retain the commitment to methodological rigour demanded by its tools, but the emphasis would be less on maintaining a correspondence or a fitness between method and goal, and more on the need to present methods in a fully transparent manner" (Ramsay 2008). See also Smithies (2017, pp. 165-171).

by nature, are pragmatic, but more importantly here is the fact that by using the term *pragmatic modelling* in DH we intend to emphasise an understanding of the act of modelling as anchored not only to theory but also to practice and language.

1.3.1 Why Pragmatics?

The word *pragmatics* (from the Greek *praxis*, action), was first introduced by the ideal language philosophers under the distinction between syntax (the study of relations among symbols of a language), semantics (the study of the relations between symbols and their *designata*), and pragmatics, defined as the study of the relations between symbols and their users (cf. Morris 1938; Carnap 1942). Ideal language philosophers were interested in formal languages, structured and designed to capture and express mathematical truths. Therefore, the syntactic structure of any well-formed sentence of a formal language was believed to be defined by strict rules of formation. Semantic values "are assigned to the symbols of the language by stipulation and the truth-conditions of a sentence can be mechanically determined from the semantic values of its constituents by the syntactic rules of composition" (Jacob 2011, p. 8 ff). Within this perspective, some features of natural languages, such as their context-sensitivity, the metaphorical and metonymic transfers of word meanings, and their flexibility, were conceived as imperfections. On the other hand, philosophers of ordinary language have been interested in exactly those features which distinguish natural languages from formal ones, among which the most important are how the context-dependency of the content is expressed ("the circumstances" in which the utterances take place) and the fact that languages are not used only for describing objects or states of affairs (what Austin called the "descriptive fallacy"): by using natural languages, speakers do not simply describe something, but perform actions (Austin's *speech acts*). Therefore, in this theoretical framework, an important role in human use of language was given, first by Grice and then by Sperber and Wilson, to the concept of intentionality. This was intended as a pivotal element both in defining what a meaning is and in explaining communication and comprehension processes.[39]

---

39 See the discussion in AI and Computational linguistics, for example Gillis, Daelemans & DeSmedt (2009, p. 20). See the examples of "Text as Megaphone" and "Textual Atmosphere" in Chapter 5.

Although focused mostly on the elaboration of a model of human communication, this approach can also be fruitful for our discussion around modelling in DH due to the key role attributed to the *subjects* involved in what is called *speech acts*. Our assumption is that an act of modelling can be compared to a speech act: as we have already seen, one important element is the involvement of the subject and the context-dependency, but to these we should add the role of intentionality, the role of interpretation and the role of language. These categories, belonging to linguistic pragmatics, are useful for clarifying core notions of modelling without reducing it to a verbal act.

In a DH context (Ciula and Marras 2016) models have their grammars, and semantics within a processual consideration of the use of language that is not purely functional or descriptive, but also metaphorical (see Chapter 2), i.e., models are at least capable of adaptability and negotiability. Moreover, pragmatics and modelling share some key concepts such as context, intentionality and interpretation.[40]

Context. It is a core notion. We are not adopting here a cognitive and internalist conception of context, or a situational and externalistic one. The notion of context[41] covers quite a broad territory; it means different things for different research paradigms and disciplines.[42] We refer here to a dynamic and interactive notion of context as 'event'; recalling the Latin root of the term meaning "joining together", we assume an articulate notion that helps us to identify the phenomenon/object being contextualised, to look and take into consideration all the 'other' elements that are embedded or that feature in that 'event' (physical, linguistic, social and epistemic contextual aspects). The context is a frame (not a container) surrounding or underpinning the event in which the *observer* and the *observatum*, the modeller and the object or phenomenon being modelled, dynamically interact.[43] The context is not just an isolated object constructed by the modeller, but rather a mode of praxis, as discussed in Chapter 3.

---

40   See Allan & Jaszczolt (2012). On the pragmatic aspects of research (and their epistemic value) in the field of DH, see also Malazita et al. 2020.

41   It is worth noting that an insightful (frequently forgotten) contribution to the reflection on the role of *context* originated in the first half of the twentieth century in the fortunate convergence of several disciplinary fields, such as anthropology (Malinowski 1923), philology (Gardiner 1932) and psychology (Bühler 1934).

42   For a discussion on the notion of 'spurious context' in natural language and in knowledge representation, see Hirst (2000).

43   See Sperber and Wilson (1986).

Intentionality. Models are intentional in that they offer a representation of some features considered relevant *vis à vis* specific purposes. Modelling is not a mere act of describing an "object/phenomenon" (*observatum*) but a process of goal-oriented selection of features, motivated by the aims and the purposes of the modeller. Any model can only establish a partial mapping between the model and the object being modelled, otherwise modelling would merely result in a duplication of the objects/ phenomena under study (the map is not the territory). Modellers aim for their models not only to be understandable and useful, but also meaningful. Some of the key aspects defining pragmatics which strictly correlate with intentionality as it is intended here, are:

- Variability – the range of choices in the use of language cannot be seen as static in any respect;

- Negotiability – such choices are not made mechanically or according to strict rules or fixed form-function relationships, but on the basis of highly flexible principles and strategies, thus also implying the indeterminacy and unexclusiveness of the choices being made;

- Adaptability - such negotiable choices can be adapted based on specific needs and contexts according to a variable range of possibilities.

These aspects (of language use) are relevant especially in the selection or identification of features, properties, and elements of the object being modelled. They are related to each other, and they direct the choices of the modeller and contribute to it. Therefore, a model incorporates both semantic aspects and the intended implicated 'messages'. Although we are not implying here that intentionality is a pure *act of communication*, specifically related to the speaker's intention, we can say that modelling is also a communicative act, as further discussed in Chapter 4.[44]

----

44 Paul Grice (1957) argued that word and sentence meanings are based on the speaker's meanings, and these in turn are based on speakers' intentions (*M-intentions*). "What he conceived as a study of the ontology of semantic notions has been received, however, as a characterization of communicative intentions, the mental causes of communicative acts, and those that the hearer has to understand for the communicative act to be successful" (Korta & Perry 2020). Communicative intentions have three fundamental properties: they are always oriented towards

Interpretation. Within the perspective explained above, modelling can be defined as a process of translation (see Chapters 2 and 4) and in particular of interpretation in the sense that it makes understandable facts and data correlated by the model. In this way interpretation is inherently integrative. The pivotal components of the act of modelling selected above (the context, the language, the actors, in essence: its pragmatic nature) in the field of DH operate dynamically and therefore the structural polarities of object *versus* model can be overcome. Therefore, adopting an interdisciplinary perspective, we can talk of models as 'mediated objects', mediated by the conditions and constraints under which perceptions, as well as the language that expresses them, are derived.

In Figure 1.4 we summarise the interplay between all the discussed categories, and how it unfolds in the modelling act.

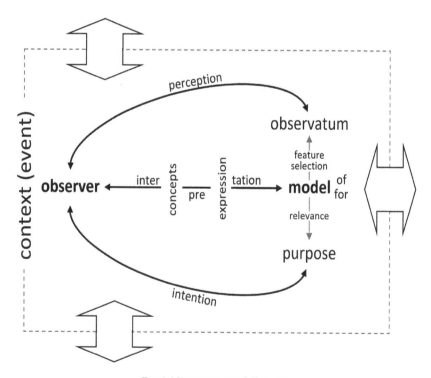

Fig. 1.4 Pragmatic modelling act.

some other agent — the addressee; they are overt, that is, they are intended to be recognised by the addressee; their satisfaction consists precisely in being recognised by the addressee (cf. Pacherie 2006).

1.4 The Language around Modelling in DH

In this chapter, we have sought to turn our attention to the multifaceted and polysemic range of the terms belonging to the semantic field of *model* and *modelling*. We have drawn a complex scenario (based on dictionaries, vocabularies, lexicons and encyclopaedias) resulting both from decades of theory and practice in modelling and the history of these terms. Such a terminological discussion and analysis allows us to reflect on the current metalanguage on models and modelling and to acquire a deeper understanding of the practices of modelling and the related processes of conceptualisation, representation, and visualisation.

A pragmatic understanding of modelling, as we adopt it in this volume, can facilitate the recognition that modelling operates within relational and dynamic cycles which are elicited via negotiations over the use of modelling languages (e.g., by narrowing and broadening categories of analysis, or borrowing categories from other disciplines).

Three dynamic aspects of modelling in DH make it pragmatic:

1. the dependency on the contexts within which modelling practices occur – e.g., research project, teaching module

2. the dependency on how the modelling workflows are used – e.g., to conceptualise a data model, to deliver a course assessment

3. the reliance on forms of expression of modelling – e.g., the constraints of a programming language, the capability of a Virtual Reality kit, and the diagrammatic expressiveness of models, as will be seen in Chapter 4.

Pragmatic modelling is a conceptual device which enables us to position the study of modelling in critical scholarship,[45] away from a mechanical and positivistic application of technical methods. A pragmatic vision of modelling implies awareness of the complexity of the objects being studied; of the multiple perspectives of analysis under which they are studied; and of the recurring conceptual schemes in structuring knowledge (metaphorical language, see Chapter 2). It also clarifies how a pragmatic understanding of modelling enables the manipulability

---

45 See for example some of the approaches emerging in Critical Infrastructures Studies: https://criticalinfrastructure.hcommons.org/session-description/.

of models via heuristic processes of formalisation (models are made computable) and translation (models take the form of media products). Indeed, pragmatic modelling combines formal and experimental modelling techniques with a constructive use of verbal and visual languages.

The interplay between the object of analysis (for instance texts) and the model, as well as across different levels of the interpretative process (e.g., close and distant reading, symbolic/paradigmatic and semantic/syntagmatic levels of text analysis), exemplify some of these dynamic aspects. Knowledge about the domain provides the means for inferring connections between objects and events that are often left implicit in natural discourse. It also creates the basis for inferring new knowledge from known facts. The problem is therefore to further develop the language (and a metalanguage) adequate for this approach to modelling in DH. A discussion and an analysis on metaphorical language and conceptual metaphors used in modelling in DH can certainly help in the definition of a renewed language for modelling.

2. Metaphoric Reasoning and Pragmatic Modelling

2.1 Metaphoric Reasoning

In this book we assume a definition and a practice of modelling that take into account the integration of interpretative[46] and computational approaches. In a Digital Humanities (DH) context, models have practical implications for how data is designed, generated, stored and processed and for the ways in which data is presented and interfaces are built (cf. Ciula and Marras 2018). Therefore, we propose to consider modelling as a creative and highly pragmatic process in which metaphors assume a central role and where meaning is negotiated through the creation and manipulation of external representations combined with an imaginative use of languages with different levels of formalisation and modes of expression (Ciula et al. 2023).

Thus, metaphorical expressiveness constitutes an irreplaceable part of the lexicon of modelling. Metaphors themselves are models of knowledge and they define the field within which knowledge and specific concepts operate (Marras 2017). In the history of ideas, metaphors evolved at the intersection of a reflection between language and thought on the one hand, and a reflection on the relation between rhetoric, poetry and ordinary language on the other; metaphors have been recognised as essential not only in ordinary discourse but also in scientific language;[47] they are a pervasive aspect of every genre of text and

---

46 See for example the use of interpretative conceptual networks for the history of ideas as explicit "framework models" (cf. Betti and van den Berg 2014).

47 See Skouen and Stark (2014, p. 148); Burkhardt and Nerlich (2010); a negative approach to metaphors in the early modern philosophical tradition is that of John

  https://doi.org/10.11647/OBP.0369.02

every register of speech. Metaphors, given their cognitive and creative resonance, are much more than an episodic linguistic phenomenon; they are also a cognitive tool which helps its users and creators understand and express their world and knowledge.[48] Although there is a broad consensus regarding the fact that metaphors lead to changes in and enrichment of knowledge, the mechanism of how these changes occur is still under discussion (Gentner and Wolff 2000[49]); investigating the role of metaphors in modelling (not only) in DH is also a contribution to this debate. In particular, the concept of pragmatic modelling discussed in Chapter 1 is connected to how metaphorical language operates in DH as well as other (mainly interdisciplinary) modelling contexts. Furthermore, it exemplifies how metaphors themselves are models of knowledge, as they define the schemes within which specific concepts operate and knowledge is established and expressed.

Given its regulative function in fixing and creating boundaries around the knowledge domain of reference, natural language plays a crucial mediating role in designing, expressing and contextualising models. By observing the use of language in modelling activities, the understanding emerges that the act of modelling, and in particular its representative and descriptive functions, make use also of metaphorical language.[50]

In our work we refer in particular to metaphors as conceptual (conceptual metaphors), because we want to specifically address how metaphors shape and model the way we think, speak, and act. When attempting to make sense of abstract, intangible phenomena, we draw from embodied experiences and look to concrete entities to serve as cognitive representatives. Conceptual metaphors have been discussed, especially in the late '90s in the field of cognitive linguistics, starting with the seminal work of Lakoff and Johnson, *Metaphors We Live By* (1980).

Locke "all the artificial and figurative application of words eloquence hath invented, are for nothing else but to insinuate wrong ideas, move the passions, and thereby mislead the judgement" (Locke 1690, Book III, Chapter X, Of the Abuse of Words).

48 See Nerlich and Clarke (2001); Leary (1990); Thibodeau and Boroditsky (2013).

49 See Gentner (1983) and Gentner and Stevens (1983).

50 An interesting example is the analysis of the observational data carried on by Michela Tardella and Niels Geissler on the language and metaphors used to encircle the concepts of model and modelling in the international workshop Thinking in Practice (see Geissler and Tardella 2018, pp. 213-214). For metaphors in scientific modelling see Wolynes (2001).

This approach considers metaphors as a 'mapping' of a source domain onto a target domain. It challenges more traditional positions that see metaphors as transportations or projections of similarities from one object to another or as a language component separate and distinct from the literal one, and rather highlight that they belong to the aesthetic and rhetorical aspects of language. Metaphors are conceived as a conceptual integrating activity.

Metaphors do not just adapt to the contextual language; they also transform it. However rich they may be, the lexical resources of a language cannot always satisfactorily capture the totality of the speaker's expressive needs. Some common linguistic phenomena, such as the proliferation of lexemes (neologisms) or the fact that they increase their range of meanings (neosemy), barely enhance the linguistic ability to satisfy these needs. Metaphors and other figures of speech become, in this respect, indispensable means to nurture the 'creative' direction of the use of language without expanding its system in a strict sense. For centuries, scholars relied on metaphorical conceptual models to 'visualise' science, worlds, and processes.[51] From the Porphyrian tree, to Darwin's corals, to Peirce's diagrammatic reasoning, to mention just a few well-known examples, metaphorical models via visual representations have been employed and developed along with the more accredited discursive forms or mathematical equations, and have recently been developed further thanks to computer graphics.[52]

---

51   See Rothbart (2007). There is a large number of visual images available on the web trying to reflect on the complexity of the visualisation of spatial metaphors to represent knowledge across disciplines and domains. See for example the figurative system of human knowledge, i.e. the tree developed by Diderot and d'Alembert (http://www.visualcomplexity.com).

52   See Averbukh (2015 and 2019); the aesthetic dimension of scientific illustration is not discussed here, but see Baigrie (1996).

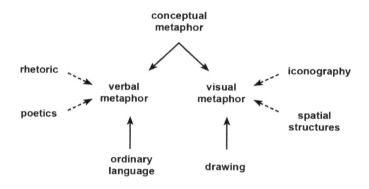

Fig. 2.1 Verbal and visual metaphor schema.

Metaphors play a fundamental and structural role in organising and modelling our conceptual systems. Conceptual metaphors condense complex ideas in simple terms and, as we saw in the previous paragraphs, are frequently used to understand how scholarly theories, models, objects, and knowledge emerge as a result of embodied physical and social experiences. According to Lakoff and Johnson, when attempting to make sense of abstract, intangible phenomena, we draw from embodied experiences and look to concrete entities to serve as cognitive representatives.[53] Conceptual metaphors map a target domain (i.e., the conceptual domain that we seek to understand) by the source domain (i.e., the conceptual domain from which we draw metaphorical expressions); in other words, metaphors map meaning from one knowledge domain on to another. This mapping process organises and conceptualises information and properties in domains and 'models' used in reasoning and acting as 'image-schemas'.[54] An example of an image-schema is 'IDEAS ARE OBJECTS', where the source frame is OBJECT and the target frame is IDEA. In mapping these two domains, the

---

53   Lakoff and Johnson's theory of conceptual metaphor posits that the nature of human cognition is metaphorical, and that all knowledge emerges as a result of embodied physical and social experiences (Lakoff and Johnson 1980). Similar findings have been documented in other disciplines: see Levinson (2003) for language and cognition and for clinical psychology, an overview is in Tversky (2019).

54   This idea paves the way for recent discussion on computational models. See for example: Veale and Keane (1992a); Veale, Shutova and Beigman Klebanov (2016); Way (1991); Weiner (1984). A comparable concept "map schemata" is used in cartography, see MacEachren (2004).

conceptual metaphor gives rise to a series of entailed metaphors, such as 'THINKING IS MANIPULATING OBJECTS' or 'UNDERSTANDING IS GRASPING' and so on. In this way, the image-schema, emerging from utterances, enables us to comprehend and express intangible matters.

The risk and the limits of this approach are the potential for confusing the content of a metaphor with the intended effect of a metaphor, and in a top-down approach which radicalises the focus on thought/ abstraction/image-schemas (Zoltán 2008), neglecting the linguistic dimension/words/objects and cultural experience:

> Metaphor is centrally a matter of thought, not just words. Metaphorical language is a reflection/expression/translation/transmediation/ mediation of metaphorical thought. Metaphorical thought, in the form of cross-domain mappings is primary; metaphorical language is secondary. (Lakoff and Johnson 1999, p. 123)

At this point it is important to underline that the approach to conceptual metaphors should not be reduced to the unidirectionality (namely from concrete to abstract) but should be better understood in its bidirectionality and processuality. We should note that a conceptual approach also includes another kind of mapping, and in this case, it could be better to talk about conceptual integration or blending (Fauconnier and Turner 1998; 2002). The concept of blending treats metaphors as conceptual rather than a purely linguistic phenomenon; it involves systematic projection of language, imagery and inferential structure between conceptual domains, but it includes an entrenched conceptual relationship. Conceptual metaphor theory is primarily concerned with metaphoric associations between concepts, and blending theory focuses on the ability to combine elements from conceptualisations into new and meaningful ones.[55] In these views, metaphors are not only carriers of meaning, but actually construct meaning itself.

An epistemology of modelling even in the metaphorical dimension in DH must depart from the specificity of its objects of study. The understanding of the nature of objects of experience in science and in the humanities has evolved substantially in the Western tradition from Galileo onward (Floridi 2011; Bod 2013; Marras 2013). Partially due to this evolution, it can be stated that in DH:

---

55 See Grady, Oakley, Coulson (1999).

[...] the objects that take part in an act of modelling [...] feature both an element of *factuality* (an experienced substance) and one of *fictionality* (they presuppose some rules of artifice). This implies that in a DH modelling activity, a process of making explicit both components and their interaction is paramount. (Ciula and Marras 2018, p. 38)

To *create* models we need to *formulate,* in the sense of giving a form and of constraining by rules (Morgan 2012) and *operationalise* concepts (see Chapter 3, note 8; see also the examples of "Text Mining as Knowledge Process and Argamon: Burrows' Delta Formula" in Chapter 5), is a process of formalisation[56] (i.e. to give a form, a schema, or a formal deductive frame, see the example "Text Sequence Formula" in Chapter 5). Expressions, each with a certain form, are generated as part of this modelling process and hence will also constitute part of its documentation. When these formulation and operationalisation processes are based on multiple (often interdisciplinary), rather than single pre-existing conceptualisations or models, they are documented in some form via computational tools and other artefacts.

2.2 Metaphorical Models

Metaphors integrate both linguistic expressions and conceptual mappings and visualisation[57] (Marras 2017; 2013); they describe novelties and facilitate the understanding and interpretation of theories. This expansive and heuristic force has made metaphorical language particularly suitable and fruitful in modelling activities and in science generally. Recognising this force contributes also to overcoming the distinction between a rhetorical use of metaphors and a cognitive one. Moreover, metaphors function as a vehicle to understand scholarly theories. Since the mid-twentieth century, philosophers have accepted that metaphor and analogy permeate all discourses, are fundamental to human thought, and provide a basis for mental leaps (Black 1962; Goswami 1992; Johnson 1981; Lakoff and Johnson 1980; Schön 1983).[58] For

---

56 For the process of formalisation see for example: Zimmermann, Ley, Budanov, Voitsekhovitch (2002).
57 Shiffrin and Boerne (2004); an historical overview on metaphor and conceptual mapping is found in Trim (2011), Parts I and IV.
58 Note that rhetorical treatises, as well as classical Renaissance tradition authors (e.g., Pellegrini, Pallavicino, Tesauro) advocated the complementarity of rhetoric

example, machine metaphors are still deeply rooted in Western culture. Their (directly observable) interacting parts and causal operations are used as the most powerful model for explaining the patterns underlying natural events and they became one of the most used conceptual metaphors in the history of science and philosophy (Haken et al. 1985). The concept of machine is frequently used to interpret complex systems in nature and in society.[59] For example, in biology, living creatures have long been described through metaphors of machinery and computation: 'bioengineering', 'genes as code' or 'biological chassis' (Vaage 2020). Comparably, we see the use of fluid mechanics to explicate and describe electric energy (Harré 1995, pp. 289-308).[60]

Both metaphors and analogies are central to Western scientific thought. Analogies are more specific than metaphors and both are largely used in everyday communication and reasoning (McCarty 2015). Consequently, researchers have been and still are interested in the form and function of analogy and metaphor in learning (and teaching) science, in how they can be used to promote higher-level thinking and yield new tools for advancing science education research.[61] Analogy can be distinguished from metaphor in the sense that in a metaphor,

---

and dialectics. Focusing on the rhetorical notion of ingegno, these authors stress its cognitive aspect, suggesting the existence of a specific intellectual role of the imagination that cannot be reduced either to pure eloquence or to pure logic, therefore the use of natural language's resources becomes fundamental. It is in this context that the intersection between the theory of language and the theory of knowledge takes place – an intersection in which the metaphorical praxis is a crucial, albeit so far neglected, component.

59   Haken, Karlqvist, Svedin (1993), see Introduction, pp. 2-4. For the clock metaphor in science see Pulaczewska 1999, pp. 163-168. These views on metaphor are, for example, quoted in a letter published in the *Journal of Natural Philosophy, Chemistry and the Arts* in 1805, p. 8, mentioning the Scottish philosopher Dugalad Steward: "Now, it is pretty obvious, that the terms power, force, &c. when used in mechanical science are purely metaphorical; for, as Professor Dugald Steward remarks, (Elements of the Philosophy of the Human Mind [1792], p. 202) 'All the languages which have hitherto existed in the world, have derived their origin from popular use; and their application to philosophical [and that includes scientific, BN] purposes was altogether out of the view of those men who first employed them.' Language commenced amongst simple men, who had little, if any acquaintance with what is now called science....". This comment refers to a debate that had lasted for decades on the scientific status of the common language and on the heuristic potential of metaphors as they are linked to ordinary language.

60   See also Harré 1960 and 1970; Bailer-Jones 2000, pp. 181-198; Gentner and Gentner 1983; Gentner 1983.

61   See for example Bonderup Dohn 2018.

A is said to be B (a meaning is created out of this comparison), while in an analogy, *A is like B* (an explicit comparison is made between two things).[62] Both have been largely used by scientists in building the foundations of experimental and theoretical sciences, in representing and describing a domain, and in promoting understanding of scientific investigations (Marras 2006).[63] Indeed, as recognised for decades now, a metaphor, given its cognitive and creative resonance, is much more than an episodic linguistic phenomenon and is not a mere linguistic embellishment. In addition, basic conceptual metaphors are never fully cashed out in a non-metaphorical language; in other words, it is rare that basic conceptual metaphors shaping our scientific language and rooted in the tradition of thought are 'retranslated' into their literary meaning. For example, consider the case of the concept of genes as "blueprints" in molecular biology. This metaphor was not deemed adequate for conceptualising and guiding the recent research and advances in scientific understanding by some biologists who rejected the blueprint metaphor for the nature of genes; as Barbara Katz Rothman suggests, "recipes" are more accurate for conceptualising gene-environment interactions.[64]

The predominant tendency of seeing precise definitions of all terms as *a sine qua non* for rigorous scientific and philosophical discourse strives to minimise the use of tropes to a role as mere ornamental or 'eloquence' devices.[65] Unlike formal languages, natural languages evolve and tropes play a central role in semantic evolution, their productive role, in turn, is the essential background against which rigorous formal definitions can be engendered. In this way, rather than being strictly separated, formal

---

62   See Chapter 5; McGann 2014; Gentner 1982.
63   Taylor and Dewsbury 2018.
64   See Condit, Bates, Galloway, Givens, Haynie, Jordan, Stables, West 2002; Taylor and Dewsbury 2001.
65   In the twentieth century the point of departure from the discussion of scientific models as metaphors can be traced back to Max Black's interaction view of metaphor (1962) and Mary Hesse's seminal work *Models and Analogies in Science* (1966). For a discussion on metaphor and thought, see the contributions collected in Ortony (1993). "To draw attention to a philosopher's metaphors is to belittle him – like praising a logician for his beautiful handwriting. Addiction to metaphor is held to be illicit, on the principle that whereof one can speak only metaphorically, thereof one ought not to speak at all. ...do not accept the commandment, "Thou shalt not commit metaphor" or assume that metaphor is incompatible with serious thought". (Black 1962, p. 25).

languages and natural languages (including tropes) complement each other in their epistemic functions.

DH is not exempt from metaphorical language, even in the overarching discourse about its definition (i.e., McCarty 2005; Marras 2010). Metaphorical expressiveness constitutes in our view an irreplaceable part of the linguistic lexicon of modelling. As we will see below, metaphors pervade both Computer Science and DH discourse, where technical terminology and metaphors are intertwined, as they do also in the discourse about computing in a wide sense and in other areas of society. In DH, metaphors are also used for structuring concepts at a macro-level, as for example in the use of "infrastructure" and "ecosystem" or the cartography and landscape metaphors used to organise contents and visualise knowledge. Nevertheless, there is something specific related to the modelling of processes and language in DH that we would like to stress here. Indeed, a metaphorical language is not only present in the DH discourse, but it also has a heuristic function. In the analysis, acquisition, and storage of data, DH applies established techniques also used in other domains where digital tools are used, along with more refined presentation and visualisation methods (i.e. charts, graphs, interactive maps, network analysis, timelines).[66] In both cases the natural language describing and conceptualising the process of modelling should take into account and grasp the interpretative activities at stake (What are the data? How are they created and understood? What is the relationship between sources and data?) as well as the dynamics of the relations between data/objects being analysed/mapped and the model/conceptualisation based on it (see Chapter 3). The interpretative dimension embedded in the modelling process as intended here is also related to some aspects of what is nowadays defined as digital hermeneutics, namely the computer-mediated interpretation and understanding of texts or corpora of texts, or about a text's reading-inspired attitude towards digital elements such as the code (see Chapter 5). The point here is not to attribute to digital technologies an autonomous interpretational agency,[67] but to

---

66   See Thompson 2010, pp. 18-24.
67   See Romele, Severo, Furia (2020): "Would it be possible to pave the same path for hermeneutics, inverting an anthropocentric attitude that has characterised most of its history? Is there any room for what might be called a non-anthropocentric or

foreground the heuristic nature of the process of modelling as well as its contingency, away from a mechanical and positivistic application of technical methods and to preserve the pragmatic aspects of modelling, in research and teaching as well as in community-based activities.

The key point is that metaphors assume a complex role and function and are themselves models of knowledge (or of a specific conceptual space under study). They define what knowledge is, what the approaches to and visions of knowledge being adopted are, and the schemes within which knowledge or a specific concept operates. In short, metaphors generate the cognitive and operational reasoning path. For example, we can identify metaphors that conceptualise a broader disciplinary approach and guide data collection or acquisition (upload, data silos, etc.).

There are many conceptual metaphors used in the domain of knowledge organisation, to model classification and acquisition in DH (as well as science in general): for example, architectural metaphors are used to conceptualise and model information and knowledge in the organisation of libraries (Van Acker and Uyttenhove 2012) and construction of enterprise infrastructures. Improvements and changes are related to the idea of a tree, usually a growing tree, which needs care; specific content and topics are presented in terms of buildings, bricks, milestones, nodes, and nets; the process of acquiring knowledge is described in terms of walkways, paths, and roads, requiring a long journey from darkness to light that can either be straightforward or involve "detours". Or we might mention mapping, which is creating metaphors for representing information. Geography and cartography are not related to a simple enumerative and descriptive approach, but they allow for the possibility of elaborating upon models of representation in which description and discovery are strictly related. Therefore, it should be stressed that as maps are made redundant by new discoveries, mapping knowledge requires new ways of sharing maps and of identifying places by names. Mapping implies and embeds spatial-territorial metaphors in terrestrial and aquatic environments. The presence of these two conceptual domains is evident, for example,

---

posthuman hermeneutics?" See also Capurro (2010). Machine-learning algorithms have already been considered as (responsible) moral agents; see for example the discussion in Floridi and Sanders (2004).

in the contemporary use of the metaphor of navigation and in the spatial terminology used to describe activities related to the web. If we look at the language used for describing these land- (or sea-) scapes, we note a large metaphorical use of marine terms such as the following: *ocean* (the vast amount of information); *navigator, explorer* (tools to navigate the net); *pirates* (who steal intellectual property and illegally download copyrighted materials); *navigating* (accessing sites, searching); *surfing* (moving from node to node in the net); *fishing* (finding data), *hits,* and many others. These metaphors are used in a complementary way to the use of literary terms such as *websites, site maps, IP addresses, visiting sites, following links* (terrestrial), along with the persistence of the use of book metaphors like *webpages* or *browsing.*

Metaphors are also embedded in web interfaces. They shape and orient the presentation of texts, images, access, and queries, and they contribute to the creation of new knowledge. Moreover, interfaces for online access to text may help scholars/users in the interpretation of the documents;[68] in this case, for example, the metaphor of zooming (Armaselu and van den Heuvel 2017) and more generally "optic metaphors"[69] are recurrent. The two metaphorical domains/spaces: tree/terrestrial and sea/aquatic, are the most recurrent scientific metaphors in relation to knowledge (Mazzocchi and Fedeli 2013) and they illustrate the observable change in recent decades of the classification and management of scientific knowledge. They also capture the current interdisciplinary scenario strongly influenced by the adoption of ICT technologies in the sciences, helping us to cope with and to somehow understand its complexity. The new digital means of mapping, accessing, and organising scientific knowledge are more correlated with the properties of aquatic metaphors than with terrestrial ones. Nevertheless, the aquatic and terrestrial metaphorical domains complement each other: beyond these metaphors of knowledge organisation and their related metaphorical fields lies the fundamental leading idea of fluidity, travel, movement, and journey. Independently of the specific grammar of each scientific field and sub-discipline, the complexity of this scenario requires categories and

---

68   See van den Chiel et al. (2011).
69   See Armaselu and van den Heuvel (2017); Armaselu and Florentina (2010). See also McCarty (2012); the reverse telescope was also the title of the AIUCD 2017 Conference (Rome, January 26-28 2017 (https://web.archive.org/web/20191230160752/http://aiucd2017.aiucd.it/).

models capable of describing, interpreting, and organising the many dimensions of scientific knowledge organisation.[70]

If we start to use the aquatic metaphors along with the terrestrial ones, knowledge emerges as a progressive aggregation of many different atomic parts. In turn, each part is a complex, multilayered object, tightly interconnected to a number of other parts, without a directly identifiable *a priori* fixed structure. Wikipedia, and all the "wikis", is one example of the complex, multilayered organisation of knowledge, combined with the complexity of multidisciplinary, scholarly contributions. These aspects rendered Wikipedia an interesting case study for collaborative web-based encyclopaedias as complex networks.

The dynamic set of nets, threads, maps, and links used in digital domains articulate a vocabulary and a use of language able to capture integrated and complementary perspectives, static and structural information, and changes over time and space. This rich and blended use of metaphors invites us to rethink the taxonomy and assessment generally used to classify disciplines and subdisciplines. It is necessary to create innovative environments in which plural access to individual disciplines and topics enables individuals to create, manage, and preserve information in personalised, idiosyncratic spaces.[71] Of course, these are also related to different approaches, methods, tools and areas of application or study: for example, there are digital humanists who apply computational linguistics methods, do quantitative text analysis, and do computational semantics; we have editing scholars who engage with text markup following the Text Encoding Initiative Guidelines (TEI) and abstract model. Software has also been developed to explore

---

70 The most pervasive knowledge metaphors are spatial metaphors (interesting in this regard is a 2012 issue of *Library Trends*, "Information and Space: Analogies and Metaphors", edited by Van Acker and Uyttenhove), and the most common approach used to work on knowledge is to map knowledge. Knowledge in fact is usually mapped, and a map is a metaphor and an analytical tool for writing and reading locations and relations between disciplines, concepts, issues, and terms. We map knowledge as we map the Earth. Otlet (1934) was certainly a pioneer for the use of the map in relation to new technologies and their primitive formulations. But the map, spatial instrument *par excellence*, is a metaphor largely used in the Western philosophical tradition. D'Alembert (1995, p. 157; originally published 1751), for example in the "Preliminary speech" to the *Encyclopédie* said: "and the end of our genealogical distribution (or if you will, our world map) of science and the arts." See van den Heuvel (2015).

71 See Borgman (2003a and 2003b).

and represent current knowledge configurations, i.e., the "Knowledge Atlas"[72], a network of maps, diagrams, texts, peritexts, and perimaps, combined together to describe the space of research in its multifaceted aspects in a sort of "knowledge cartography".[73] Charting, mining, analysing, sorting, enabling navigation, and displaying knowledge are tools and methods used in the mapping of knowledge domains.[74]

Information technologies transform the boundaries of disciplinary research and foster new areas of investigation. This requires people to set flexible tools and services to gather information from multiple sources, and to manipulate them for their own purposes. A deep change occurred in the access to information since Schiffrin and Börner (2004, p. 5183) wrote:

> The changes that are taking place profoundly affect the way we access and use information. Scientists, academics, and librarians have historically worked hard to codify, classify, and organize knowledge, thereby making it useful and accessible. The day is fast approaching when all this knowledge will be coded electronically, but mixed in a vast and largely disorganized and often unreliable sea of mostly recent information. Fishing this sea for desired information is presently no easy task and will continue to increase in difficulty. However, the speed and power of modern computation gives hope that this daunting task can be accomplished. In addition, and perhaps even more important, the new analysis techniques that are being developed to process extremely large databases give promise of revealing implicit knowledge that is presently known only to domain experts, and then only partially.

This process of knowledge organisation, which most recently has been described metaphorically as the emergence of a new landscape,[75] requires a growing ability to access and organise complex information and this landscape metaphor designs the model for a paradigm shift

---

72 See http://www.visualcomplexity.com/vc/project.cfm?id=288.

73 http://www.knowledgecartography.org/

74 See the research carried out on the community of scholars working in the "spatial humanities": http://spatial.scholarslab.org/project/. Spatial humanities is a tentative answer to the necessity of mapping the scenarios and the fields that scholars are currently experiencing. Particularly interesting are Minard's numerous maps from the nineteenth century where he visualises all sorts of data in his "statistical graphics": https://papress.com/products/the-minard-system-the-complete-statistical-graphics-of-charles-joseph-minard.

75 For example: Svensson (2010).

that moves from the dichotomic interplay between bottom-up and top-down approaches to a middle-out model of knowledge; examples include collaborative websites, content management systems, and online reference management services.[76] In a DH context the use of metaphors can have practical outcomes for how data processing, storage, and design are structured, and for how data are presented and interfaces are built (Ciula and Marras 2018).[77] Furthermore, metaphors themselves are models of knowledge and they define the schemes within which specific concepts operate and knowledge is established and expressed (Marras 2017).[78] One example are the metaphors used to represent the relationships between data, information, and knowledge, such as the pyramid of DIKW (Data, Information, Knowledge, Wisdom) or the chain, or the graphs.

2.3 The Factoid Example

An example originally reflected upon in Pasin and Bradley (2015) and Ciula and Marras (2016) comes from DH modelling applied to prosopography, an historical methodology for the study of pre-modern societies to collect systematically and analyse information about individual persons as attested in disparate historical sources. "Factoid" is the name associated with the prosopographical model used in several DH projects based at King's College London and elsewhere since 1995.[79] The name evidently mirrors the "historian's worry" (Bradley and Short

---

76 Cf. Colburn, Shute (2008).
77 A similar approach was used in the establishment of CIDOC-CRM (Conceptual Reference Model) in the museum world, http://cidoc-crm.org, and of LRM in the library world, https://www.ifla.org/publications/node/11412. For the CIDOC CRM see https://cidoc-crm.org/ and for the International Federation of Libraries Associations (IFLA), see https://www.ifla.org/resources/?oPubId=1141.
78 Recent reflections on modelling practices are at the King's Digital Lab (KDL), see Ciula et al. (2023).
79 For a detailed discussion on the digital model and access to the associated semantic web ontology, see Bradley et al. (2020). See also the example of Records in Contexts-Conceptual Model (RiC-CM), which aims to integrate into a single conceptual model the descriptive standards developed over the last two decades by the International Council of Archives, and provide the prerequisites for an application of the semantic web technologies to the archival world. The conceptual model is accompanied by a specific ontology, RiC-O (https://www.ica.org/en/egad-ric-conceptual-model).

2005, p. 8) that what they record as assertions in the historical sources under study are not the same as facts. A factoid is an assertion made by historians (in a DH context, usually a project team) that a source 'S' at location 'L' states something ('F') about person 'P'. It reflects a context-aware approach to history used in prosopographical projects spanning ca. 2000 years of history. The factoid, with appropriate extensions, has been a reusable concept successfully operationalised in DH projects. The historical narratives around which prosopographical studies are built are very nuanced (multidimensional, complex, non-linear), hence not easily translatable to the unambiguous language of databases: "[...] factoid approach can show that formal structuring if designed correctly need not impose, as Veltman implies, a single perspective on the data it models, but is capable of accommodating a range of views from the different sources." (Pasin and Bradley 2015, pp. 89–96). Via its operationalisation, the factoid concept embeds the historical approach being used but also structures the digital resources being produced. The data structure of the factoid model is operationalised as the linking of different sorts of entities (e.g. persons, places, sources, possessions etc.) and was tailored to several project cases.[80]

1. The factoid model can be considered a metaphoric model which structures the digital resources it originates at least on the following three levels (see Pasin and Bradley 2015):

2. Data acquisition, by acting as a guiding metaphor to conceptualise a broader historical approach outlined above and the corresponding data entry;

3. Data storage, by acting as a practical, flexible and sustainable schema for designing databases;

4. Data presentation, by acting as a notion around which to build user interfaces.

Pasin and Bradley (2015) suggest that rather than a systematic application of formal structures to a specific knowledge domain (in this case the prosopography of specific pre-modern societies), the factoid model can rather be considered as a process of conceptualisation and

---

80   See for example Rachel Stone (2014).

formal structuring designed to accommodate a range of views on a certain society from the perspectives of different sources.

DH scholarship requires adaptable models like the factoid model to grasp domain-specific concepts. These models stem from the specificity of DH theories and objects of analysis, as they are seen in the context of specific disciplines in the humanities (mediaeval history, historiography and prosopography in this case) with potential applications beyond those contexts (e.g. modelling historical persons across time and space). They grow more or less organically during the modelling process, in connection to, rather than just as an effect of, the observational contexts in which they are immediately applied (Ciula and Marras 2016).

In highly computational settings, the intrinsically metaphorical component of the DH modeller's use of language – whether verbal, as in documented descriptions of the model, or visual, for example in the forms of diagrams illustrating the model – is what makes the objects generated out of the application of formal and functional languages interpretable in the first place. The act of interpretation is also an act of translation (*transferre*) implying an act of transportation from one language, domain, context, or culture to another. In the perspective we adopt here, the concept of translation is the 'engine' of the modelling process. It allows us to bridge the dichotomy between formal and informal, object and theory, physical and mental. The process of modelling in DH is a translation between domains; it suggests a reconsideration of the notions of faithfulness, adequacy, and equivalence. It contributes to a non-dualistic perspective, to a de-dichotomisation of the polarities between object and subject, *explanans* and *explanandum*, observer and *observatum*.

2.4 The Pragmatic Metaphorical Modelling

To sum up, a multilayered notion of metaphor is particularly productive in understanding acts of modelling as non-restrictive. The process of signification within which modelling activities operate implies translation, negotiation and transformation of meaning, which will be discussed further in Chapters 3 and 4 and exemplified in Chapter 5. Operationalisation formalises models into, for example, programming language source code and software components, but the process of abstraction of target historical and cultural objects or complex phenomena into rule-based procedures is contingent and cannot be reduced to strict formalisation only. It is an aim in the development of DH software that the models be formalised to a level where they can be implemented and usable, e.g., as software modules, but still respect enough of the variation, peculiarity, and context awareness of the data to make them adequate to address research questions in the humanities. This is an example of the trade-off between computability and acceptance of the complexity of modelling targets that we find in all scholarly and scientific modelling. Furthermore, the notion of metaphor and the metaphorical conceptual modelling we use does not correspond simply to the use of a metaphor in an analogy-based model, but it merges different aspects: cognitive, conceptual, heuristic, relational, and metalinguistic; indeed, in DH modelling, as elsewhere, metaphors work transversally at the experimental, theoretical and practical levels. We can therefore list a few points to sum up the characteristics of metaphorical modelling:

- Metaphors assume a complex role and function. Metaphors themselves are models of knowledge and define what knowledge is, what the approaches to and visions of knowledge being adopted are, and the schemes within which knowledge or a specific concept operates.[81]

- Metaphors enable the grasping of the unknown via what is known, both by making implicit knowledge explicit and by drawing on unexpected connections with other semantic domains. For example, in a DH context, the process of abstraction (which is usually called 'analysis' or 'design') translates the idiosyncratic data of interest into thematic clusters and categories, which in turn can be used to make sense of, classify and eventually ingest new data.

- Metaphors define their own semantic fields, which have the potential to expand across related domains. In a DH context these have practical implications, for example with respect to

---

81   In the area of knowledge management, computer systems are often claimed to store and manipulate knowledge. It is central to the argument here that this is a related, yet different meaning of the word 'knowledge' from that we use when we describe metaphors as models of knowledge. Metaphors have a privileged relationship to human knowledge and meaning that knowledge management systems lack.

how data is processed and stored, and is used when designing data models, data presentations, and interfaces; very often the labelling of entities and their relations makes use of the semantic fields opened by guiding modelling metaphors.

- Metaphors structure meaning and senses. In a DH context, this is where data-model and data-structure (also at the level of presentation of the data) are organised and expressed by a metaphor. So for example, a hierarchical object oriented model will define a specific idea of relationships between entities, including inheritance of properties. A relational model expresses the connections between entities differently from a graph model, even if, at some level, the "same" system (logical model) can be represented using either type of implementation (physical model).

- Metaphors lead narratives and reshape their contexts of production and use. In a DH context, the metaphorical language used in a project influences the core data and software structures as well as the presentation of the data and the design of interfaces. Of course, it also influences the narratives in more traditional publication formats, partly directly, and partly through the implemented systems.

As noted in Chapter 1, pragmatic modelling is conceived as being anchored in theory and language, and implies at least a solid understanding of the objects being modelled as complex objects, for which both elements of *factuality* and *fictionality* must be made explicit along with an adequate language to theorise and inform the practice of modelling in DH (see Chapter 3). In contrast with the life sciences and physical sciences, objects being modelled in the humanities are usually cultural constructs (whether artefacts or concepts) made by humans. The importance of metaphors in structuring knowledge and hence in modelling processes in DH can explain the integration of practices of 'analogue' modelling with practices of modelling oriented towards a digital implementation.

Furthermore, a theorisation and a reflection on metaphorical language in modelling can explain how patterns and/or principles are formalised by accounting for the integration of practices of 'analogue' modelling with practices of modelling oriented towards a digital implementation. As discussed in Chapter 1, pragmatic modelling is also intended as a research and learning strategy that takes into account the complex intellectual, social, and cultural dimensions within which DH operates. Metaphors, in terms of their cognitive and structural power, can help us to rethink disciplinary borders and reshape the terms of a debate about the nature of scholarly research, evaluation, and publication related to new knowledge organisation. A metaphorical pragmatic vision of modelling implies awareness of the complexity of the objects being studied and is therefore needed in order to further explain how it is possible to imply the multiple perspectives of analysis under which models are studied (meta-modelling) and clarify some recurring conceptual schemes in structuring knowledge (metaphorical language). Moreover, it clarifies how the manipulability of models is achieved via heuristic processes of formalisation (models are made computable) and translation (models take the form of media products).

3. Modelling as Semiotic Process[82]

3.1 Introducing a Semiotic Framework

Digital Humanities (DH) is a field of research engaged in exploring how humanities scholarship is transformed and extended by the digital and *vice versa*. This mutual transformation and extension concerns tools (technology) as well as epistemologies (how we come to know). One of the core practices of DH research is modelling (McCarty 2005, pp. 20-72; Buzzetti 2002; Flanders and Jannidis 2015; 2018), which implies the translation of complex systems of knowledge into models to be manipulated (processed) computationally.[83]

In this chapter we contextualise DH practices within a semiotic conceptualisation of modelling adapted from Kralemann and Lattmann (2013) and complemented by intermedia theories on iconicity (Elleström 2013). Despite being neglected or relatively unexplored in DH, a semiotic framework allows us to see modelling primarily as a strategy to make sense (signification) via practical thinking (creating and manipulating models). From a semiotic perspective, modelling is a process of signification enacting a triadic cooperation between object, *representamen* (form of a sign) and *interpreter* (*significate* outcome of a sign or the thing that is signified). A semiotic framework is therefore instrumental in stressing that modelling and models are dynamic by

---

82 This chapter is built extensively on: Ciula and Eide (2017) and Ciula and Marras (2018).

83 From 2009 to 2013 the working group "Reference Curriculum for the Digital Humanities" worked towards defining a common methodological core for the field. In essence, it identified exactly these two aspects as core areas that are central to all work in DH. First, "modelling" is defined as making explicit and computable research questions, their domains and pertinent data, and second "formalisation" as finding algorithms and software solutions to process these models and their data. For more details see Sahle (2013, p. 20).

   https://doi.org/10.11647/OBP.0369.03

nature and to understand modelling as an open process in renewed terms. Referring to Peirce's classification of hypoicons,[84] in this chapter we will reflect on some DH examples of modelling in the form of images, diagrams and metaphors. We claim that a semiotic understanding of modelling could ultimately allow us to further investigate the duality of object vs. model (as well as sign vs. context). This is central to the overall argument of the book, as outlined in the previous chapter where we proposed to consider modelling as a creative and pragmatic process of thinking and reasoning in which metaphors assume a central role and meaning is negotiated through the creation and manipulation of external representations combined with an imaginative and faceted use of formal and informal languages.

This chapter has two parts: in the first part (Section 3.2), some core concepts around the ontology and epistemology of modelling are introduced to explain the argument which follows; in the second part (Section 3.3), DH and semiotics are put in dialogue with one another to discuss what a semiotic model of modelling entails in relation to two other central concepts, namely iconicity and reasoning.

3.2 Modelling as a Process of Signification

As discussed in Chapter 1 and in Ciula et al. (2018), the complexity of the concept of modelling is not only the result of decades of theory and centuries of practices in modelling, but is deeply embedded in the roots and history of the term itself. Therefore, it is not surprising that there are multiple, often discipline-dependent definitions of modelling.

In the last two decades there has been a significant development of theory (with due connections to interdisciplinary research e.g. in McCarty 2005; 2009) that complements the practice-based tradition of DH as a field. The practice of modelling in DH is mainly theorised

---

84 'Hypoicon' is a technical term introduced by Peirce in order to define 'iconic signs/representamen' which rely on shared rules to be decoded and understood as distinct from 'pure icons' (which, if that were possible, could be understood without referring to any cultural or conventional rules): "But a sign may be iconic, that is, may represent its object mainly by its similarity, no matter what its mode of being. If a substantive be wanted, an iconic *representamen* may be termed a hypoicon. Any material image, as a painting, is largely conventional in its mode of representation; but in itself, without legend or label it may be called a hypoicon" (2.276).

around understandings of modelling adopted in the techno-sciences and computer science in particular (Flanders and Jannidis 2018; Mahr 2009). This theory builds especially on an analytical understanding of modelling inherited from computer science (e.g., the practice of data modelling instrumental to system development), but also more widely on the consideration that modelling is an heuristic strategy of coming to know, which spans multiple scientific cultures and epistemic traditions. Recently, model-making was theorised within a semiotic framework, whereby modelling is presented as a process of signification (semiotic process of meaning-making; see Kralemann and Lattmann 2013; Ciula and Marras 2016; Ciula and Eide 2014; 2017).

Taking stock of these approaches and their intersections by modelling, we mean mainly two things:

1. A creative process of thinking and reasoning, where meaning is made and negotiated through the creation and manipulation of external representations;

2. A research strategy intended as a process by which researchers make and manipulate external representations ("imaginary concreta", Godfrey-Smith 2009) to make sense of objects and phenomena (Ciula and Eide 2017, p. i33).

In line with Nersessian's (2008) *continuum* hypothesis adopted in her cognitive-historical account of modelling, (2) (modelling in research and science) is a specification of (1) (modelling in life), in the sense that it is constrained and enhanced by the idiosyncratic contexts and purposes of research endeavours in science and scholarship at large. Figures 3.1 and 3.2 are examples of historical models developed to study molecular structures.

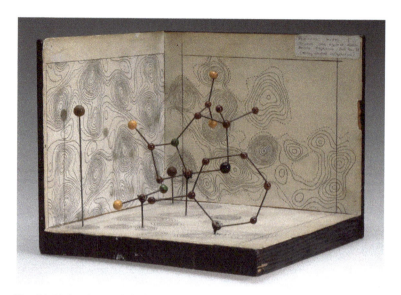

Fig. 3.1 Molecular model of Penicillin by Dorothy Hodgkin, c.1945, who used large punch-card operated tabulators to help analyse the patterns cast by reflected X-rays. Science Museum Group Collection © The Board of Trustees of the Science Museum.

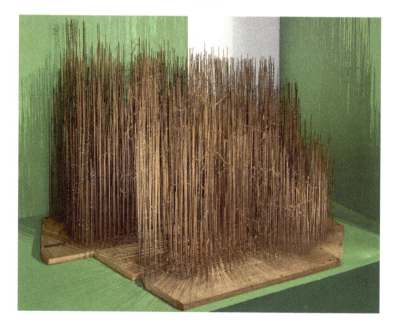

Fig. 3.2 Model of myoglobin ("forest of rods") constructed in 1960 with mecano clips to represent the molecular structure of a compound that stores oxygen in muscles. Science Museum Group Collection © The Board of Trustees of the Science Museum.

At a rather abstract level and in line with sense (1) mentioned above, a model provides a shareable language through which to talk about and understand (hence communicate, as we will see in Chapter 4) existing or possible realities. Historical analysis of scientific practices backs up this understanding and accounts for model-based reasoning (in sense (2) above) as a social problem-solving strategy grounded in everyday signification (sense (1) above). At a more concrete level, cognitive sciences and the philosophy of scientific modelling contribute to the understanding that cognition is distributed and shared through external mediations—of which formal and informal models are but instantiations (see Chapter 4)—in modelling acts of everyday life (1) as well as in scientific contexts (2).

Whether generic as in sense (1) above or more specific as in sense (2), the process of signification that unfolds in modelling activities implies translation and negotiation of meaning. Within a scientific or scholarly context, these translations and negotiations occur both in modelling processes engaged with abstraction of complex phenomena into rule-based procedures — what Gooding (2003, p. 280) calls "reduction" — and in modelling directed at the re-integration of the results of that abstraction or reduction into interpretative frameworks such as explanatory diagrams and data visualisations — what Gooding (2003, p. 278) calls "expansion".

As a process of translation (see Chapter 2 on this concept) and negotiation of meaning, whether in its reductive or expansive role, modelling has therefore both terminological and semiotic implications. In addition, modelling is strictly related to foundational ontological and epistemological issues concerning the nature of the objects being modelled (when we encounter the *model of* an existing object, for example) or 'created' (when we encounter a *model for* an object to be)[85] and the relations between modeller, modelling and model.

---

85 Models for and models of are Janus concepts discussed extensively in the literature (e.g. Geertz 1973 and, in DH literature, McCarty 2005). According to Mahr (2009) they embed relational aspects present in all models, even if the respective emphasis varies: "[F]rom the perspective of creation, the model object may be viewed solely as a model of something, whereas from a perspective of application, it may be viewed solely as a model for something. However, this does not affect the circumstance that the judgement on model-being is justified only if the model object is linked to both constructive relationships, at least in a mental sense" (p. 372).

If we assume that in a humanities research setting, the "Modelling process is part of what is being modelled" (Flanders 2012), it becomes crucial to ask what model of modelling can be 'adequate' to DH. So, for example, if a text (which as an external object can only occur in the form of a document or an acoustic stream) becomes the object 'text' only when we entertain the idea or a representation of a model of it, how that model comes to be is of paramount importance to guide any further analysis or computational processing. It is precisely to address the question of 'what model of modelling can be 'adequate' to DH' that we reflect below on three constitutive elements of humanities research: objects of study (Section 3.2.1) and practices of modelling (Section 3.2.2), followed by a semiotic perspective on modelling acts operating as languages of signification, reasoning, and DH scholarship (Section 3.3).

3.2.1 Factuality and Fictionality of Objects

Rooted in the history of science and philosophy, the discussion concerning the nature of an object of experience has been led by crucial epistemological and philosophical questions such as: How can objects pertaining to the physical world (causally determined) have an effect on the human mind (generally considered as a free entity)? Under which conditions can the existence of external objects be processed?

Within the history of science, the problem is framed as a struggle to reach an accurate representation of nature and to find an adequate language able to provide the link between external objects, belief, and knowledge (Daston 2000). Encompassing discussions spanning from the language of God to the 'language of nature' (Galileo Galilei), natural philosophers have traditionally addressed the problem by questioning the truth and falsity (*in senso lato*) of the objects of scientific knowledge and of the mathematical entities explaining them. Especially in the early modern era in the Western world, the making and the use of microscopes, telescopes and lenses changed the perspective, the distances, and the accessibility to the smallest entities as well as to those objects farthest away. A process of approximation based on analogy, directed at identifying relational abstractions, at mapping the structure of the object, at defining, analysing and measuring, rather than at 'directly' observing objects, was introduced. Consequently, the perception of the nature of the object changed radically from what could be directly measured and touched to something that is somehow 'created' via mediated observations. In early modern times, the object of experience assumed a complex profile and was often conceived as the result of a cultural process and activity[86] (Daston 2000).

A still common and affirmed image of science today is that of an activity based on the experimental gathering of facts, a mathematical modelling of results deduced from facts, and the framing of hypotheses and theories.[87] This process of development and construction of scientific objects is dependent on the intrinsic interweaving of perception, representation and consciousness in a multilayered socio-technical environment; it has its counterpart also in scholarly debates in the humanities, ranging from questions around the nature of consciousness (Palmieri 2012) and the nature of cognition, to the definition of the ethnographic object, just to mention a few.

Semiotics has contributed to this discussion with its theory of signs whereby a semiotic object is generally intended as what a sign represents (or encodes) within a generative interpretative process. Historical, anthropological, sociological and ethnographic disciplines within and outside the humanities consider cultural artefacts - spanning, for example, from weapons to inscriptions, from folk dances to theatre productions—as their objects of analysis. In the last century, material culture approaches have evolved across those disciplines to inform object-based analyses aiming at unpacking artefacts, writing their biographies, their stories, shaped by use ("thick descriptions", Geertz 1973). Within this perspective, artefacts are considered intentional, cultural releasers "animated by their passage through the lives of people" (Graves-Brown 2000). While the total meaning of an artefact might be unattainable, the claim is that there are clues to the ways of thinking and living of those who made it. Similarly, in the realm of textual scholarship, theories connected to material culture approaches, such as the social theory of texts, recognise texts as open objects to be understood in the dynamic

---

86 A multi-disciplinary approach to the early modern world of material culture can be found in: *Early Modern Things: Objects and Their Histories, 1500-1800*, ed. by: Paula Findlen (2012); The point of view of the science in the definition of the objects and the role of the (disappearance) of the observer in Gal and Raz (2012).

87 An example of how such processes can be understood and analysed in the light of media transformations can be found in Chapter 4.

condition of their creation, formulation, and media production (see Chapter 4) on the one hand and their use, reception, and interpretation/ understanding on the other.[88]

DH research[89] has tended to prefer texts as objects of recurrent modelling activities. In line with a social theory approach, by texts we mean dynamic cultural objects (material documents as well as conceptual objects) contingent on the contexts of their production and reading or fruition, expressed in a wide range of manifestations from linear to discontinuous narrative, from manuscripts to printed editions, from analogue codes to digital re-coding, encompassing hybrid modalities.

Taking into consideration the evolution of the understanding of the nature of objects of experience outlined above, the objects that take part in an act of modelling—whether they are the texts (or other objects) being studied or the models being created—feature both an element of factuality (an experienced substance) and one of fictionality (they are construals that presuppose some rules of artifice). This implies that in a DH modelling activity, making explicit both components and their interaction is paramount; this means making explicit the perspectives of study towards the analysis of an object both in interpretative and technical terms. Making explicit the facts of modelling—the contexts in which models are created, how they are used and what forms they take— as well as its fictionality—the constraints of the discipline or knowledge domain that determine the creation and use of those models and the rules of the technical systems according to which they are created and used—go hand in hand. For example, unpacking various theories of text (as exemplified using visual and descriptive languages in Chapter 5) is a way of making explicit the fictionality of a modelling act as important as algorithm criticism. Similarly, describing the material realisation of a model (its size, production process, language of expressions, materials, modalities, context of use) is useful for the observation of its factuality and practical 'affordances' (in the sense used by Norman (1988) as fundamental properties that determine how a model could be used).

---

88 Jerome McGann has articulated this framework extensively over the years and made it relevant also to a DH research context (e.g. McGann 2014).

89 Note that we are implying a DH informed mainly by textual scholarship and *de facto* excluding other traditions, for example in computational archaeology, a community that mostly does not recognise itself under the DH label. Some examples from archaeology are included in Chapter 4.

3.2.2 Modelling Practices

If acts of modelling are used to make sense of our cultural objects, they are meaning-making practices and hence in themselves objects of study for the humanities.[90] Therefore the modelling process can also be posited as something to be modelled, as outlined above.

Modelling is considered to be one of the core research methodologies in DH, particularly in its earlier incarnation as humanities computing (McCarty 2005).[91] In DH-specific research and teaching, modelling has mainly been embedded within a techno-scientific approach with connections to multifaceted conceptualisations of modelling as used and understood by other disciplines and practices.

In very sketchy and simplified terms: as modellers, we behold a certain understanding of a cultural phenomenon of some sort. By way of (often informal) external models of aspects of such understanding (e.g., sketchy graphical representations such as *ad hoc* diagrams not compliant with formal languages or conventions), formal[92] and computable models of components of that understanding are generated and manipulated in an iterative cycle, which progressively—often via repeated and adjusted trials and errors—make us gain a more nuanced analysis of reduced portions of the phenomenon from which we originally departed. Sometimes the analysis we develop is in conflict with our original takes on that phenomenon. These iterative experimental cycles have been extensively theorised within design and development practices engaged with making things and building methods.[93] In connection with digital

---

90 This is the case if we accept a wide definition of what the objects of study for the humanities at large are: "The humanities study the meaning-making practices of human culture, past and present, focusing on interpretation and critical evaluation, primarily in terms of the individual response and with an ineliminable element of subjectivity." (Small 2013, p. 57).

91 Modelling as a research methodology is deeply intertwined with DH research. Statistical analysis of texts, the development of experimental tools to study visual objects, critical mapping, and many other important parts of DH research all include modelling as an important methodology together with other practices and approaches.

92 As in Chapter 2, we refer to Morgan's definition of 'formal' which she applies to modelling studied within the social science context of economics. Models are formal in at least two senses as proposed by Morgan (2012, pp. 19–20): (1) models give form and shape to ideas; (2) models make ideas rule-bound.

93 For example, in an interactive design context: Cooper, Reinman and Cronin (2007); see the comprehensive overview of process models in design and development by

modelling in literary criticism, Moretti (2013) talks about the well-known process of 'operationalisation', whereby concepts of humanistic inquiry (e.g., Hegelian pathos in Greek tragedies) are literally operationalised, made measurable, hence creating empirical objects of study which bear theoretical consequences for the discipline of literary study as a whole. Bode (2020, p. 100) enriches the discussion further by stating that in quantitative literary studies "modeling is the means by which literary concepts and artefacts are both made computable and computed".

The epistemic value of modelling in research is ascribed in particular to the operationalisation aspects of modelling. The reconceptualisation of a theory used in a specific field can occur via the process of making humanistic objects or phenomena of computable enquiry; in parallel, during modelling interactions, the computational methods themselves are subject to critique (e.g., in the form of algorithmic criticisms), to phases of refining and re-building, as part of one or more modelling cycles. A pragmatic approach to modelling practices accounts for different levels of analysis and for the recognition of gaps and bias (Bode 2020) embedded in the operationalisation (inevitably a reduction) of a theory or a conceptual device, but also in the construction of datasets (inevitably partial) and of the models used to compute them.

A domain often used to explain modelling practices in DH is digital textual editing. In this context, one might adopt the Ordered Hierarchy of Content Objects (OHCO) model combined with a Text Encoding Initiative (TEI) document abstract model and schema (if unfamiliar with this, see "The OCHO Model" in Chapter 5). During the modelling process itself, the OHCO model as well as the TEI categorisations might be questioned deeply, for example, because of their inadequateness to represent the modeller's theory of the historical documents at hand or because of the constraints the models force on the specific objects of interest:

> [The modeller] will most likely go back and forth in her modelling efforts to match – based on her knowledge and scholarly language – what she would like to elicit in the document (e.g. the organisation of the diplomatic formulas, the occurrence of names of witnesses in certain locations in the document, the abbreviations occurring in the

---

Wynn and Clarkson (2018).

date clauses) with the formal hierarchical structure proposed by one or more of the TEI guidelines chapters on the encoding of primary sources. Once this mapping reaches a certain stability and she is able to actually process that model, her interpretative activity will likely have to zoom in and out of these manifestations (e.g. between single cases and emerging patterns). She will often puzzle over exceptions that will allow her to iteratively refine the original mapping or require a total rethinking of categories and of the OHCO model being adopted. (Ciula and Marras 2016)

We shall add that even in empirical, technical, or highly implementation-focused settings, formal (e.g. computationally rule-bound) and informal (e.g. narrative, story-based) models coexist and interact to give sense to our modelling efforts.[94] For example, while parts of the documentation to accompany code for a computational implementation has the main purpose of making the source code understandable in a narrow sense, best practices in documentation aim also at making the system understandable in the context of specific use cases, in the relevant research setting and activities. This sort of documentation is expressed mainly in informal language. Ciula et al. (2023) illustrated how modelling can occur at every phase of the Software Development Lifecycle in a Research Software Engineering DH laboratory and across its operational methods of design (or designing), building, maintaining and monitoring (Smithies and Ciula 2020). They showcase how in that setting, one of the core functions of modelling practices is "to support the translations of cycles of analysis and design". Building on the idea in Génova et al. (2009) of modelling activities as trajectories in the multidimensional space along the axes of purpose, reality and abstraction, the examples of modelling practices they bring to the fore are "all but linear", evolve organically and intersubjectively with the agency of multiple actors (team members and project partners) and the mediation of a diversity of languages of expression. The resulting models are "artefacts of different kinds including but not limited to

---

94 For an in-depth discussion on the role of formal models and stories in economics, see Morgan and Knuuttila (2012). In computer science and user-centred design, the methodology connected to user's stories is an example of a similar phenomenon. For reflections on modelling iterations combining different levels of formality in a DH research software engineering context, see Ciula et al. (2023).

computational models" expressed via "verbal descriptions, graphical representations following more or less standardised conventions, code":

> Each modelling cycle produces one or more models which can contribute to bridging building phases and increments (analysts ← models → developers ← models → designers). This process is far from linear and unidirectional. Its epistemological value can be limited to one role (for example an analyst sketches a model of a domain of knowledge for her own understanding and to inform requirement elicitation at a later stage), to more than one role within the engineering team or indeed to the overall research team including partners outside KDL. It facilitates communication, shared understanding and ultimately the building of a final product charged with meaning sedimented in more or less ephemeral intermediary products (widely defined here as models). More often than not, models are also shared outside the research team of a project with other users and researchers (e.g. in focus groups and workshops as part of user research and testing or dissemination activities). (Ciula et al. 2023, p. 271)

Modelling is a pragmatic activity framed within the complex cognitive, social, and cultural functioning of DH practices affected by cross-linguistic and interdisciplinary dimensions. As introduced in Chapters 1, 2 and further discussed in Section. 3.3 and elsewhere (Ciula and Marras 2016), a pragmatic stance highlights how the relational and dynamic aspects of modelling operate. Pragmatic modelling is anchored to theory and language, while at the same time claiming indeterminacy and some level of independence from both.

3.3 Semiotics of Modelling in DH

In this section we would like to draw attention to some key intersections between DH and semiotics and to how, in some cases, semiotic conceptual tools applied and used in a DH context acquire a specific meaning. In addition to modelling itself, at least two key cross concepts emerge as particularly relevant, namely iconicity and reasoning.

Recently, Kralemann and Lattmann (2013) proposed a semiotic model of modelling which they claim pertains to modelling in the sciences as well as in life more generally (semiosis). We maintain that DH practices of modelling can also be contextualised within this semiotic conceptualisation of modelling, albeit complemented by additional semiotic and intermedia theories on iconicity (see Chapter 4) as well as a pragmatic understanding of the importance of a creative use of language in modelling. As discussed in Chapter 1, a pragmatic understanding of modelling, as practised in DH research, can facilitate the recognition that modelling operates within relational and dynamic cycles which are elicited via negotiations over the use of modelling languages (e.g., by renaming categories of analysis or adopting neologisms).

Considering modelling as a process of signification and reasoning in action does not mean that we leave aside its role in human-machine communication, or its implementation-oriented purpose of creating working digital artefacts in software-intensive DH research.[95] Contextualising modelling within a semiotic framework is an attempt to provide a wider framework of analysis to account for the multiple facets that modelling takes in a DH context, from the translation of concepts into formulas (see for example "Argamon: Burrows' Delta Formula" in Chapter 5), to the use of metaphors in constructing a project language; from the integration of design workflows into evolutionary development of a technical solution, to the construction of a narrative used to make sense of a clustering graph. A view of modelling as a meaning-making process sees very different yet integrated workflows included in the remit of modelling acts and, consequently, diverse populations of models ranging from conceptual schemes describing and depicting a theory (as amply exemplified in Chapter 5) to artefacts resulting from data modelling and interface design activities.

The challenge is therefore to see whether modelling intended as a sense-making strategy (signification) via practical thinking (creating and manipulating models) is an adequate lens through which to study modelling as research and teaching strategies in DH and to complement other perspectives, for example in the philosophy of computing or software engineering.[96]

---

95 On Software Intensive Research in DH, see Smithies (2017), pp. 113–151.

96 See for example Guarino, Guizzardi, Mylopoulos (2019) and Mayr and Thalheim (2021) as recent excellent references on conceptual modelling in these respective areas.

3.3.1 Models as Signs and Grades of Iconicity

Modelling as a general strategy of creative reasoning and as a scientific methodology has been fruitfully related to the semiotic concept of iconicity as a form of extended similarity (Kralemann and Lattmann 2013; Ljungberg 2018; Lattmann 2018). The semiotic theory proposed by Peirce identifies three types of signs based on the relationship between the object and the sign:[97] symbols (e.g. conventional names in lexicons of languages used to denote objects via arbitrary association), icons (e.g. onomatopoeic words such as 'splash'), and indexes (signs used to point directly to their meaning, such as 'there'). The general semiotic meaning of iconicity is resemblance or analogy between the form of a sign (*representamen*, source) and its object (target):

> Representation based on resemblance generally falls under the heading of 'iconicity'. When something is understood to be a sign of something else because of shared, similar qualities, it is referred to as an iconic sign. (Elleström 2013, p. 95)

The discussion on iconicity and modes of reasoning is one of the leading themes in semiotics since its beginnings in Peirce's theory and is still the subject of ongoing interdisciplinary inquiry (Giardino and Greenberg 2015): "it is by icons only that we really reason" (Peirce 1933, CP 4.127 [1893]). Kralemann and Lattmann (2013, pp. 3399–3400) claim that models are icons, because the dominant relationship with the objects they represent is one of similarity, as shown in Fig. 3.3. In Peircean theory, such an iconic relationship of similarity is what makes icons signify. Icons act as signs based on how the relation of similarity is enacted: via simple qualities of their own in the case of images; via analogous relations between parts and whole and between parts in the case of diagrams; via parallelism of qualities with something else in the case of metaphors (Olteanu 2015, pp. 77 and 193).

Different grades of iconic similarity between sign and object as theorised by Peirce correspond to three kinds of models in Kralemann and Lattmann:[98]

---

97 Note that there has been a significant development over time in Peirce's thinking, with further extensions of the system presented in very simplified form in this chapter.

98 The distinction between the three types of hypoicons is not ontologically clear-cut. We follow Elleström (2013) amongst others in seeing these types as grades in a

- image-like models, for example, real-life sketches where single qualities such as forms and shapes enable them to act as signs of the original objects they represent in given circumstances;

- relational or structural models, for example, diagrams such as the relation exhibited in the graph of a mathematical equation, where the "interdependence between the structure of the sign and the structure of the object" (Kralemann and Lattmann 2013, p. 3408) enables the modeller to make inferences about the original by manipulating its model;

- metaphor-like models which represent attributes of the original by a non-standard kind of parallelism with something else which generates further models (in this generative sense metaphors are considered meta-models; (Kralemann and Lattmann 2013, p. 3409).

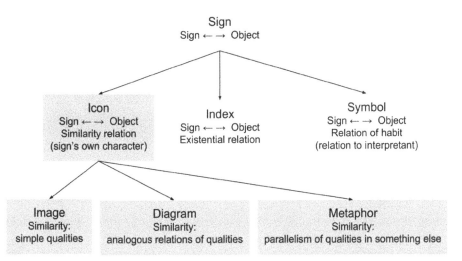

Fig. 3.3 This is a reproduction of Ciula and Eide (2017, Fig. 2), based on Kralemann and Lattmann (2013, Fig. 2). Highlighted in grey is the Peircean sign type of icon associated with models by Kralemann and Lattmann. Based on how the respective similarity relations signify, pure icons or hypoicons are classified further by Peirce into images, diagrams and metaphors.[99]

'continuum' or even as a development rather than separate categories.

99 For a recent detailed and comprehensive overview of Peirce's categories and taxonomy of signs, see Olteanu (2015, pp. 61–79).

In Figure 3.4 below the object is the apple and the models (icons) are the three different apple icons exemplifying the grades of iconicity:

The representamen of an image is perceptually close to its object, which means that the object may be sensuously perceived in much the same way as the representamen (this is a conception that is close to Peirce's own few remarks on the image). The *representamen* of a metaphor is at a greater distance from its object, which means that the interpretation of a metaphor includes one or several cognitive leaps that make the similarity between representamen and object apparent (Ellestrøm 2013, p. 104).

A semiotic understanding of modelling shows clearly how the analytical dichotomy of objects vs. models is useful, but also misleading. Indeed, the semantics of an object changes when the model changes; the meaning of the apple in the metaphorical example is different from the apple in the diagrammatic example. The context of the interpretation changes the sign, but the sign also changes the context of interpretation. In modelling, ontology (of objects and models) and epistemology (how we know objects via models and modelling) are entangled.

objects and models

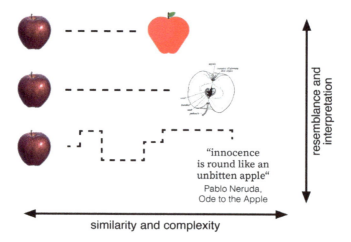

Fig. 3.4 Three grades of iconicity: apple sign in a grocery shop (image), schematic visualisation of the apple in a botanical handbook (diagram), apple as a sign of innocence in a poem (metaphor). We are well aware of the fact that 'the object' (as a concrete exemplary object) on the left of the diagram can itself not be represented in any other way than through 'some' mode of representation (here: photographic).

Elleström claims that Peircean iconicity in the form of images, diagrams and metaphors expresses a *continuum* of interpretative engagements from the immediacy of resemblance to highly creative cognitive leaps (Haley 1988, p. 34). If we accept this view, it follows that grades of iconicity can function as additional operative semiotic components.

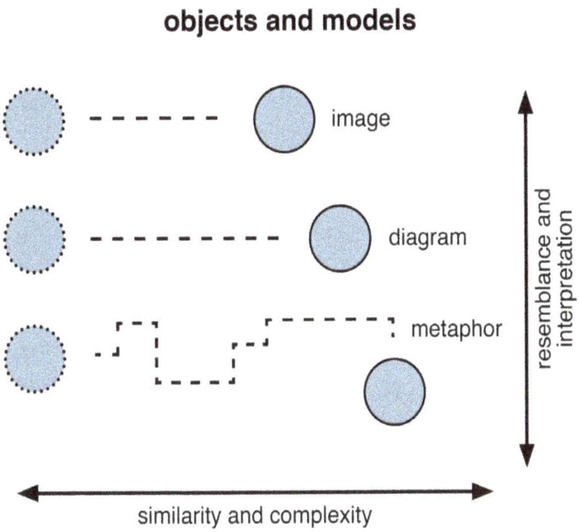

objects and models

Fig. 3.5 Three grades of iconicity: icons form a scale with varying degrees of conceptual complexity. Along the scale of similarity, metaphors feature the greatest 'distance' from their objects compared to the structural similarity of diagrams and the immediate resemblance of images (cf. Ciula and Eide 2017, Fig. 3).

In Peirce's original theory and in Kralemann and Lattmann's theory, signs and models as signs do not act as signs in virtue of themselves. What establishes the model as a sign is the interpretative act of a subject, whether in the role of creator, reader, or user. Each act of modelling connects a model to its interpretation, that is, to its specific semantic content in a given social and institutional context (Kralemann and Lattmann 2013, pp. 3402–3403). The modeller's judgement depends on his or her presuppositions connected to 'theory, language or cultural practice' (Kralemann and Lattmann 2013, p. 3417). Models are contingent. The iconic relationship between the model and the objects or processes being modelled (often referred to as the target of modelling) is partly externally determined (it relies on the similarity between the model and the objects or processes) and partly internally determined (it depends on theory, languages, conventions, scholarly tradition, etc.). Based on this duality, they stress, on the one hand, the subjectively determined dependency of models on prior knowledge and theory (what we above called 'the fictionality' of models) and, on the other, their independence from these in light of the specific conditions of what is being modelled and of what is produced in the act of modelling (which we describe as 'the factuality' of models and objects).

3.3.2 DH Context and Examples

As outlined above, models as signs relate to the interpretation of the objects they represent in different ways, from the immediacy of visual similarity on the image end of the iconic *continuum* to the conceptual similarity on the metaphorical end. In order to understand the inferential, epistemic and heuristic roles of models as sign-relations, one needs to look at both how they come to be—their context, including how we make our prior knowledge explicit and often formalised—and how the similarity with the object is used to create meaning and new knowledge. Of special interest in the discussion around modelling in DH is how iconicity can be used to unpack the nature of the relation established between sign (model) and object (often also referred to as target). As further discussed below, it can be characterised as a sort of 'mirroring relation' based on similarity intended broadly to encompass analogy and metaphorical thinking. When contextualised within modelling practices in DH, iconicity and its associated wide spectrum of graded approaches to reasoning seems particularly productive. Indeed, the notion of iconicity is not only about how models (as signs) appear with respect to similarity to their objects. It also encompasses the possibility (affordances) of reasoning (see Key term Model/s 2) with models while making and manipulating them.

If modelling in DH implies the translation of complex systems of knowledge into models to be processed computationally, it follows that every DH model is a diagram in that it embeds a structure, a formalism of logical and mostly mathematical nature. A digital image or a 3D model of, for instance, a historical monument can act as a surrogate of the monument or a substitute for a physical reconstruction of the real object. A diagrammatic version of the same model could be the mathematical equations underlying the graphical 3D model (Ciula and Eide 2017, p. i39). Furthermore, any operationalisation, as discussed above, formalises models into rules, from algorithms to software systems and applications; however, as discussed in Section 3.3.2, the process of abstraction (Gooding 2003, p. 280) of target objects or complex phenomena into rule-based procedures cannot be reduced to strict formalisation only. Indeed, even if the functioning of the source code of a software system through its compilation into machine code is rule-based, the design methods and data modelling processes, the writing of the source code itself, and the interactions with the interfaces experienced by the user are not. Even more evidently, the re-integration or expansion (Gooding 2003, p. 278) of modelling efforts into interpretative frameworks relies on verbal and visual language to document code and to explain the results of an experiment.[100] The variations between formal representations in modelling processes can be ascribed to a more or less conscious, context-dependent adoption of defined iconic systems of representation "with determinate rules of interpretations" (Giardino and Greenberg 2015, p. 16) and "replete with rules of construction, interpretation, and even proof" (Giardino and Greenberg 2015, p. 12) which can vary in their rigour, explicitness, expressiveness, applicability and readability. Chapter 5 showcases an arbitrary selection of this variation expressed with different iconic systems which range, for example, from "Terras: Levels of Reading" and "Pierazzo: Dimensions of Text" to "Text as Expression and Content", "Stokes: Text as Script", "FRBR Group One: Hierarchy of Textual Entities", "Witmore: Text as a Vector", and "Argamon: Burrows' Delta Formula". While formalisation into computable models is prominent in DH research and teaching, the variation across levels of formality is less specific to DH but endemic to individual and socialised iterative modelling processes. This variation arguably contributes to the epistemic and creative potential of modelling across its contexts of use.

---

100 These are also media transformation processes. What can be expressed varies in the different media, as discussed further in Chapter 4.

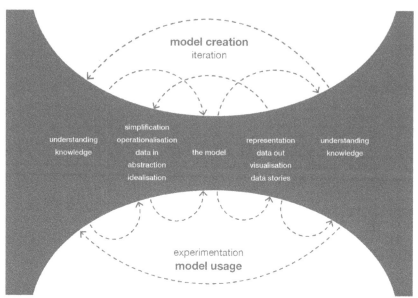

Fig. 3.6 Inspired by Gooding 2003 (Fig. 13.4) and McCarty 2018 (Fig. 1), this graphical model serves to generically illustrate modelling as an iterative process of reduction of complex phenomena to enable quantification and manipulation on the one hand (via simplification, abstraction, etc.) and as a process of expansion (via visualisation of findings, data stories, etc.) to make the models interpretable on the other hand. It shows how computational approaches in DH can be considered analogous to other processes of abstraction, measurement and contextual interpretation in experimental settings, whereby reduction of complexity is followed by expansion in the guise of a double funnel-shaped process. Iterations occur both at the level of creation as well as usage of the model.

Building on previous work (Ciula and Eide 2017; Ciula and Marras 2019) we will exemplify how different grades of iconicity corresponding to the three model types mentioned above, namely image, diagram, and metaphor, can be identified in DH modelling activities. Three specific examples are used below to map Kralemann and Lattmann's trichotomy of models as icons to examples of digital modelling in DH research dealing with historical artefacts. These examples are drawn, respectively, from: (1) digital palaeography research for the image-like model; (2) research on generating digital maps from historical texts for the relational or structural (i.e., diagrammatic) model; (3) a fictitious example of modelling networks of characters (person entities) featuring in art historical objects for the metaphor-like model. These prototypical cases were chosen in order to investigate how model types relate to the cultural objects they represent and how modellers reason with those models.

If we accept Kralemann and Lattmann's argument, it follows that in modelling, we link models to qualities and relationships that may already exist in and between the objects being modelled. Such linking is based on choices which are made for a certain end, informing and motivating the act of modelling. As discussed in Chapter 1 (see also Key term Model/s 5), models are contingent, created in actual scholarly situations of production and use. A model is partially arbitrary in that the same inferences drawn by manipulating one model could have been reached in other ways, for instance using a different model.

In this framework, models operate as sign-functions, initiating a sign-relation (model-relation). To understand their epistemic role, we need to look at both how they came to be and how the similarity relation with the object is realised. By analysing the association of syntactic attributes of the source object with the attributes of the model, we focus here mainly on the latter. The focus on this representational correspondence is part of what we defined above as factuality of the models and is useful in explaining how the similarity relation is realised via the creation of objects to be experienced. To explain the semantics of the model, however, the analysis of the similarity relation needs to be complemented with an analysis of the overall sign relation (looking also at the fictionality of the model) in which production and use of models are enacted. Three examples are discussed below to analyse the three types of sign-functions and relations in a DH context.

Example 1: Image-like model.

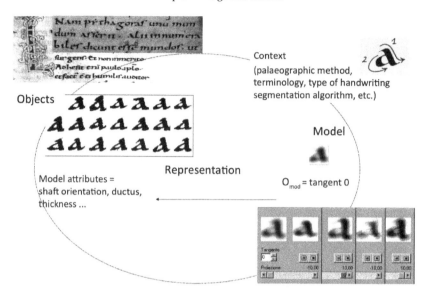

Fig. 3.7 Image-like model. Morphological features of segmented letter forms are modelled into an average morphing letter. Inferences on the manuscript handwriting are based on the analysis of the morphing letter-models by virtue of an 'immediate resemblance' between the original letters and the model.

The first example is taken from digital palaeography research (Ciula 2005; 2009), where the abstract model letter acts as an image-like model of the samples from which it was algorithmically generated. What we can learn about the objects of analysis (the mediaeval handwritten letterforms) depends on the features selected in the modelling process. The inferential power of this specific palaeographical model is mainly based on a strong immediate similarity (or resemblance) between model and object.[101] The 'a' of the model looks very much like the 'a' of the handwriting in the manuscript, they have the same spatiality. The sign-relation hermeneutical power relies, however, on a difference in temporality between object and model. Anchoring the reasoning on

---

101 In Chapter 4, we will see how this could be unpacked further by stating that the similarity is first and foremost of a spatial nature: the handwritten letter is a two-dimensional spatial object as its spatial model is. However, their temporalities are different. We encounter single instances of letters in the manuscript pages, while the morphing models as shown in Fig. 3.7 incorporate variants that can be visualised in sequence.

spatial similarity enables us to go beyond it and learn new things about the object. Indeed, new inferences are fostered by the availability of an 'actual' temporal element in the morphing of the model.[102] While we have to look at all single instances in the manuscript, we get a model which incorporates all variants, and by sliding from left to right, we can 'see' those variants in real time. The object itself, however, is not temporal in this sense. So while the model is an abstraction—a fuzzy image which loses the precision of the instances from which it was generated (the representation is indeed asymmetrical) while maintaining a basic (symmetrical) similarity—it still gains an actual temporal mode that the single-instance objects do not hold. The ability of the modeller and user of the letter models to make inferences is also based on their awareness of scribal variants and of which morphological traits are more revealing of different dating and locations than others. So context and prior knowledge are important, not only for the creation of models but also—not surprisingly—for their use and interpretation.

Example 2: Relational model.

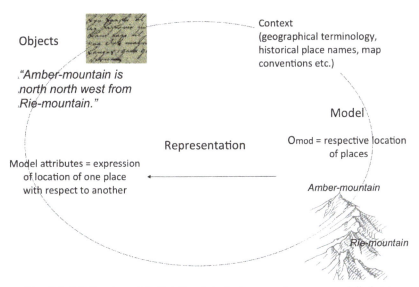

Fig. 3.8 Relational model. Relational textual expressions are modelled into geometrical relations. Inferences on space as expressed in the text are drawn by virtue of the corresponding spatial structure on the map.

---

102 This morphing model expresses a 'less fixed temporal mode' than the object it represents (cf. Chapter 4 Sections 4.2 and 4.4).

The second example is taken from models of landscapes described in historical sources, where information read in texts is modelled in the form of maps (Eide 2015). The inferential power of the model relies on the analogous relational structure between the object (here: text) and the maps as model. When the text says 'A is north of B' it makes a claim about a geometrical relationship between places denoted in the text. A map showing A north of B makes a claim expressing a similar geometrical structure. What new knowledge we can gain about the object of analysis depends very much on the correspondence between the structuring of the textual expressions in the modelling process and the structure of the map model.

The model–object relationship here is not between an expression and a landscape but between two expressions in different media as shown in Fig. 3.8 (more on this in Chapter 4). These media express structural relationships in fundamentally different ways. To see the structural similarity, one needs to understand the written language being used in the text, the schemas used in topographical maps to convey meaning, and to have experience of real landscapes. These elements define the context of the model.

In this example, 'similarity' is not an immediate resemblance. The digital model—the map—looks completely different from the source object—the text. There is, however, a structural similarity with a strong hermeneutical potential between the two. It can be used to reveal gaps; there are things expressed in the text that cannot be put on the map. Examples of things that cannot be expressed include open, borderless expressions such as 'the area north of the river' and ambiguous expressions such as 'Either A or B is on the border'. The analogy breaks at some point; the examples show how the signification of rich expressions in the text cannot be communicated via the structure of the map. This realisation can lead to new knowledge and a need to renegotiate what a text can mean. Based on the structural correspondence and non-correspondence between the virtual geographical space of the text and the geometrical geographical space of the map, the map makes the 'virtual space' 'visible' and in so doing reveals a dissimilarity. As explained in Chapter 4, a virtual space is the space a competent reader can establish in her mind when encountering a text. The dissimilarity between these virtual and visible spaces pinpoints the degree to which the text is spatially underspecified, that is, how open the virtual space of the text is. This forces our understanding of the text to change.

Example 3: Metaphor-like model.

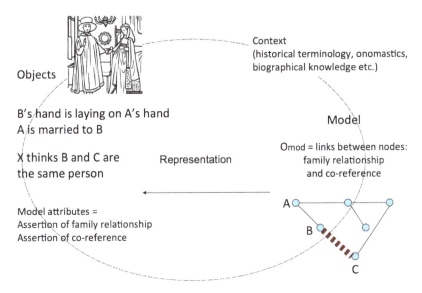

Fig. 3.9 Metaphor-like model. Person names and their relationships as referred to by a document (artwork) are modelled respectively as entities (nodes) and properties connecting them (links). Assertions of co-reference are also modelled as properties connecting entities. Thus the net is used to model social relations as well as assertions about people.

The third example is a network model designed to capture information about references to persons in historical sources. Even if this specific case is fictional (i.e., not used as it is in a research context), similar models are often used in DH research to tie specific objects (e.g., textual passages) to real-world historical entities. It is also used to form parts of co-reference networks (Eide 2009). The use of things shaped as woven networks (e.g., leaf venation, a spider, or a fishing net) or of technical networks (e.g., in telecommunication) to describe relationships between people is metaphorical. The inferential power of the model relies on a deep conceptual similarity between the model (the topography of a network) and the object (e.g., kinship of historical figures). It can generate unexpected connections between the objects it represents, which exist 'only' metaphorically in the context of a network-like model.

In the example in Fig. 3.9, we see the sketch of a historical picture by Jan van Eyck of a woman laying her hand on a man's hand. The literature on readings of this fifteenth-century painting is vast. For example, one interpretation of this image sees it as a claim that the two individuals depicted are married; another suggests more subtly that the joining of arms is rather an act of presentation by the man of the picture of the child to be borne in the woman's womb to the destinatary in the mirror, hence exhibiting the fatherhood of the painter (Lancioni 2012). Whatever the symbolic link between the figures, the physical link (the joint hands) establishes a bond between them. This bond can be associated with, and hence expressed as, a link between two nodes in a network.

There are also other types of links deduced from historical documents that can be expressed using a network model. One is co-reference, which occurs, for instance, when two person references expressed in two different statements, such as names in texts or pictures of identifiable persons, refer to the same person. A source can for instance claim that B, the person in the image, and C, a name in a text, refer to the same person. Such claims of co-reference can also be expressed as links between nodes in a network.

Both these types of links (marriage or child presentation vs. co-reference) are metaphorical. There are no strings attaching occurrences of names referring to the same historical characters to each other, and there are no familial or sentimental connections between historical persons that bear any structural similarity to the topography of a net. The social network in the model is a projection of a conceptual framework. Concepts from our understanding of social relations are combined with a sequential object, such as the textual document attesting to a wedding, and a two-dimensional painting, to form a spatial network model. Aspects of this process can be understood as a complex media transformation from the media products of the basic media types of textual document and painting to a media product of the basic media type of network, as discussed further in Chapter 4 (Section 4.5).

But the development and use of such models change our view of history; we start to see relationships as networks. The network gains hermeneutical power and makes visible as well as quantifiable aspects of a past family network or societal relations. However, different types of relationships (family vs. co-reference) easily lose their particularity and become merely links. The chain of signs becomes greedy and takes over another cognitive space or plane, which in fact deals with relations of a different semantics, in our example moving from the plane of assertion of social relations to the plane of assertion of co-reference.

One meaning can trigger others; for example, the links between entities not only connote a relationship (e.g., kinship), but their length or thickness might also be interpreted as more or less the distance between those entities (i.e., more or less related); in this sense the sign (model) takes on a life of its own. In Chapter 5, this cognitive and creative resonance in the use of metaphorical visual and verbal languages is exemplified by, amongst others, "The Keyhole Model, Frozen Text", "The Staircase of Text", "Text is like the Coast of England", "Text as Kintsugi". A link in the net is just a link, and a documented co-reference relationship becomes a supposed marriage. Context and prior knowledge influence the construction and interpretation of the model, but in turn are also influenced by it.

Reasoning Approaches

Common to all three types of model is the inferential power operating at the interplay between their "intrinsic structure" and their "extrinsic mapping" (Kralemann and Lattmann 2013, p. 3409). Indeed, the features being selected in the modelling process are influenced by contextual elements of different kinds, including hypothesis, scholarly methods and conventions, sample selection, and the technologies being used. However, the inferential and epistemic power of the model relies both on extrinsic and intrinsic aspects of the model relation. In the former case (extrinsic), the examples show us how—sometimes with vivid immediacy—a similarity of existing verifiable qualities between object and model enables DH modellers to manipulate models to make new sense of those objects. In the latter case (intrinsic), the examples show us again how models are conducive to new meaning and further modelling through our exercising of a certain imaginative freedom in selecting salient qualities to model and associating concepts.

These three examples can be matched to the following reasoning approaches:

- Morphing reasoning. In the case of the image-like model, the model is an average morphing letter generated from a semi-automatic process of selection of specific morphological features of segmented letter forms of mediaeval manuscript image samples. Inferences on the manuscript handwriting with respect to dating and localisation were based on the analysis of the morphing letter-models by virtue of an 'immediate resemblance' between the original letters in the manuscripts and the model.

- Corresponding reasoning. In the case of the relational model, relational textual expressions (e.g. location A is north of location B) were modelled into geometrical relations, which in turn were rendered into geographical maps. Inferences on space as expressed in the text were drawn by virtue of the corresponding spatial structure on the map.

- Metaphorical reasoning. In the case of the metaphor-like model, person names and their relationships as referred to by an art historical object (a painting in the example) are the hypothetical salient objects modelled respectively into entities (nodes) and into properties connecting them (links) in a network graph. As it happens in real DH models of social networks, the metaphor-like model of the net was used both to model the morphology of the painting (e.g. B's hand is laid on A's hand), the inferences on social relations (e.g. A is the wife of B) as well as the assertions of co-references about historical people (e.g. A in painting X is the same person as C in the historical document Y). This example illustrates the power of metaphorical models to extend creatively across domains, but also the potential risk of applying them inaccurately to make assumptions spanning instinctively different contexts and semantics.

3.4 What Comes Next

3.4.1 From Icons to Mediated Expressions

While many more angles that intersect DH with semiotics exist in the literature or could be explored, our argument in this chapter has addressed the following basic questions: Do models work as icons? If so, what kind of study of modelling could allow us to overcome the apparently implicit dichotomy between observer and *observatum*, sign and object, subject and object?

To address these questions, we followed two complementary paths: we presented modelling as a form of reasoning in practice, in alignment with Nersessian's (2008) *continuum* hypothesis that modelling in science and scholarship is a special case of modelling strategies that humans adopt in everyday life; the other argument we have followed is based on semiotics, whereby models behave as icons and hence support reasoning based on a faceted notion of similarity. We have shown how both paths can be applied to DH practices and contexts. To this aim, we have placed DH and semiotics in dialogue in order to consider the central concepts of iconicity and reasoning approaches as they relate to modelling in DH. We have contextualised DH practices within a semiotic conceptualisation, which presents modelling primarily as a strategy for making sense (signification) via practical thinking (creating and manipulating models). In particular, we have focused on some aspects highlighted in Kralemann and Lattmann's semiotic theory of models with respect to the role of 'context' in modelling and the nature of the 'representational relation' between objects and models through practical examples. We believe that these two *foci* point to where modelling practices in DH productively meet with a specific semiotic framework. In particular, they are useful in explaining the form or factuality of models (intended both as morphology and topology of models in addition to rule-based formality of models) and the contexts where formal (in the sense of rule-based) modelling practices are integrated with interpretative visual and verbal languages (to take account of the fictionality dimension of models). We contextualised this framework with specific examples of image-like, relational, and metaphor-like modelling in DH research. Prior knowledge is a *sine qua non* to create models in the first place and to use them as interpretative tools with respect to the objects they signify (Ciula and Eide 2014). The relationships between modelling processes and interpretative outcomes are neither mechanical nor directly causal (Ciula and Marras 2016); however, the type of similarity on which modelling relies shapes the interpretative affordances of those 'anchor' models. Modelling processes bring about investments and burdens with respect to our knowledge of the objects we model. In particular, models as signs relate to the interpretation of those objects in different ways, from the immediate similarity on the image end of the iconic *continuum* (Elleström 2013) to the imaginative ramifications of conceptual similarity on the metaphorical end. To understand the inferential, epistemic, and heuristic role of models as sign-relations, we need to look at both the factual and fictional aspects of models, at how they come to be and how the similarity relation with the object is used to create meaning. In summary, studying the "single respects" (Kralemann and Lattmann 2013, p. 3401; in Peircian terms "the ground of the representantem") by which a model becomes a sign for an object is useful for explaining both the logic and syntax of DH models within specific contexts. The next chapter integrates this overarching semiotic perspective on modelling with concepts from intermedia studies. It focuses further on how models are built as well as how the relation with the object is realised by discussing models as media expressions made up of modalities and exploring modelling as a media transformation process. Before we explore these elements further, a few reflections on what we are leaving out are needed.

3.4.2 The Role of Technical Objects

First of all, the selection of salient qualities or features to exhibit in the models plays a crucial role both in the creation and interpretation of these models. However, such selection is not necessarily exclusively human-driven. In DH, we increasingly use computing algorithms to facilitate and even propose such selection, especially in complex environments where variables are manifold and interconnected (e.g. pattern recognition in image processing or textual similarity in stylometry). In deep learning systems, the complexity of, for instance, classification networks goes beyond what can be understood, explained, and made explicit with human methods of analysis because of the reliance on algorithmic modelling and computer systems as *de facto* black boxes even for those who develop them (see Fazi 2021). Our examples have shown how the relationship of iconicity between the model and the object being modelled is partly extrinsically determined (it relies on the similarity between the model and the object) and partly guided by intrinsic choices (it depends on theory, conventions, imaginative associations, and prior knowledge). Indeed, we have shown how the inferential power operates at the interplay between the models' "intrinsic structure" and their "extrinsic mapping" (Kralemann and Lattmann 2013, p. 3409)[103] favouring, however, a human-centred perspective.

From this exploration of the semiotics of models we have gained a different way to look at and analyse models: models as a type of sign mediating between the impressions of experience and freedom of association. While we have left out a more granular view of the socio-technical contexts of these mediations in the examples we used, a holistic, semiotic and pragmatic understanding of modelling imply that humans, technical objects (Smithies, ffrench and Ciula 2023) and computational agents co-exist in, have agency in (Fazi 2021), and therefore co-create this environment.

By reflecting on some DH examples of modelling, we have shown that a semiotic understanding of modelling could ultimately allow us to surpass the duality of object vs. model (as well as sign vs. context). Semiotic concepts applied and used in a DH context acquire a specific 'meaning' and a semiotic approach gives high prominence to a dynamic view of models and modelling which reinstates the understanding of modelling as an open, indeterminate process in renewed terms, as a creative process of thinking and reasoning where meaning is made and negotiated through the creation and manipulation of external (mainly iconic) representations, combined with an imaginative use of formal and informal languages. Different styles of reasoning and modes of thought, including algorithmic modelling, can contribute to this process but their incommensurability in terms of human explanation (Fazi

---

103 A challenge for a research agenda in this area would be to explore how the interplay between intrinsic structures of models (selection of salient qualities) and extrinsic mapping (their iconic ground) develops in the creation of scholarly arguments in the humanities.

2021) remains unresolved and at the moment more or less critically integrated via processes of human signification and interpretability (corresponding to Gooding's expansion efforts). Ultimately, a semiotic approach facilitates the integration of a "techno-scientific" perspective on modelling with a "humanistic" one. Indeed, if acts of modelling—inclusive of the technical apparatus via which they are operationalised and interpreted—revisited from a semiotic perspective are used to make sense of our cultural objects, they are meaning-making practices and hence in themselves objects of study for the humanities.

3.4.3 Variety and Creativity

Compared to other contexts,[104] in DH, 'models and stories' coexist and are not in opposition; formal and experimental modelling techniques are combined with a constructive use of programming, verbal, and visual languages. We touched on how metaphorical modelling can lead to the creation of project narratives in Chapter 2. In Chapter 5 we collected examples of visual models which in some cases inspired, influenced or directly resulted in computational models. In Section 3.2.2 and elsewhere (Ciula et al. 2023), we have reflected on how modelling iterations typically adopt different levels of abstraction and different languages of expression within a collaborative setting such as a research software engineering team. However, a focus on the variety and creativity potential of models is a line of enquiry that would require further research.

---

104 This aligns with the discussion about metaphorical models in the sciences (e.g. Wolynes 2001) and models as fiction in natural science modelling. See Suarez (2009) for an overview with different positions represented.

4. Modelling as Media Transformations

4.1 Models Are Media Products

Models are created and used in modelling activities to express selected aspects of their targets in a specific and usually formalised way. In so far as they are concrete, shareable expressions, what Godfrey-Smith (2009) calls "imaginary *concreta*", they are expressed in some medium. As discussed in Chapters 2 and 3, the concept of translation could be considered the 'engine' of the modelling process, in the sense that the process of signification that unfolds in modelling activities implies translation, negotiation, and transformation of meaning. The process of signification was explained and exemplified in Chapter 3. In this chapter, the mediality of models will be discussed; as Gelfert pointed out, this is central to what we can learn from them:

> If it is indeed the case that specific encounters with models always require some concrete format or representation—be it a set of diagrams scribbled on a piece of paper, or an elaborate three-dimensional model that mimics the 'look and feel' of a target system—what we can learn from a model will fundamentally depend on how we encounter the world through it or in it. (Gelfert 2016, pp. 21–22)

We will base the discussion on the terminology proposed by Lars Elleström (2010; 2014; 2019b) to describe mediated expressions and media transformations. His approach to the study of media does not depart from the concept of media itself, but rather from the building blocks of mediated expressions, that is, from modes and modalities. It gives us a clear language with which to talk about media—a highly useful approach for us. His attempts to base the discussion on a more

    https://doi.org/10.11647/OBP.0369.04

general understanding of media than 'text' and 'reading' fits well into the complexities of models. Indeed, what is often called 'reading,' including of non-textual media products, is by Elleström replaced with 'perception' (Elleström 2018, p. 282, cf. p. 277) to give prominence to the sensory input and its fast interpretative connections.[105] The following three concepts are fundamental to this chapter:

- A media product has a material form and is defined by the processes in which it can be involved—it is necessary for communication to take place. It "enables the complex transfer of cognitive import from one (or several) producer's mind(s) to one (or several) perceiver's mind(s)" (Elleström 2019b, p. 22).[106] The media product has some sort of materiality, but its form does not have to be solid. Some media products may be interactive, evolving partly from or fully based on signals from the perceiver. One and the same mind can be both co-producer and perceiver of a media product. Examples of media products include a public reading of a poem, a drawing of a ship, an essay, a mathematical formula, a comforting smile directed at a nervous presenter, and an art performance.

- A technical medium is "the entity that mediates; it is the material presence that is actually perceived" (Elleström 2014, p. 49). Thus, it is what is used for the actual distribution of a media product. Technical media such as a television screen or a whiteboard can be used for many different expressions but also put limitations on the form of what can be expressed.[107]

---

105 Perception is, like reading, strongly connected to meaning-making. "[A]n act of perception 'between' the media product and the perceiver's mind" is always initiated by the perceiver's sense organs and always, to some extent, followed by and entangled with interpretation. [...] Thus, compared to the potentially extensive act of production, the act of perception is brief and very quickly channelled into interpretation, which of course occurs in the perceiver's mind. Nevertheless, the type, quality, and form of sensory input provided by the media product, and actually taken in by the perceiver's sense organs, are absolutely crucial for the interpretation formed by the perceiver's mind." (Elleström 2018, p. 283).
106 See further elaborations in Elleström (2018; 2019b).
107 In agreement with the long tradition of media studies (see, e.g., McLuhan 2001) and as shown for modelling in Eide (2014), the technical medium also influences the content of what is said.

- Qualified media denote "media categories – artistic and non-artistic – that are historically and communicatively situated, indicating that their properties differ depending on parameters such as time, culture, aesthetic preferences and available technologies" (ibid, p. 19). They include well-known media and genres such as music, painting, and news articles.[108] "A qualified medium is constituted by a cluster of individual media products" (ibid.).

Shareable models are media products. Important parts of the nature and usefulness of models can be fruitfully explored through an approach based on media studies. Our aim in this chapter is to show how this approach can clarify certain aspects of models and modelling, complementary to other approaches used in this book. In order for a model to be shareable it has to be expressed through a medium. This shareable form has a certain configuration, which can be received and understood as meaningful by those involved in modelling acts. Study of these media configurations contributes to a more holistic understanding of modelling in Digital Humanities (DH).

There is no guarantee that the intention of the model is understood by all receivers, or even that a transfer of intention is possible at all in a strict sense. But as explained in Chapter 1, modelling is a pragmatic act in which a model is created by someone with a specific purpose. An intention, in principle and to some extent, is understandable for users of the model, provided that they have the necessary competence and share enough of the cultural background with the creators of the model. This includes speaking the same language in a broad sense and is connected to the concept of 'modelling literacy'.

A popular and well-used model changes over time, both through flexible interaction, as when parts of a stage model used to prepare a theatre performance are being moved, and through permanent modifications, as when new parts are added to the stage model. Studying the model as a media product enables us to understand both processes and products of modelling as creative interactive acts used as a basis for new knowledge—new in the sense of being new for at least some of the participants in the communicative act of sharing models.

---

108 According to Elleström, genres are submedia (2019b, p. 117).

In this chapter we will discuss media modalities and how they influence modelling processes in general, and then illustrate the mediality of models and the analysis of their modalities through a number of examples. We will then proceed to show how the modelling activities can be seen as media transformations.

4.2 Media Modalities

Media modalities[109] is a set of analytical categories which can be used to understand media products better. In Chapter 3 we saw how describing the material realisation of a model (its size, production process, language of expressions, materials, context of use) is useful for observing its factuality and practical affordances. Thus, the focus in this chapter is on the factuality of models, although the entanglement with the fictional aspects (see Chapter 3) will also be important to bear in mind. The four modalities defined in Elleström (2010) give us a language with which to talk about media.[110] Thus the intended use of these categories is explorative rather than prescriptive. All four modalities apply to all media products and there is no assumed development in time from the first modality to the last, either for production or for reception of media products. They are parts of a complex intertwined process of signification. All media products of all types include all four modalities. Each modality has a number of possible modes, that is, a way to be or to do things. For each media product these modes are configured in a specific way for each modality. The level of similarity between these mode configurations for two media products is a criterion for deciding whether they belong to the same qualified and/or technical medium or not.

A media product has a (1) *material* interface which meets the (2) *senses* of the recipient in a (3) *spatiotemporally*-based interpretation leading to a (4) *semiotic* understanding of the meaning of the media product in the specific case under study. The first three modalities are

---

109 This summary is based on Elleström (2010) and Eide (2015).
110 Note that Elleström explicitly uses the word 'model' in his subtitle: "A Model for Understanding Intermedial Relations".

pre-semiotic, in that they lay down the material basis for the meaning-making, which takes place in the semiotically-based understanding of a media product.

1. *The material modality* is "[t]he latent corporeal interface of the medium; where the senses meet the material impact" (Elleström 2010, p. 36). This modality is the potential for media interaction held by all objects, in all forms and formats. It is not the physical substance of the medium, but rather the potential which is in need of something to be expressed, that which is capable of being manifested through it.

    Important modes via which material modality manifests itself include:

    a. Human bodies. Examples include bodies dancing or performing in theatre plays.

    b. Other demarcated materiality. Examples include statues, books, and TV sets.

    c. Not demarcated materiality. Examples include sound and smell.

2. *The sensorial modality* is "[t]he physical and mental acts of perceiving the interface of the medium through the sense faculties" (ibid.). Some sense-data from objects, phenomena, and occurrences meet the receptors in our cells to create sensations, that is, some sort of experienced effect. *The central modes* of this modality are the five senses: seeing, hearing, feeling, tasting, and smelling. In addition to what directly meets the senses, the sensorial modality also includes complex sensory connections, where stimulation of one sense triggers experiences in other senses.

3. *The spatiotemporal modality* is: "[t]he structuring of the sensorial perception of the material interface into experiences and conceptions of space and time" (ibid.). This modality qualifies the connection between the sensorial interaction with material media expressions and the meaning-making in the mind of the receiver. Thus, it is a complex and many-faceted modality. The focus on space and time stems from all media products

being in some sense spatial and temporal. The spatiality of a media product varies greatly, from a free jazz jam or a firework show to a handwritten manuscript or a computer game. In modelling, it is interesting to study how and to what extent the media product changes, and what steers the changes in form. We will come back to this point later, for instance, in the difference between a drawing of a ship and a VR (Virtual Reality) system for the interaction with digital versions of paper puppets.

Space and time can both be manifested in the material interfaces of media products. Examples of space include document pages and dancing bodies, examples of time include the sound of audiobooks and dancing bodies. Time can be more or less fixed, as we saw in Section 3.3.2 with the letter-form model example. In any encounter with media expressions, there is always a cognitive space and a perceptual time. These are structurally similar but quite different from one another as the cognitive space is a space of expression and the perceptual time is the time of experiencing the media product. Virtual space and time can be experienced at a more abstract level than the space and time of the material interface. Examples include a room and the human bodies moving around in it, as they are expressed in a novel. The page of the book or the reading device is the space manifested in the material interface, while the room described in the novel is the virtual space. Creating a model of places in novels, for instance by putting them on a map, is based on the virtual space, not on the space manifested in the material interface. In models based on visual media this can be different.

The spatiotemporal modality involves a transformative process from the materiality of the media product as it is met by our senses in time, to an understanding of the possible (and often intended) space and time of the mediated expression. When played out in narrative, this modality is a complex area strongly linked to the chronotope,[111] where the direct space and time as we experience it through sensorial impressions based on the material interface mix with virtual time and space to create experiences and understanding. The spatiotemporality of the model has

---

111 Bakhtin (1981). See Eide (2015, pp. 195–198) for a discussion related to modelling and media modalities.

an important role in creating the iconographic relationship to the target, as pointed out in Section 3.4.1.

> *The central modes* of this modality are thus:
>
> a. space manifested in the material interface
>
> b. cognitive space (always present)
>
> c. virtual space
>
> d. time manifested in the material interface
>
> e. perceptual time (always present)
>
> f. virtual time

4. *The semiotic modality* is intertwined with and necessary for the other three modalities; it epitomises the meaning-seeking activities of humans as semiotic animals. It is "[t]he creation of meaning in the spatiotemporally conceived medium by way of different sorts of thinking and sign interpretation" (ibid.). The semiotic modality enables sign-grounded meaning which is based on the distinction between symbol, icon, and index that we know from Peirce's semiotics.

> *The three main modes* are
>
> a. convention (symbolic signs)
>
> b. resemblance (iconic signs)
>
> c. contiguity (indexical signs)

The first three modalities (material, sensorial and spatiotemporal) are pre-semiotic and give the material basis for the meaning that emerges in the semiotic modality. The spatiotemporal modality is essential for enabling meaning-making based on the materiality of the media product that meets our senses, whereas the semiotic modality is where the arrangement of signs happens in the process of understanding the media product. An expression will include all four modalities in a form which is specific for that expression, but still classifiable according to general rules. The modes of each of the modalities may or may not be active and are mixed in various combinations. Finding out how the modes mix in the various modalities for a media product can tell us something about the medium to which the product under study belongs.

Doing this more generally for classes of media products is one strategy for better understanding the ontology of qualified media. Following up on the discussion in Chapter 3, an important focus for us is to better understand how applying this classification system to modelling also has an epistemological bearing. In the following section we will outline how this understanding of media can be applied to models and modelling.

Elleström does not dwell on different kinds of signs and we will not systematically distinguish between types of symbolic or indexical signs. However, as discussed in Chapter 3, it is the iconic dimension of models in particular that enables reasoning in an interpretative context (such as the use of models in DH research and teaching). The same distinction across image-like, structural, and metaphorical icons outlined in Chapter 3 is therefore recalled here.

4.3 The Modelling Function

In previous works, including Ciula and Eide (2016), specific areas of model-based research have been explored in order to develop an epistemology of modelling in DH based on analyses of concrete modelling activities. In Chapter 5 of this volume, we illustrate a number of modelling examples taken from the humanities. Many are focused on the modelling of various phenomena of text as a target object, but in order to illustrate how media modalities work, it is also important to extend the diversity of the modalities beyond text.

We assume all models to be media products, used in modelling activities. In a modelling activity one or more modellers (human beings using various tools)[112] use a media product (the model) as a means to: a) understand the targets of the modelling better (model of), and b) create new modelling targets (model for). All modelling includes both a and b, but often focuses more on one than the other.[113] Thus, modelling can be seen as a combination of three elements:

modelling = (modeller+, model (mediaProduct+), target+)

---

112 The role of agency in modelling and the possibility for non-human agent driven modelling was discussed in Section 3.4.2.
113 See Section 3.2 on the model of/model for distinction).

The triadic structure of this definition is in line with Minsky (1965, p. 1).[114] In semiotic terms, the targets align with the object, the media products with the representamen, and the modellers with the interpreter. Modelling is an activity in the creation of models as well as in their use. As pointed out in Chapter 3, what makes the model a sign is the interpretative act of a subject, whether in the role of creator, reader, or user. Modelling is the signification function which defines the relationships in the sign triple. A media product is a model when it takes part in a modelling activity and is perceived as a model. Thus, no object is in itself—disconnected from its use—a model.[115] The targets of modelling processes in DH can feature different levels of complexity. They can include single objects of art or literature as well as large historical and cultural frameworks or concepts such as 'feudalism' or 'text,' cf. the examples in Chapter 5.

Modelling is a pragmatic activity, encompassing the modeller, the tools used, and associated creative processes of selection. Combined approaches from semiotics (see also Chapter 3) and media studies are useful to account for the materiality of modelling and understand both its epistemological and operational aspects. Trying to decide which medium a model belongs to is problematic in many cases—what is the medium of the text wheel in Chapter 5? It consists of some diagrams, some pages of German text and some interpretation and application by others.[116] Can we get anything more fruitful than that out of questioning media modalities of models?

---

114 The definition of a model in Metasystem Transition Theory, http://pespmc1.vub. ac.be/MODEL.html, includes the relationship between the target (the modelled system) and the modelling system (what is here called a media product is the model). However, the representation function found in MTT is here complemented by a modelling agent, the modeller/s. That means that our definition extends MTT by replacing representation as a relationship with an active process of pragmatic modelling, including making choices and learning, as discussed in previous chapters. See Orlandi (2019) for a more general discussion of MTT in relation to digital humanities.

115 This is parallel to media products generally: "As being a media product should be understood as a function rather than an essential property, virtually any material entity can be used as one" (Elleström 2018, p. 281).

116 The text wheel model is—textually and visually—originally developed and explained rather loosely in Sahle (2013) as part of a more general discussion of textuality. As an object of scholarly discourse, it 'took a life of its own' and is more often adopted on the grounds of the reception, adaptation and re-presentation by others, be it through journal articles (Fischer 2012), conference lectures (cf. https://

In Chapter 3, an iconic understanding of modelling is used to better understand the relationship between intrinsic and extrinsic features, related to the interplay between factuality and fictionality in modelling (Section 3.2.1). Indeed, clarifying the relationships between the different configurations of modalities that models assume is crucial to the understanding of modelling as a process of *formation*—as we saw above, this is a process of giving form and it is strongly connected to the affordances of the technical medium and the modalities of the media product, linked to the historical and cultural understanding and habit expressed in qualified media. Understanding the levels of interaction between these configurations is also important, as is understanding aspects of control and how media systems steer modelling processes. There is always mutual control between a tool and a modeller. Echoing early communication and media studies theories (Culkin 1967) which assert a mutual shaping between media and subjects, we control the model we make; yet, we are also controlled by technological affordances of the (formal) language, tools, and systems we use for modelling.

All mediated models are media products in Elleström's terminology. This claim hinges on the concept of mediation and the understanding that anything mediated implies physical carriers and display devices, be it a computer disk, a paper scroll, or two screens emitting light and two loudspeakers producing sound as in the case of VR head-mounted displays (HMDs). Still, modelling understood in this way cannot be disconnected from human thinking activities. Models as media products materialise conceptual objects, enabling sharing and negotiation of them. Indeed, the models-as-media-products are in constant interaction with models-in-the-mind as they mutually shape each other.[117] We find an example of this in Chapter 3, where the combination between a reading of a text as a sequential object and a two-dimensional painting was used to form a mathematical, but also spatial, network model (Section 3.3.2). This is in line with the basic assumptions we saw in Elleström's view on the role of media products as a sort of cognitive transport device used in communication between producing and perceiving human

---

twitter.com/torstenroeder/status/1174223317764661249) or training events (e.g., Ciula 2016).

117 On different materialities of models in life sciences, consider the difference between synthetic models and model organisms, see Knuuttila and Loettgers (2018).

minds,[118] bearing in mind how the modalities of the transport device strongly influence the process. The mediated materiality of the three pre-semiotic modalities meets the meaning-seeking mind of a human (the interpreter) in the semiotic modality.

A digital model can also be experienced in a non-digital (analogue) way, but the manipulation of the digital form and examining how this relates to different modalities lies at the core of digital humanities research. Clarifying the relationships between—and the levels of interaction with—the different configurations of modalities that models assume is crucial to the understanding of modelling as a process of analysis, formalisation and translation.

4.4 Modelling and Media Modalities

Example 1 (Figure 4.1) is a digitised version of a drawing made during the excavation of the ninth-century Oseberg Viking Ship in 1904–1905 (Eide 2018). This is a descriptive or illustrative model of an assumed configuration of the ship in the mound where it was found—but not at the time of the excavation. It is a hypothesis for how the ship was placed originally. It also includes traces of a later event, namely, a mediaeval plundering of the burial. What is shown on the drawing are two different idealised views of a speculative position of the ship that were never seen by the archaeologists doing the excavation but are hypothesised (modelled) based on material evidence. The drawing is a model of two specific events: the burial and the plundering. It is also a model of an idealised state of the buried ship in the mound extended in time from burial via plundering to excavation.

As a digitised version of a paper drawing, the model is easily accessible online and can be studied in great detail. One can zoom in to see the fine details. As the drawing is scaled, one can also read out measurements of the whole as well as the parts of the ship as assumed by the modeller. The texts add a basis for interpreting the drawing based on scholarly assumptions: it is depicting the ship "som det oprindelig maa ha staat i haugen",[119] indicating that the model is well founded but not based on direct visual observation.

---

118 See also Nersessian (2008).
119 "As it originally must have stood in the mound".

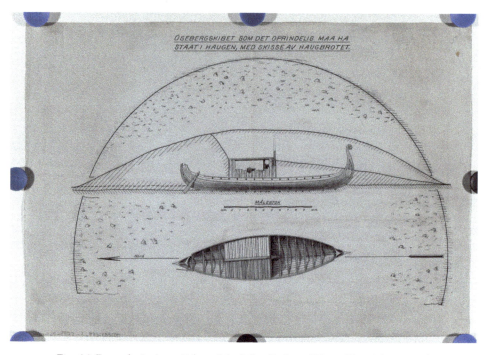

Fig. 4.1 Example 1: A spatial model of the Oseberg Viking Ship. Museum of Cultural History, University of Oslo, Saksnr 05_8823_2_835_C55000.

Example 2 (a fragment is included as Figure 4.2) is a predictive model of the same Viking ship discussed in Example 1 above (Hørte et al. 2005). This so-called strength model of the ship is based on input from many different sources, including 3D scans, manual surveys of damage, testing of material properties of the ship itself, other items uncovered during the excavation, as well as other studies of preservation of wooden constructions as they are known from the literature. The development of the strength model was supported by consultation with experts in archaeology and preservation as well as the skills of the engineers who wrote the report, including extensive experience in writing reports used in the certification of modern ships. The strength model is also called a calculation model, which highlights its dynamic aspects. The model is illustrated in Figure 4.2 reproducing a figure from the report, which "illustrates the implementation of material category 0, 1 and 2 with material properties being assigned to different elements in the model" (Hørte et al. 2006, p. 17).

Category 0: Green ("good")
Category 1: Yellow ("average")
Category 2: Red ("very poor")
Category 3: Black lines (cracks through entire
   thickness)
(White: Cavity/opening where samples for dendrochronological
dating have been removed.)

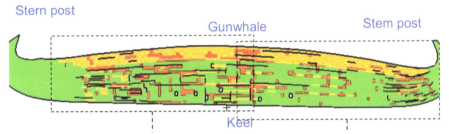

Fig. 4.2 Example 2: "Implementation of material category 0, 1 and 2, plus through-thickness cracks. The figures indicate the position of the ribs" (Hørte et al. 2006, p. 19).

The model is created as a so-called 'element model' consisting of a large number of elements representing parts of the ship, that is, parts of planks and other wooden structures. Each element is spatially connected to other elements; each connection is modelled as a separate link connecting the elements. The model is used to evaluate the current stress situation for the ship and make predictions of its future stability, linked not only to the need for better physical support but also to a possible future movement of the ship. The predictions have been used, also politically, as a basis to justify certain actions. The material form in which the model is made available is a written report with illustrations and mathematical formulas available as a PDF document in two versions: Norwegian and English (ibid.).

Example 3 is the text wheel in Chapter 5. This model tries to explain what text is. The simple starting point takes up the production of texts, where a message is conveyed first through expression in a certain language and then through communication by means of some form of media. Within the modelling process, questions of identity arise: how can a model ensure that it leads to functionally identical or equivalent representations of its target? For the example of text: how can a model guide us in representing a text (the target) so that the result can be accepted as being "the same text" (an instance or application of the model)?

Obviously, the identity criteria depend on single textual features that are claimed to be either essential or arbitrary. To the three understandings of text as content (as message), as verbal expression (in language) or as physical object, further notions can be added. Text as work, as a certain version, or as a complex visual sign can be placed in between these three textual axes. With this, the model names, marks, positions, and relates stances towards text, perspectives on text, and strategies of representation of text.

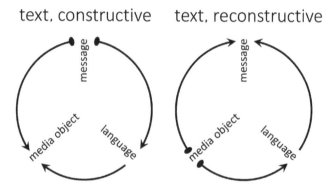

Fig. 4.3 Reduced basic model for the text wheel model.

As a map visually depicting six prominent understandings of text, the model allows for further differentiation and the location of other notions of text. It is basically a map to locate other understandings (or models) of text and thus mainly a metamodel in the sense indicated in the Introduction to this volume. It may conceptually recall/resemble an understanding and model of text which includes different forms of textual representation on a scale between originality (close to the material artefact) and usability (close to the interests of a reader) – see Chapter 5. This model has to be circular in order to connect the two perspectives that are positioned at the extremities of the scale and thus could suggest a naïve understanding which is actually questioned by the model itself: that the message (the semantics) of a text is closely related to its visual appearance when it comes either to the expression or the reception of a textual message. The choice of a circular form of the visual model provokes questions around distance from/to a core essence of text (what is the core?), inner and outer orbits, or the exact place and distance between named positions. In the transformation from verbal description to diagram, it emerges that the model is essentially a map that allows for locating and relating items (which are themselves models); therefore, our literacy in reading diagrams, and indeed our modelling literacy, may also bring about/trigger further unintended (yet potentially productive) interpretations. The text wheel represents a more complex example of models, as media products materialise and interact with conceptual objects. It is further discussed as a use case for modelling studies in Chapter 5.

Example 4 consists of an interactive model of two puppets (the *Frenk* and the *Karagöz* figures (Figures 4.4 and 4.5) used in Turkish shadow theatre. They were initially scanned by Enes Türkoğlu from the original object, held in the Theatre Collection of the University of Cologne. The idea behind the modelling of these objects was to move beyond the traditional digital online museum catalogues, which include descriptions of objects with static illustrations, in order to give prominence to the cultural and expressive context of the objects (Türkoğlu 2019). The Frenk figure (Figure 4.4) is a wannabe European, which is reflected in his looks, based on the historical and cultural context surrounding the development of this specific shadow theatre tradition in Turkey. He is often depicted as greedy and open to lucrative deals. The target of this digital model (i.e., the physical puppet in the museum) has a hidden hand which, with the right level of momentum, can be swung out. This hand is used to quickly close a deal or demand money. This effect does not work with the original figure as the mechanism is partly damaged and interventions to repair it are not feasible due to the fragility of the object.

Since its establishment, the Theatre Collection has sought to act as a laboratory for interaction with real objects connected to theatre. Given the fragility of the objects, this aim is hard to fulfil. In order to re-establish the main original purpose of the collection, it was necessary to create new objects, that is, to transfer their functionality to new objects. The decision was made not to make a physical replica, but rather to establish the new object in another medium.

The model was developed by Enes Türkoğlu in the computer game engine Unity and can also be manipulated using that tool.[120] The simulation was created partly based on the affordances of Unity, the sprite system, and the configurability of that tool. It was also based on scholarly knowledge and personal experience of interacting with such objects in the cultural setting in which they are used.

Figs 4.4 and 4.5 Reproduction of two digitised Turkish shadow puppets in performance modus in Unity. The Frenk figure is to the left and the Karagöz figure to the right.

Employing this platform, the active and creative play with the puppets in shadow theatre can be simulated. This is accomplished not just by modelling the objects themselves, but also by modelling the joints which are the axes of movement. The joints of the figures can be configured and also restricted, as shown via the green semi-circles and circles in Figures 4.4 and 4.5. The development of collision rules, that is, when parts of the figures can move on top of other parts and when interaction leads to a collision and halts movement, was based on knowledge of physical theatre. When two figures interact it has to be decided what is a collision (thus blocked) and what is not. The hands do not collide, which makes handshakes possible. Also the centre of gravity had to be developed through trial and error until a good level of functionality was reached.

Thus, the physical hand movements made by the puppeteer are modelled as a movement steered by the computational input devices.

120 Unity Technologies: Unity Website, 2022, https://unity.com.

In principle, performances can be staged and recorded in Unity, and users can explore different interactions with the puppets in the digital interface. The movements available in Unity include a reconstruction of the hand movements that no longer work in the original due to damage. Thus, the possible interactions of the digital model go beyond what is currently possible with the original, implementing movements assumed to have been possible in the past. Light and sound effects are not included in this model but there are no technical reasons prohibiting them – these are done with other digital models used in theatre studies.

Example 5 is a data model of manuscript KBK 2869, 4°, 2 held by Det Kongelige Bibliotek in Copenhagen, representing a draft of Henrik Ibsen's play *Peer Gynt* (first published in 1867). The focus of the example is the modelling behind the digitally transcribed and encoded text, which is complemented by a scanned facsimile of the manuscript and which is published as part of a digital documentary edition (Pierazzo 2011) on the webpage of the project Henrik Ibsens Skrifter.[121] The name of the actual XML file which can be downloaded from this site is DRVIT_PG PG42869.xml.

Data modelling of textual documents based on the TEI Guidelines[122] is a well-understood process which has been central to discussions on digital scholarly editing for decades. For an overview and visualisation of TEI abstract model, see Chapter 5 ("Digital Humanities: Text according to the TEI"). The adoption of TEI as a modelling practice was also discussed in Section 3.2.2 above. The actual data model for the specific manuscript under examination is expressed by the XML structure found in the document itself, that is, in the file DRVIT_PG PG42869.xml. This structure is in line with a grammar expressed in an XML formal description. The formal description was developed as a customised TEI schema based on TEI P4 in SGML and later converted, first to TEI P4 in XML and then to TEI P5 in XML.

The extended XML schema created by the Henrik Ibsens Skrifter (HIS) project and its concrete implementation in the XML file DRVIT_ PG PG42869.xml can be defined as a TEI conformant schema and a

121 https://www.ibsen.uio.no/DRVIT_PG|PG42869.xhtml.
122 https://tei-c.org/ See also Chapter 5. See for instance the introduction to Flanders and Jannidis (2018) for a summary with further references as well as Ciula and Eide (2014) for some reflections on the historicity of the TEI abstract model.

TEI document, respectively. The model as it is expressed in this XML document is used to show a scholarly understanding of how the draft manuscript for Peer Gynt is written and clarifies the structure of the text of the manuscript as it is understood by the editors. The relationships between this manuscript and the other versions of the text edited by the HIS project can be explored in the user interface which was developed in order to publish the XML document.[123] As of today, the project website presents the model through a text with various typological elements. It features an interactive system which can be used to compare two or more versions of the text, in the form of facsimiles as well as a digital text, and to show details about the complex manuscript. The many alterations of the manuscripts, visible via the interface, are based on what is encoded in the XML document. This is an example of current standard procedure for the publication of complex digital document collections in the form of digital documentary editions (Pierazzo 2011). The structure of the model expressed in the TEI-XML file is in line with the OHCO structure described in more detail in Chapter 5 ("Information Science meets Electronic Texts: Renear et al.") in which encapsulation in an ordered hierarchy is the structural basis for the model ("The OCHO model", Chapter 5).

Figure 4.6 shows a fragment of page 7r of the manuscript, where Peer Gynt and his mother Aase are talking. The fragment is structured as a dramatic text with verse lines, some of which are shared between the speakers. It includes changes to the text within single lines, as well as larger parts that have been removed and replaced. It also includes an added part written in the margin.

The XML coding, partially shown below, includes both standard TEI elements such as 'speaker', 'app', and 'l', and extensions/alterations to TEI which are in the HIS namespace (starting with 'HIS:'). The dramatic structure of speeches and speakers, the line structure with verse lines, as well as the alterations, are all recorded in XML, using XML elements from TEI and from the HIS extension.

---

123 The relationship between the different manuscripts and editions of Peer Gynt was not encoded within the HIS project. Given the differences between the draft manuscript discussed here and a later manuscript called the print manuscript ("Trykkmanuskript", KBK 262, 4°, I.2) used as basis for the first edition, this would be a significant task, which might be enabled by tools which were not available at the time of the project.

Based on the information from the manuscript modelled and expressed in the XML-TEI file as well as the stylesheets used to convert it into HTML, the web system shown in Figure 4.7 is generated. The encoding in the XML files are used to generate the formatting of the dramatic structure as well as the line structure and the modifications made to the manuscript. This is a typical way of using data modelling in order to make editions with TEI-XML. The letters and words found in the manuscript are transcribed into the XML document. The organisation of the play, with verse lines and the dramatic structure, are encoded, and the modifications made to the manuscript are encoded according to criteria and a level of granular detail agreed by the project team. Not all words can be easily read; in some cases, certain letters or words are tagged with 'unclear'.

By modelling the manuscript in this way, the project achieves its operational goals: the text can be presented online and in print with variations; it can be connected to other versions of the same text, and the encoding can be used for some forms of text analysis and indexing. At the same time, the different levels of information are formalised in a way which clarifies certain aspects of how Ibsen wrote his manuscripts, while distinguishing those parts of the manuscripts which at the time of encoding were considered not to fit with any existing elements of TEI (the additional elements preceded by the 'HIS:' prefix). As discussed in Section 3.2.2, the modelling typically takes place in cycles, leading to models fulfilling the ever-refined and often shifting goals of the project, as well as to a deeper understanding of the form and structure of the manuscript and how it establishes meaning. In this case, this process of modelling is not made explicit in the online edition, but is documented in the 'revisionDesc' element in the TEI header of the document through notes about changes, corrections, updates, validation, re-coding, etc.

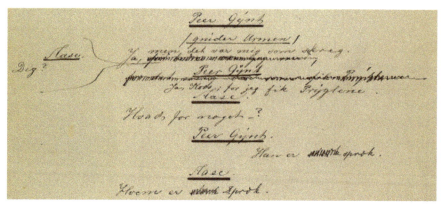

Fig. 4.6 Fragment from KBK 2869, 4°, 2, page 7r.

Part of the XML encoding of the fragment above:

```
<HIS:hisSp who="PEERGYNT">
   <HIS:spOpener>
         <speaker>Peer Gynt</speaker><lb/>
         <HIS:hisStage>(gnider Armen)</HIS:hisStage>
   </HIS:spOpener><lb/>
   <l>Ja,
   <app type="alteration">
         <lem>
               <HIS:hisAdd place="offline">men det var mig som
               skreg.</HIS:hisAdd>
         </lem>
         <HIS:hisRdg>
               <HIS:hisDel rend="overstrike">Gud bedres – var
               jeg med</HIS:hisDel>;
         </HIS:hisRdg>
   </app>
   </l>
</HIS:hisSp>
<HIS:hisAdd place="margin"><lb/>
   <HIS:hisSp who="AASE">
         <HIS:spOpener>
               <speaker>Aase</speaker>.
               </HIS:spOpener><lb/>
               <l part="I">Dig?</l>
   </HIS:hisSp>
</HIS:hisAdd><lb/>
<HIS:hisSp who="PEERGYNT">
```

```
<HIS:hisAdd place="inBetweenLines">
<HIS:spOpener>
        <speaker>Peer Gynt</speaker>
        </HIS:spOpener>
</HIS:hisAdd><lb/>
<app type="alteration">
        <lem>
                <HIS:hisAdd place="infralinear">
                        <l part="F">Ja, Kors; for jeg fik Pryglene.</l>
                </HIS:hisAdd>
        </lem>
        <HIS:hisRdg>
                <l>
                        <HIS:hisDel rend="overstrike">for det
                        <unclear>mig</unclear> var
                        <unclear>som</unclear> fik Pryglene</
                        HIS:hisDel> –</l>
        </HIS:hisRdg>
</app>
</HIS:hisSp>
```

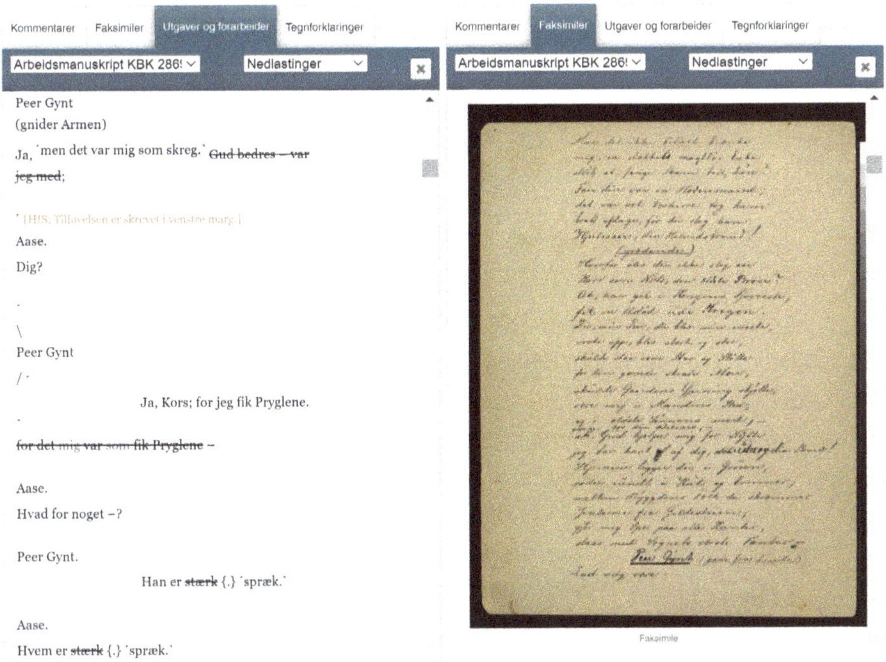

Fig. 4.7 Web version of the fragment from above, showing the text with amendments in a so-called parallel view, with the facsimile next to the text. Note that all parallel views also include the edited text, which is omitted here.

In all these examples, modelling processes resulted in media products, that is, in the models. The technical medium of the model has a number of characteristics which influence what can be expressed by the model, but it does not determine the function and meanings of the model. Indeed, aspects of the qualified medium also have a role in the creation and use of models. The concept of the technical medium relates to the technical limitations and possibilities (affordances) of the model, while the concept of the qualified medium encompasses the cultural expectations, or the modelling literacy, of those creating and using the model. Such expectations are based on our media experience and can always be challenged; technical limitations can change over time too. We see that computer-based models have possibilities for interaction that paper-based models do not have, but also that a 3D model has affordances that a scanned drawing does not have. Thus, the affordances are only partly dependent on whether the media product is digital or not. In what follows, we will organise some of these affordances based on the modalities of the media products.

There is no general quality or value hierarchy in which to order types of models based on their technical or qualified media. The stress model in Example 2 was costly—the job was paid for by the museum—so it is more valuable than the drawing in Example 1 in the sense that the financial cost of making it was higher. However, the drawing provides a clear overview of the burial setting that the stress models do not offer. In cases where such an overview is needed, the drawing has a higher value. As our understanding of modelling as pragmatic acts makes clear, a model value may be assessed in light of the purpose of the modelling activity from which it originated as well as the context of its use.

Models seen as media products are analysable using the system described above. This approach can be used for single models as well as for classes of models. In some cases, classes of models could be linked to or even establish qualified media. In Fig. 4.8, the media modalities are used to analyse and compare the five examples. For each of the modes introduced above, a plus or minus sign indicates whether a modality is present or not, while a pair of parentheses indicates that the presence of that modality is partial or reliant on specific conditions or perspectives. However, presence or lack thereof does not in itself show how a mode functions. The specific ways in which the modes are used will be discussed further below.

Modality	What the modality is	The most important modes of the modality	Oseberg drawing	Predictive model	Text wheel	Puppet in VR	Ibsen manuscript
Material modality	The latent corporeal interface of the medium; where the senses meet the material impact	1. human bodies	–	–	–	–	–
		2. other demarcated materiality	+	+	+	+	+
		3. not demarcated materiality	–	–	–	–	–
Sensorial modality	The physical and mental acts of perceiving the interface of the medium through the sense faculties	1. seeing	+	+	+	+	+
		2. hearing	–	–	–	–	–
		3. feeling	–	–	–	–	–
		4. tasting	–	–	–	–	–
		5. smelling	–	–	–	–	–
Spatiotemporal modality	The structuring of the sensorial perception of the material interface into experiences and conceptions of space and time	1(a) space manifested in the material interface	+	+	+	+	+
		1(b) cognitive space . . .	+	+	+	+	+
		1(c) virtual space	+	+	(–)	+	(+)
		2(a) time manifested in the material interface	–	–	–	+	–
		2(b) perceptual time . . .	+	+	+	+	+
		2(c) virtual time	+	+	–	+	(–)
Semiotic modality	The creation of meaning in the spatiotemporally conceived medium by way of different sorts of thinking and sign interpretation	1. convention (symbolic signs)	+	+	+	+	+
		2. resemblance (iconic signs)	+	+	+	+	+/–
		3. contiguity (indexical signs)	+	(+)	–	(+)	–

Fig 4.8 Overview of the four media modalities (Elleström 2010, p.36) applied to five examples of models.

In the material and sensorial modalities, all five of our examples engage the same modes. All of them are documents on paper or on computer screens and thus have materialities that connect primarily to sight.[124] This is not just common to these five examples: models in many parts of the humanities tend to be conveyed via flat spatial documents consisting of texts, illustrations, etc. This is different in areas such as architecture, design, musicology, theatre, and performance studies. In modelling activities as communicative acts where models are shared and critiqued, moving human bodies and body parts, hands, fingers and human voices have a role too (Nersessian 2008; Ochs 1994). But they are not generally seen as parts of the models. Media configurations such as dancing bodies and live music are important in specific areas such as choreography studies. Such modalities are also used for public outreach and teaching. Turnbull describes scientific modelling as a process of collective visual communication utilising diagrams and other media products. This shows how performative aspects of modelling are parts of the development of models as a social activity more generally.

A hodological understanding underpins two revealing approaches to the role and use of diagrams; one ethnographical and one analytical. Ochs et al. looked at how experimental physicists work collaboratively and found that they use "visual representations and models to create a virtual space in which they can travel as a hybrid construction of themselves and the objects they are attempting to explain and understand" (Ochs et al. 1994, p. 151). Osborn describes diagrams as "tools for learning how to see, how to reason, and how to narrate" (Turnbull 2007, p. 144).

In the spatiotemporal modality there are some differences between our five examples. In all five of the examples, space is manifested in the material interface. In three of the examples virtual spaces are also created, but this is not the case for the Text wheel example, which instead spans a "conceptual space". The occurrence of a virtual space mode can be argued for the Ibsen manuscript example, as XML documents represent

---

124 One could claim that a model with which one can interact on a computer includes, as part of the intended interaction, the sense of feeling one has when using, for instance, a keyboard or a mouse. These devices are however dependent on individual setup and circumstances; issues of accessibility are not really addressed here either. A more rigorous application of the modelling function outlined above would require the examination of the circumstances of the interpreter (e.g., how would a deaf subject experience the modes of these models?).

tree hierarchies with specific culturally and scholarly agreed upon visual forms expressing the structure of the schema and the document. Furthermore, the spaces manifested in the material interfaces and the present virtual spaces are different, in ways that relate strongly to the semiotic aspects. Indeed, the spatiotemporal modality works here as some sort of transfer mechanism from the material modality met by the senses to the meaning.[125]

Only the puppet model has time manifested in its material interface; the other four examples are static documents, with the nuanced case of the web interface for the Ibsen manuscript, which also has interactive elements, manifesting time in the material interface. The time is not fixed in the puppet model nor in the web publication of the manuscript; the movement patterns included in the interfaces of these two models rather imply that movements can be played out in time. While the reading of a PDF document, and indeed of a printed book, includes browsing from page to page, this movement is a fundamental part of the activity of perception and is part of the perceptual time of the spatiotemporal modality only. The interactivity of the VR interface is essential to the perception itself, in that the actual message is changing with the interaction, rather than the interaction being necessary to get to content that is static. The interactivity of the web interface of the manuscript might be less essential to the use of the model (one could still read the static document without engaging with other elements of the interface), but it is still a core aspect of the usability of the system. These movements in time can be seen on a computer screen or, in the case of the puppets, also in a head-mounted display (HMD).

The models afford different types of interaction in time—perceptual time is present in all cases but is experienced and used differently. In virtual time we see further differences. The Oseberg drawing manifests two different periods, as expressed in the caption: the state of the ship in the mound and the shaft used for the plundering, which took place over a much shorter period. The predictive model describes both the past and possible futures of the ship in the museum. Thus, it functions as a model telling stories, also about the future, which creates a virtual time.

---

125 Transfer here does not suggest a movement from modality to modality. The transfer is an analytical link between the two other parts of the modalities (Eide and Schubert 2021, pp. 189-190).

The text wheel refers to textual objects without laying out a specific development over time; therefore, the time here is mainly perceptual. While there might be underlying synchronic aspects, these are not central to the model. The wheel suggests an arbitrary sense of order of reading in time: you start somewhere and then proceed to other places on the wheel, creating and negotiating relationships between the different positions. In fact, the sight of a material object, the reading of words and sentences, and the construction of the meaning of a text based on the reception all happen reciprocally, alternating between senses that are different, but still connected and mutually interacting. In some uses of the wheel, arrows are added to show a specific reading order, indicating an intended direction of the perception. The puppet model has the potential to be used to perform theatre plays. Thus, a non-fixed, virtual time is inherent to the interactive potential of the model. The XML structure of the manuscript model is not in itself time-based, but the order of the XML elements is connected to the time inherent to the narrative.

Semiotically speaking, all of the models use symbolic aspects of signification, both in textual and graphical form. The puppet model also represents personal and cultural aspects of a stereotypical person through visual resemblance and convention, in addition to what digital puppet theatre players manipulating the model can do, for instance, in describing the character as part of the storytelling dimension of the model.

In the Oseberg drawing, the iconic aspects are in some sense creating an image-like link to an assumed reality—but it also has clear structural aspects. The text wheel is a structural icon (a conceptual map or a diagram) with metaphorical aspects. The predictive model expresses complex iconic relationships through its pictorial and diagrammatic representations as well as mathematical formulae. The focus is on structural similarities, but there are also clear image-like aspects, as well as some level of metaphor. We also saw a similar example of structural similarities in the text–map example in Section 3.3.2. The puppets in VR manifest an image-like similarity with the originals, both in the static form and in patterns of movement. The XML structure of the TEI model of the manuscript is iconic to a tree structure and the general abstract structure of a graph.

The scale of the Oseberg drawing enables a map-like index where the metre scale indicates an implicit indexical grid. As for the predictive model, it includes 3D scans and digital photographs which can arguably be seen as indexical (Lister 2007). The modelling of the puppet creates a similar potential for indexicality.

4.5 Modelling as Media Transformations

The perspective taken in the previous section clarifies that the process of modelling is not simply a free selection of features from the target, but rather a process where the chosen set of features in their selection and form are partially steered by the affordances of the medial form used to express the model. The affordances of the medium contribute to the definition of the factual aspects of the model. This is the case for all modelling, also in the sciences, and is closely linked to how tools shape senses, knowledge, and actions. Indeed, the process of creating a mediated model by translating selected aspects from the model target is at the core of research processes, as discussed in Chapter 3.

To get one step further towards an understanding of the mediality of models we can ask how the modelling process itself can be analysed using the language of intermedia theory. Insofar as the target of the model is itself a media product or a technical or qualified medium, the process of modelling can be conceptualised as a media transformation based on the same framework from intermedia studies.

The degree to which it makes sense to see the target of modelling, the objects and/or processes being modelled as some sort of medium varies. In the humanities, we often make models based on one or more expressions which are clearly media products.[126] In those cases, the modelling activity is not just influenced by the modalities of the model but also by the modalities of the target and the relationship between the two sets of modalities. The process of modelling can be seen as an act of translation between two or several media products, or between a

---

126 This is not exclusive to the humanities. Also, in the sciences targets of modelling are selected and understood by human scientists or other agents (cf. Section 3.4.2) and it can be argued that a mediation takes place in this process (Daston 2000). However, a discussion of media products in the context of the targets of scientific models is beyond the scope of this book. See Fanjoy et al. (2012) and Shin et al. (2018) for discussions of the use of diagrams.

qualified medium and a media product: a model can be based on one or more works, or on larger groups of works. In the context of intermedia studies, using the theoretical framework introduced in the beginning of this chapter, such translations are called media transformations (Elleström 2014). While media transformation processes are *studied* in intermedia studies, they are *performed* in scholarly modelling.

Media transformation is not a process of transformation in the sense that the source is being modified into the result, as in the case of transforming a block of marble into a statue. It is rather a process of creating one media product based on aspects taken from either another media product or from a qualified medium. Here, we will introduce a model for media transformation based on Elleström (2014) and its application to modelling in Eide (2015, pp. 195-198) showing how it can be used to better understand modelling.

Media transformations are analytically divided into two groups: transmediation and media representation. Transmediation denotes the creation of an impression in one media expression, the *target*,[127] based on another expression in another medium, the *source*. A typical example is film adaptation, where the narrative structure from, e.g., a novel is recreated in a film. Other examples include a painting of a crying man picking red flowers being reproduced as a scene in a film, without showing the painting itself.

Media representation takes place when one media product is represented in another medium. A typical example is when a painting is seen in a film. Textual descriptions can also be the result of processes of media representations, as we see in the long tradition of ekphrasis, where works of visual art are described in poetic texts. The source of media representation does not have to exist in reality: a novel describing a photograph taken by one of the fictional characters is also an example of media representation. Transmediation and media representation are often mixed, except for in cases of pure media representation, where no transmediation between the two media expressions takes place.

In the context of scholarly and scientific modelling we also find media transformations not directly connected to the target of the modelling

---

127 This is a different use of 'target' than that which we find in discussions about modelling (a 'model target' is intended usually as the object being modelled or in fact as the source of modelling), and elsewhere in this book.

process. Often, modelling includes a series of representational stages. Three examples will show how this works; the first is taken from mathematical modelling, the second from philology, and the third from modelling in media studies. These examples also relate to the discussion about the relationship between reduction and expansion in modelling (Section 3.2) and the integration of formal (rule-based) modelling with interpretative visual and verbal expressions (Section 3.4).

In the work of Gregor Gassner and colleagues on numerical modelling of real-world phenomena,[128] one of the application areas is Tsunami warnings. While this research is based on a natural condition as a starting point, it goes through a number of models, each building on the previous one. This series is an example of what we intend here with modelling as media transformations. The natural phenomena (target) forming the basis for the chain of models is open sea with water, landforms, variation of sea floor elevation, etc. This is expressed scientifically in the form of a physical model of relevant aspects of the environment. A mathematical model is then created, which represents the aspects of the physical model—and thus also of the physical environment being modelled—needed for the research. As this mathematical model cannot be used in real-time simulations while volcanic activity is taking place, a numeric model based on it is made, with enough details to give useful predictions, but still limited enough to make calculations possible within the timeframe. This numeric model is then used in a simulation where predictive results are obtained, which can then be communicated to authorities in charge of counter-measures along the coast in the form of visualisations, accompanied by recommendations in writing. Thus, what we see is a series of models, each based on the previous one, which are all transitive, so that the end result is also a model of the real-world environment and processes therein:

(world →) physical model → mathematical model → numeric model → results from modelling → visualisation

---

128 The description here is taken from a presentation by Gregor Gassner in the lecture series of the Centre for Data and Simulation Science at the University of Cologne on 8 May 2019, http://cds.uni-koeln.de/en. The research which formed the basis of the aspects highlighted here is published in the 2018 PhD thesis of Niklas Wintermeyer, https://kups.ub.uni-koeln.de/9234/.

As in the stress model of the Oseberg ship, the main purpose of this model is to influence future actions.

A visual series of stepwise formalisation, which is basically a media transformation from mediaeval manuscript writing to interpretative and explicit vector graphics (SVG), can be found in an ongoing project of one of the authors (Sahle) shown in Figure 4.9. Here, a representation of Noah's Ark in a manuscript of Peter of Poitiers' *compendium historiae* is converted stepwise to a form which is visually similar (in the sense of image-like resemblance discussed in Chapter 3) but most of all structurally isomorphic. The Ark here is basically and conceptually represented as a 'three-storey-thing' with three top sections (mild animals, humans and birds, wild animals), two mid-sections (store, dump) and one lower (bilge) section and a door (to the left). If formalisation is the distinction between arbitrary and essential features of the target, which is a specific historic media expression in this case, then 'stepwise' involves eliminating, abstracting or normalising specific features or properties one by one. This regards, for example, historic and individual expression and aims at the general conceptual structure which then is valid not only for this manuscript but for the conceptual understanding of the Ark according to certain textual sources.

Fig. 4.9 Critical stepwise formalisation of a diagram of Noah's Ark from Peter of Poitiers, *Compendium Historiae*, here detail from British Library, Ms. Harley 658, fol. 33r (c. 1200/1225).

A similar approach can be observed in so-called critical stepwise formalisation, in which a media expression is studied via the process of adapting it into a new expression in another medium step by step (Eide 2015, in particular Chapter 3). The main structure is in line with what we just observed in the example from mathematical modelling above. The starting point is the media products under study. Based on this starting point, a model is created, and refined through steps which are expressed in different formalisms, until an end result in another medium is created. The application in Eide (2015) was a process of transforming a text to a map, as visualised in Figure 4.10. We see how interpretations of a text fragment are expressed differently in a number of formalisation steps up until the end result, which is a graphical representational expression: a map. A large number of such expressions linked together make up a model of a terrain as it is expressed in a text, with the spatial information in the text as the starting point (or the source in Elleström's terminology) of these transitive modelling steps.

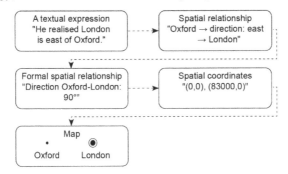

Fig. 4.10 Critical stepwise formalisation example (Eide 2015, p. 43, Fig. 3.1).

Unlike the tsunami warning modelling above, the main aim here is not the end result—the last model—but rather what can be learned from the process. Modelling as media transformation works differently in different research contexts, and the goals can be quite different, but in all cases each of the models is a media product with a set of media modalities different from the models it is based on and from the models based on it, and the process is transitive, so that the end result is taken as a model of the starting point. This does not mean that the process of creating and using such a modelling structure can be seen just as a directed and linear series of stages. According to a media transformation-based view on modelling, each stage can also be seen as part of a larger modelling effort consisting of phases and iterations of reduction and expansions as expressed in Section 3.6.

One important part of such modelling in the humanities, as exemplified in the map example, is to identify and interact critically with aspects of the objects and processes of study that are difficult to formalise. What are meaningful media products for a competent human are symbols to be shuffled for a computer. The lack of understanding on the side of the computer system on which we develop and run our models makes many tasks hard to automate, but can also be seen as a positive affordance in that it has the potential to make the specific steps in the processes of decoding media products more visible to us. The process is often glossed over in human meaning-oriented interaction with media products. Using a computer-based modelling tool, we are forced to make explicit steps that are often glossed over in the internalised processes of establishing meaning that humans apply when they interact with media products.[129] "In digital humanities we exploit the fact that computers are less goal oriented than we are, less framed in sympathetic exchanges with desire for meaning, so they can help us to find other readings than the ones we see" (Eide 2015, p. 57 footnote 24).[130] As pointed out by Gelfert (2016, p. 113), such a view on models as concrete objects is different from seeing models just as mediators, for instance, between theory and data. The mediality and thus also the materiality of models (their factuality) can be used to reason with and learn from in relation to their fictionality and agency, a point also noted by Knuuttila:

> [I]n the recent discussion on models, the earlier emphasis on representation has been replaced by the attempts to approach modelling from a mediative and productive perspective. A central move taken by that approach is to consider models as independent entities that can be used to gain knowledge in a multitude of ways. (Knuuttila 2010, p. 168)

While all humanists engage with digital media products, it is in the digital humanities that the translations from analogue to digital forms and vice versa are problematised in epistemological terms and undertaken with the research aim of operationalising a concept. Seeing modelling as processes of media transformation pinpoints how the epistemological functions are dependent on the media modalities of the models. Where a specific piece of work is located on the scale between mass digitisation and hand-crafted modelling is not just based on technical and logistical possibilities but also on the relationship between the configurations of the media modalities in the technical media. Similarity can vary and it is not the aim here to make clear borders between what is modelling and what is not based on an analysis of the relationship between model and

---

129 There is a long discussion over this aspect of computer use in the DH literature, see, e.g., section V of the TEI Guidelines https://tei-c.org/release/doc/tei-p5-doc/en/html/SG.html, and McCarty (2005, p. 5).

130 This is also related to the discussion of agency in Section 3.4.2.

target. Rather the opposite: the context of a process of the creation of media products, with its operational and epistemological goals, is what characterises it as modelling. The choice of frame of understanding is based on production systems, media modalities, human expertise and choices, and more generally—the context of usage and analysis.

How the media modalities work in a source medium as opposed to in the target medium is important for understanding how a media transformation is influenced by the two media. Media modalities can be used to understand how transformation processes have systematically different affordances based on the configurations of the media modalities in the source and in the target media. These differences can be strongly linked to changes in the material and sensorial modalities, for instance, when written words and graphics are used to express the structures of music as it is found in audio recordings or in graphical markup languages for dance. In other cases, the differences we see in the transformation are mainly connected to the semiotic modality, as in the map example above. A further discussion can be found in Eide and Schubert (2021).

When the material and sensorial modalities are fairly stable between target and model, an integration in the same expression is quite easy, like a map modelling a text or a graph modelling the reproduction of a painting. A transfer between time- and space-based material modalities, on the other hand, can lead to documents with quite different forms, but in such cases content elements can still be translated without too many obstacles, as in the performance of a musical score or the reading aloud of a written text. That said, it is important to remember that all modalities interact in media transformation processes. More research is needed in order to move towards a classification of modelling practices along the lines of media modalities.

4.6 Mediality as Affordances in Modelling

In Chapter 3 we saw how in the example of metaphorical iconicity, model targets of two different media (text and image), complemented by contextual knowledge and other sources, result in a media product of a third medium (network). The relationship between model and model target is complex and evasive, as are the two categories themselves.

Using semiotic and intermedial frameworks, we have a richer language to discuss these concepts. This enrichment, however, does not make the phenomena and the relationships between them simple, easy to formalise, or identical across different concrete cases of modelling. The possibilities in seeing modelling as media transformations are only indicated here. A larger body of material must be studied in order to generalise the patterns we see here into a model of modelling seen as media transformations.

Our aim with this chapter was to reflect on models and modelling by analysing modelling objects and processes with a focus on their materiality as media products. Accounting for media aspects in modelling also allows us to better understand the consequences of positive and negative affordances being added to a model. The media affordances of the mediated models and modelling process include the limitations and possibilities we know from the long history of inter-art studies, with Lessing's "Laokooon" from 1766 as a central work, into the current study of intermediality, as in Elleström's publications cited above: the models are enabled and limited by the available grammar, lexicon, geometry, and other inherent properties (their factuality). These properties vary from expression to expression, but can be grouped and systematised. Elleström's work has given us a language for such a systematisation which we find useful as a complement to the other approaches presented in this book.

The discussion here is linked to the philosophy of technology and the study of how artefacts function. In the case of modelling in DH: The formal rules (e.g., those given by the computational artefacts we use or develop) and the subject matter rules (e.g., those given by a specific field or domain of knowledge), taken together, provide the means of reasoning with a model in DH research and teaching. The understanding of the model as a media product is mainly used to develop a more nuanced understanding of the formal rules expressed as model modalities. Models as concrete forms with an identifiable level of formality provide affordances to the intellectual process by enabling and constraining the development of *what* can be represented and *how* it can be represented.

This is even more evident when immersive systems such as VR are used in modelling. While such technologies are often used for computer games and more generally for art and entertainment, they are also used in simulations with the purpose of training and research. They are already important parts of scholarly modelling, as seen in areas such as medicine, chemistry, archaeology, and theatre studies. In the humanities we tend to make our models by using the modalities we have available for visual expressions based on textual data. Other modalities such as hearing, smell, and touch have been less used even if some areas of research, including musicology and archaeology, regularly use hearing and touch as ways of acquiring knowledge. Smell is also used in some areas within the humanities as well as in the sciences.

Creating an adaptable model of modelling is important not just in order to understand more of modelling as it happens today, but also to understand better how it might develop in the future. Seeing models in light of their mediality is a necessary part of developing such an understanding.

5. Modelling Text: A Case Study[131]

5.1 "Let's Talk about Text"

In this book, we talk about models and the process of modelling in a Digital Humanities (DH) (and that is an interdisciplinary) setting. Observation, description, analysis, and generalisation are some of the methods we have used to reflect on modelling and its practices. To a certain extent, a meta-analysis has to be detached from the deeper discussion of single, concrete models. This tension entails the problem of how to bind the theory work back to the actuality of models. In the previous chapters, we used several examples to explain and illustrate different approaches. But how can we demonstrate that our approach can be observed in models in and modelling of a certain domain in itself? How can we derive theoretical assumptions from the variance of models that concern a common object of study? How can we add a more empirical layer to our research? In contrast to our discursive approach towards modelling, in this chapter we present a limited case study that focuses on examples of models around an arguably singular modelling target: text. Only indirectly does this refer to the modelling process itself. This book has the subtitle "Thinking in Practice". That practice in DH and other fields can mean different things: most of all the practice of developing models by analysing modelling targets and evaluating the applicability of these models for some purpose (like research). This fundamentally iterative process usually does not start from scratch. Rather, it is based on the study of other already existing and established models which have been created in the same

---

131 This chapter was written in collaboration with Nils Geißler. Most drawings were made in collaboration with Julia Sorouri (2017-2019) and Anna Wibbeke (2020-2022).

     https://doi.org/10.11647/OBP.0369.05

or a neighbouring field. The practice of modelling is also a practice of identification and examination of other models as starting points for the particular modelling endeavour as well as points of reference and parts of the terminological and conceptual discourse.

Models are everywhere. In our daily life as well as in all scientific and scholarly domains.[132] With our point of departure in DH, which has traditionally focused on text-based studies, it is natural to start with text itself. 'Text' as an object of study and as a case for modelling is particularly interesting and suited for our purposes because text is (or texts are) a central matter in many scholarly and scientific disciplines as well as a commodity or something that is just used and processed in various fields (see Section 3.2.1 on this). Even disciplines studying other media types, such as art history or musicology, use text as a major tool for describing objects of study, analysing evidence, recording knowledge and publishing results. Indeed, even in research with a focus on non-textual objects, texts are still an important, sometimes dominant, part of what is actually studied or presented. This prevalent focus on texts allows for the observation of interdisciplinary perspectives on text, as well as of different appropriations of (the concept of) text. 'Text' is not only seen very differently in the various academic disciplines but also in their diachronic or isochronic partitions which are often referred to as schools or turns. Text is also handled very differently as an object of study (text as a cultural phenomenon to be observed), as textual content (e.g., linguistic code) or as a tool and technology (text as media). Since the late twentieth century, concepts of 'text' and 'reading' in some disciplines have even left their original scope of oral or written utterances and eventually been expanded to refer to all sorts of cultural objects—to finally end up with the broadest possible: "culture as text".[133]

As we pointed out in this book, in the DH research context, text has been one of the most common objects of modelling activities. Thus, by starting here, we can offer a basis for a wider perspective on how modelling can give us insights into the complex shapes, forms, and the

---

132 On this view see Sahle (2018).

133 The much older idea of 'culture as text' is nowadays most famous through its association with the anthropological view of Clifford Geertz, initially laid out in his chapter "Thick Description: Toward an Interpretive Theory of Culture", in Geertz 1973.

ontological status of text, and thus, on the opportunities and limitations of a model-based approach to studies in the humanities.

'Let's talk about text'. Nearly everybody (at least in academia) seems to talk about text. Or the other way round: nobody talks about text but everybody 'has text'. And nobody talks without text. At least everybody uses text(s). Therefore, everybody must have an idea of what text is. However, beyond the 'natural' treatment or use of text, even if people talk explicitly about text (as a phenomenon), in most cases they do not provide well-structured, formal or definitive definitions of text that could serve as models. Depending on the notion of model, some may say that—until today—there is no definitive model of text at all. Others may claim the reverse: that in every talk about text that is research-oriented and even in every practice of working with text (by description, representation, analysis, processing etc.), there must at least be an implicit model of text. Otherwise, one could not work with text in a rational and intersubjective manner. If that is true, then there are very many text models around. Yet, since they are implicit, it is hard to tell precisely what they are and how they differ from each other.

The nature of a thing determines what can be modelled as properties of that thing. But the perceived nature itself is shaped by the model that we have; properties are identified within the model through the act of modelling (cf. Chapters 2 and 3 of this book). Maybe objects only have these properties once they are declared in a model. One of the strange basic characteristics that text shares with other media objects is its ontological status as an abstract object that is always bound to physical items, as discussed in Section 4.5. In fact, the notions of text that we encounter cover a wide range of views on scales constituted by abstract versus concrete, idealistic versus materialistic, content versus form and other similar conceptual pairs. These rather dichotomising frames of investigation have already generated much heated debate and deserve further diligent differentiation. The basic recurring question in debates on 'text' regarding the nature of the relationships between an abstract object and its material basis is seen in many other modelling domains as well, and pulls us into underlying philosophical reflections. The simple question of whether text is the script that conveys a message or whether text is the message that is conveyed by some document can easily be debunked as too naïve and not very productive. The extreme positions of pure materialism or Platonism in themselves cannot lead to convincing models that would be useful in describing the phenomenon of text or lead to tools for working with texts. This is why the notion of purely material or purely conceptual things is much less productive in a DH context than possible layers in between, and the relations and translations between observable and describable properties of these layers.

Text as a target for modelling shows further interesting aspects, including the differences between and the duality of models of and models for. Sometimes, for instance in cultural history, a description of a text becomes a model of an observable thing in the real world. But in other domains models are built to decode, encode, represent or re-medialise text (as a category) or to make text treatable and processable as a proxy or resource for the analysis of other phenomena such as language, information, or communication. Therefore, some models are descriptive while others are oriented towards the realisation of media processes or the operationalisation of research agendas, or else they describe such operationalisations. Interests in text, and in models derived and deduced from such interests, mostly focus either on the genesis and production as well as reproduction of text, or the reception (including interpretation, understanding and processing) of text. Very few models cover more than one of these perspectives, and it is equally uncommon to explicitly refer to or integrate other models even from the same domain, let alone from other domains. Thus we clearly see the limitations of disciplinarity and purpose-driven investigations (see also Chapter 1 on this). This begs questions about relations, intersections, and the possibilities for overarching approaches. As text is probably the most important interdisciplinary information resource in scholarship and science as well as in our daily interactions, meta-models integrating the different particular views should help in stabilising a common ground for the understanding and employment of textual resources in a world that is increasingly integrated via the ubiquitous availability and reusability of data. Collecting and comparing the many models of text out there makes it clear how models of a certain object or in a certain domain are not able to, or even meant to reach the larger goal of a comprehensive representation and understanding. They are not developed in broader consensus across the single views of different persons, groups, or disciplines, and not developed in a coordinated process. Rather, they have emerged from certain specific fields of interest and application, leading to a significant diversity of model types. While this is normal for our specialised research fields, disciplines and subdisciplines, we (at least in the field of DH) also need more generalised models. With these, we pursue operational as well as non-operational goals: operational because models have to function in an interdisciplinary research agenda, non-operational because we aim to arrive at a deeper understanding of the meaning of — in this case — text. As we have argued throughout the book, these goals are inextricable: the epistemology of modelling is linked to the practice of building models. The examples here are presented with the dual aim of showing the underlying diversity we have described and also pointing towards a possibility for creating more integrative and general meta-models that may relate and map the more specialised models.[134]

Often, 'text' is also discussed in scholarship without any claim of presenting a theory or model of precisely what 'text' is. Still, we assume that one will already have some implicit understanding of text which can in principle be made more explicit. On these processes, from conceptualisations to mental models, see also Section 2.1.[135] In many cases, texts about text are long and complex. Elaborate, sophisticated and differentiated. In this case study we aim to make them comparable, to find connections and differences, and to build bridges. Thus, in translating them into graphical forms of expression, we narrow them down. We select, we extract, we simplify, often quite brutally. The excerpts and the choices are ours! Many readers will disagree with our view on the texts about 'text' that we study; some of which are already canonical. Our goal is not so much to do justice to the full depth of the authors' thoughts and expressions, but rather to create visual versions that (in future work) can be used to establish more general meta-models.

---

134 This follows up on recent work including Patrick Sahle, *Textbegriffe und Recodierung* [notions and recoding of text], Digitale Editionsformen vol. 3, Norderstedt: BoD 2013. This in turn is based on the study of various text models and first attempts for meta-models.

135 We do not trail the question from which we may speak of a model as opposed to other, less formally structured, forms of mental understanding. For a recent detailed discussion on the definition and creation of conceptual models see Guarino, Guizzardi, and Mylopoulos (2019).

This anthology approach can also illustrate a methodology for the development of meta-models.

In some cases, authors already provide visualisations of their own models. How these visualisations relate to their ideas, usually given in primarily textual form, that is, how authors express their ideas additionally through visual representations, is another interesting field of research. In Chapter 1, we talked about a new language for modelling. This refers to the concepts, the terms, and the words we use. But this may as well refer to the visual language of the diagrams that express models. Up to now, we must assume that the process of translation and explanation from verbal to visual in the literature we deal with is largely free of method and theory. Most of the authors we cite are highly skilled at expressing complex ideas through written language. Most of them will not have studied, for example, Bertin (1967)[136] and his fundamental work on diagrammatical design, and are probably not systematically and formally trained in information visualisation and design. Nor are we.

Where authors have included their own visual expression, we have used these. Sometimes we have slightly adapted them to make them fit more appropriately into the format of this book, or we have merged more than one visual expression from the same author. In the majority of cases, however, visual expressions have been created by us based on our own reading and interpretation. They are our graphical expressions of what an author wrote. In intermedia studies, media transformation processes are studied. In transformative digital intermedia studies, media transformation processes are performed, as outlined in Section 4.5. In our visualisations, we also do the latter. Sometimes the authors' verbal models already use a metaphorical language (see Chapter 2.1 on this) that suggests an obvious imagery – as with McGann's "coast of England" or Wenzel's "frozen language". But more often, we have simply created drawings that show our understanding of what authors have expressed in their texts, translating from the verbal to the visual. In doing this, we show the specific medialities of modelling languages

---

136　This book, published in several editions, is also famous in its translations (English: *Semiology of Graphics: Diagrams, Networks, Maps*). It marks the beginning of systematic and interdisciplinary reflection on diagrams as a visual language that has evolved into a robust and sustainable research field in recent years.

and in particular their intermediality (as discussed in Chapter 4). At first, models seem to be "abstract" or purely structural by nature. Still, they always come in some kind of notation and take some kind of form. And these forms, which are languages of expression, vary widely. In the end, formulas, structure diagrams, metaphorical sketches, drawings, narrative texts are always media products (cf. Section 4.1) – how else could models be communicated?

Recalling the approach towards modelling sketched by Gooding (2003) and re-visualised by us in Section 3.3.2, the examples collected here are mainly about the reduction phases in modelling. In our integrative process of collection and visualisation we use the freedom of subjective judgement and visual interpretation to clarify and strengthen the intersections between the different models. In an idealised understanding of our procedure, we unpack the core concepts as they are expressed through the terms used, as well as through the inherent structures and relations in the single models. In this way, parts of certain models reoccur and overlap, paving the way for a broadening of the modelling process and for more comprehensive overarching meta-models. The development of these meta-models is not grounded in a traditional scholarly discourse, in the exchange and weighing of arguments, which would be expressed in the verbal and narrative modes of academic publications. Rather, they are, at least until now, the results of the creative, visual and conceptual synopsis of the many single models at hand. They are also a skilled activity made possible by many years studying and questioning what 'text' really is. They emerge from visual thinking in integrative meta-modelling.

What we present here is a first licentious 'florilegium'. The examples are taken from well-known texts but they could have been chosen differently. There are of course many more implicit and explicit models of text out there. In fact, this compilation is already a selection of a wider collection with further examples that did not make it into the book. Some of our examples are obvious candidates and stand for central and important approaches (such as linguistics as a discipline, FRBR as a fundamental bibliographic ontology or ASCII as a technical format) although even here, the choice of which reference work to use can be disputed. Others are more randomly sampled to show the breadth of the field and the multitude of perspectives and approaches. The compilation might be developed further in the future as there are many more models to be considered.

This chapter is intended to facilitate research into modelling practice in mixed textual-visual forms of expression. We provide basic exemplary material and make a first attempt, mostly abstaining from analysis. We do not really question the nature, the peculiarities, or develop a scholarly system for the relationships between text and visual forms. We do not dwell on the different grades of iconicity of the selected graphical models. We do not categorise or systematise the very different forms of graphical expressions which span from table to diagram, and from formal notation to drawing. We do not systematically analyse the terms used in the models either, and we do not explicitly unpack the implicit assumptions and connotations of specific words. In this sense, our approach is rather on the playful side. Based on some experience in modelling, as well as on studies of 'text' in various forms, but without a stringent methodology, we pick up central words, relations and structures and turn our understanding into some visual expressions. We do this within a formal spatial frame by following a basic typographic rule: each model has to fit an open double page. We take one page for the model as a text–usually represented by a quote, a short summary or a comment–and its bibliographic reference, and one page for each model as a visualisation. With this we do not do justice to the authors and their models. We do not give full accounts of what has been said, we do not situate the models in their historical or disciplinary contexts, we do not talk about the process by which they were shaped on the path from intuitive starting points to sometimes highly elaborated models. Instead, we re-create and re-present these models, simplified and based on our aims for this specific study. We select and extract 'verbal icons' from the texts.

In most cases, these are central quotes from well-known texts. Sometimes it is quite difficult to find an appropriate span of text. Sometimes we give short comments on the quotes; explanatory, contextualising or as a starting point for some sort of dialogue. Sometimes, when we do not have an indicative quote, the comment is all we provide. In some cases, a relevant position for which there is not a single most acknowledged publication, we present it with our own summary statement. As we usually use authors and texts as witnesses for particular standpoints, and as the visualisations discuss bibliographic items, we give the full references on the respective pages instead of compiling them in a common bibliography.

The use case presented here is a random anthology of very different types of visualisations. They range from cartoon-like drawings to info-graphic-like illustrations to formalised diagrams and formulas.[137] We try to illuminate a spectrum of media modalities (Section 4.2) within the range of affordances and limitations of the printed page. We do not address the question of relations between texts and visualisations explicitly, so we do not deal with the nature and properties of these visualisations in a systematic way. Nor do we investigate the various functions of these visualisations in this chapter; specifically, we do not ask in which sense they are explanatory, if they make use of a metaphor, or how they express and show concepts and relations between them. The material presented here may constitute a corpus of objects for further research, but this exceeds the bounds of the present publication.

The use case starts with a model of the album itself. For every 'model', there will be some 'text' on the left and a 'visualisation' on the right. Running page titles indicate the domain of research (left page) and give a description or name for the diagram (right page). These names are either already established, suggest themselves or are our own proposals. The textual side may contain original quotations, for which we provide translations if the original language is not English. To distinguish quotes from translations, comments and explanations, we use two different fonts. On the right page (bottom right) we credit the creators of the figure: family name for those not drawn by us, initials for contributions from Nils Geissler (NG), Julia Sorouri (JS), Anna Wibbeke (AW) and Patrick Sahle (PS).

---

137 Again, this does not lead to any real taxonomy or reflected system. For at least a first attempt to differentiate different forms and terms (like picture versus diagram) see Giardino/Greenberg (2015).

5.2 Text Models: An Album

Domain: specifics

Original quote	Our own translation
Footnotes	
Bibliographic information	

Comments on text or figure

Name of the figure

Figure

Origin

An Introduction: Text as a Word

Text is a common language word. People use it to speak about and point to things. As any other word, it has different meanings in different situations. People use it differently. "The text of this song" means something other than "bring me that text from the library". We use words without the need to strictly define them or model their domain of application because we use them in context. When it comes to scholarship and science, disciplines demand explicitness and therefore engage extensively in modelling what is denoted by words. It is however not uncommon for researchers and scholars to start this process by conceding that the words they model enjoy or suffer from a pre-theoretical use ...

Text: Thought, Spoken and Written

PS, IS

Linguistics: First Impression

"**text** *(n.)* A pre-theoretical term ..."

> Crystal, David. *A [first] Dictionary of Linguistics & Phonetics*, Oxford: Blackwell, 1980, 350 (²1985, ³1991, ³1994, ⁴1996, ⁵2003, ⁶2008).

"Text ist eine vortheoretisch intuitive, weder quantitative noch qualitativ definierte Kategorie sprachlicher Äußerungen von mehr als einem Satz, die sich vorwiegend auf schriftliche Erzeugnisse unterschiedlichster Form und Funktion bezieht."

Text is a pre-theoretic intuitive, neither quantitatively nor qualitatively defined category of verbal expression of more than one sentence that mainly refers to written products of most diverse form and function.

[own translation]

> Horacek, Helmut. 'Text, Diskurs Und Dialog'. In *Computerlinguistik Und Sprachtheorie. Eine Einführung*, edited by Carstensen et al., 2nd ed., 335–347. München: Elsevier, 2004, 335 (¹2001, ³2010).

> Horacek here refers explicitly to Bußmann, Hadumod, ed. Lexikon Der Sprachwissenschaft. 2nd ed. Stuttgart: Alfred Kröner Verlag, 1990, 776 [other editions: ¹1983 (p. 535), ³2002, ⁴2008 (p. 719)] − see below on how the quote does not match exactly.

"Text[: ...] Vortheoretische Bezeichnung formal begrenzter, schriftlicher Äußerungen, die mehr als einen Satz umfassen."

Text: Pre-theoretical term for formally delimited written utterances of more than one sentence.

[own translation]

> Bußmann, Hadumod, ed. *Lexikon der Sprachwissenschaft*. Stuttgart: Kröner ²1990, 776.

The claim that 'text' is a *pre*-theoretical term can get lost in translation (here: from German to English). It seems as if, when talking about text, a theory necessarily evolves...

"text[: ...] Theoretical term of formally limited, mainly written expressions that include more than one sentence."

> Bußmann, Hadumod. *Routledge Dictionary of Language and Linguistics*. Translated by Gregory P. Trauth and Kerstin Kazzazi. London; New York: Routledge, 1996, 1187 (²1998, ³2006).

Thinking of Text

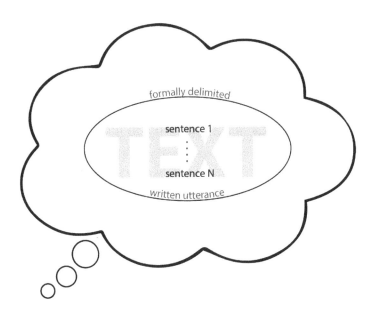

Linguistics: Short Definition

"Ein Text ist eine komplex strukturierte, thematisch wie konzeptionell zusammenhängende sprachliche Einheit, mit der ein Sprecher eine sprachliche Handlung mit erkennbarem kommunikativem Sinn vollzieht."

Linke, Angelika, Markus Nussbaumer, and Paul R. Portmann. *Studienbuch Linguistik*. 4th ed. Reihe Germanistische Linguistik. Tübingen: Niemeyer, 2001, 245 ([1]1991, [2]1994, [3]1996, [5]2004, [repr]2007).

A text is a complexly structured, thematically as well as conceptually coherent linguistic unit, with which a speaker executes a verbal action with recognisable communicative sense.

[own translation]

Text as Megaphone

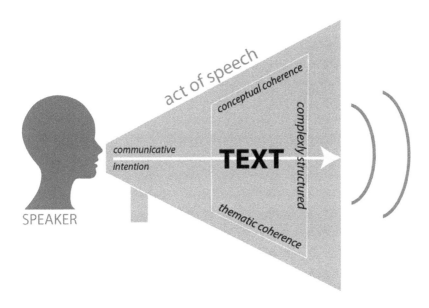

Linguistics: Extensive Definition

Texts, i.e. language units we recognise as a unity although eventually comprising more than one **sentence** (212) are a product of a union of **multiple sentences** to a whole (215). The relations between individual sentences can be associated with linguistic elements in many cases. Those elements are syntactically and semantically clearly interrelated— this is called **cohesion** (215). Text is seen as the topmost form of organisation in speech—speech understood as the particular linguistic products in **concrete communication situations** (223). A text always just directly gives access to a **surface structure**, where many—but not all—information units of a text are realised verbally and—also only partly—connected by means of cohesion (224f). The conceptual base of a text—the **deep structure**—is multi-dimensional, its distinct information units are complexly interlinked (225). "Text holes" on the text surface can be cleared by the text recipient supplementing missing text blocks. The recipients construct relations between text elements thus carrying out **text work** using extralingual knowledge (226). Where recipients lack the necessary knowledge for the completion of presuppositions (233f), they must infer sensible 'intermediate pieces of text' (234). Relevant fields of knowledge are **world knowledge** and **procedural knowledge** (227). With the term **'conceptual interpretative patterns' we** refer to a stock of knowledge that is part of and a prerequisite for our 'world knowledge' (227). The **Theme** is the core content that must not get lost even when radically shortening a text (237). **Theme** is what something is said about, whereas **rheme** is what is said (238). A text is a complexly structured, thematically and conceptually coherent linguistic unit, with which a speaker performs a speech act with recognisable communicative sense (245). **Text function** relates to **'intention types'**, which have a **societal-cultural predisposition** (246). The **communication medium** is an extra-textual criterion, which 'carries' the text (250).

[own translation of]
Linke, Angelika, Markus Nussbaumer, and Paul R. Portmann. Studienbuch Linguistik. 4th ed. Reihe Germanistische Linguistik. Tübingen: Niemeyer, 2001, 212-250 (11991, 21994, 31996, 52004, repr2007).

Textual Atmospheres

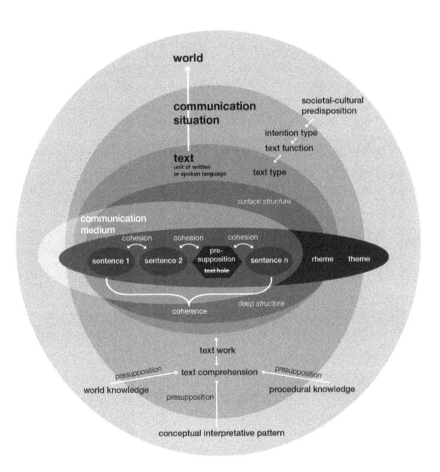

Linguistics: Communication

Text does not come without context. Text has to be 'somewhere'. It is embedded in situations where something happens. We may call this 'communication'.

"[A] text [is] 'an **ordered sequence of language signs** between two noticeable discontinuations {Unterbrechungen} of communication'."

> Beaugrande, Robert-Alain de. 'Text Linguistics'. In *Discursive Pragmatics*, edited by Jan Zienkowski, Jan-Ola Östman, and Jef Verschueren, 286–296. Handbook of Pragmatics Highlights 8. Benjamins, 2011, 288. [Original square brackets were altered into curly brackets for the sake of consistency.]

"Was aber ist ein Text? Aus den vielen möglichen Definitionen halte ich mich hier weiter an die einfachste: Ein Text ist eine **geordnete Folge von Satzzeichen** zwischen zwei auffälligen Unterbrechungen der Kommunikation. Die untere Grenze eines Textes liegt bei zwei aufeinanderfolgenden Monemen, d. h. kleinsten bedeutungstragenden Sprachzeichen, die obere Grenze ist offen."

But what is a text? Out of the many possible definitions, here I stick with the most simple one: A text is an **ordered sequence of sentence signs** between two apparent discontinuations of communication. Two consecutive monemes, i.e. the two smallest meaningful language signs, mark the lower boundary of a text, the upper boundary is open.

[own translation]

> Weinrich, Harald. *Sprache in Texten.* Stuttgart: Klett, 1976, 186ff.

Text as Discontinued Sequences of Communication

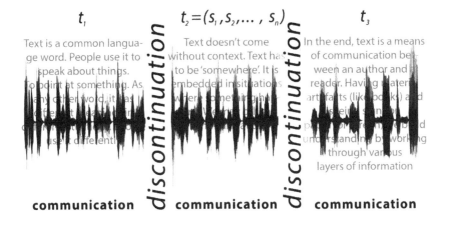

t_1 $t_2 = (s_1, s_2, \dots , s_n)$ t_3

communication   *discontinuation*   **communication**   *discontinuation*   **communication**

PS, NG, JS

Linguistics: Formalisation

"[There are d]efinitions like 'a text is a coherent sequence of utterances' (Isenberg 1970, Steinitz 1969, Weinrich 1971), a text is a coherent **sequence of language signs and/or sign complexes** which are not a priori embedded in another (comprehensive) language unit (Brinker 1979, 7) [...]"

> Viehweger, Dieter. 'Coherence – Interaction of Modules'. *In Connexity and Coherence: Analysis of Text and Discourse*, edited by Wolfgang Heydrich, Fritz Neubauer, János S. Petöfi, and Emil Sözer, 256–274. Research in Text Theory 12. Berlin: De Gruyter, 1989, 256.

> The quote refers to Isenberg, Horst. *Der Begriff 'Text' in der Sprachtheorie*. Berlin: Akademie der Wissenschaften der DDR, 1970, to Steinitz, Renate. *Adverbial-Syntax*. 1st ed. Studia Grammatica 10. Berlin: Akademie-Verl., 1969, to Weinrich, Harald. *Tempus. Besprochene und erzählte Welt*. 2nd ed. Stuttgart, Berlin, Köln, Mainz: Kohlhammer, 1971 and to Brinker, Klaus 'Zur Gegenstandsbestimmung und Aufgabenstellung der Textlinguistik'. In *Text vs. Sentence. Basic Questions of Text Linguistics*, edited by János S. Petöfi, 2:3–12. Hamburg: Buske, 1979.

"Any sequence of sentences temporally or spacially [sic] arranged in a way to suggest a whole will be considered to be a text"

> Koch, Walter A. 'Preliminary sketch of a semiotic type of discourse analysis'. In *Linguistics* vol. 3 issue 12 (1965): 5-30 (here p. 16).

"Wir verstehen unter einem 'Text' eine kohärente Folge von Sätzen[...]."   We understand "text" as a coherent sequence of sentences [...].

[own translation]

> Isenberg, Horst. *Der Begriff 'Text' in der Sprachtheorie*. Berlin: Akademie der Wissenschaften der DDR, 1970, 1.

"I use the term 'text' [...] as a synonym for '**sequence of linguistic signs**'. This should be sufficiently general and vague to be quite uncontroversial."

> Reicher, Maria. 'Objective Interpretation and the Metaphysics of Meaning'. In *Language and World. Part Two: Signs, Minds and Actions*, edited by Volker Munz, Klaus Puhl, and Joseph Wang, 181–190. Heusenstamm: Ontos Verlag, 2010, 185.

Sometimes, it is said that **text is a sequence of *language* [*or linguistic*] *signs***. This sounds like a clear definition and a complete text model. But what are the language signs? And in which way are the sets of language signs finite and well defined? For some the language signs might be sentences (se), for some they might be words (w). Some may say that language is represented in texts by characters of an alphabet (ac). Some would like to include punctuation marks in the set of language signs (pc). Some would argue that language signs in fact are realisations of characters, allographs or glyphs (gl) – making s and ſ two different language signs; as well as s and s (as being two instances and distinct on the graph level - gr).

Text Sequence Formula

$T = \{(s1 - s2 - s3 - \ldots - sn) \mid s \in S\}$

$S = (se1, se2, se3, \ldots, sen)$?

$S = (w1, w2, w3, \ldots, wn)$?

$S = (ac1, ac1, ac3, \ldots, acn)$?

$S = (ac1, \ldots, acn, pc1, \ldots, pcn)$?

$S = (gl1, gl2, gl3, \ldots, gln)$?

$S = (gr1, gr2, gr3, \ldots, grn)$?

Text Technologies: Standardisation

Probably by far the most influential text technology in our digital media environment has been (and with its successor Unicode still is) the "American Standard Code for Information Interchange" (ASCII) which paved the way for a common global representation of texts.

Every technical solution realises a (often implicit) model of its domain. Based upon the technical possibilities and limitations of encoding, the ASCII standard was first published 1963 and as matured standard in 1968. It comprises these features:

- Given 7 bits of zero and one, 128 code positions are possible. Therefore 128 codes make up the set of textual signs.

- Text is a sequence of distinct signs (characters); one position (one index), one sign. Signs themselves do not have modes. The mode "case" is realized by doubling the alphabet.

- There are normal, visible, printable characters and other, non-printable characters

  - printable characters comprise the Latin alphabet, numbers, punctuation marks and other special characters

  - non printable characters relate to the structure of the text (as a stream or as displayed in two dimensions) or the transmission of texts between devices

- Signs and Codes are inherited from the tradition of previous text technologies (mostly typewriter and teletype machines) or created due to the intended use of the standard in text encoding and transmission

- Codes are positioned in groups and in bit-shifting relation to each other (upper/lower case; numbers and special characters), following the typewriter tradition or in favour of easy sorting and computation.

The ASCII code is often visualised as a table. There is no compelling reason for this but allows for a strong compactness. Using columns for the 5th to the 7th bit as well as grouping the 16 codes of bit one to four as rows reveals some inner order of the code. Non-printable and control characters are mostly in group one and two. Alphabet characters are in four and five (upper case) and six and seven respectively. With that, there is also an inner functional logic in the positions: changing the sixth bit shifts the letter case.

The diagram (table) comes from the manual to a type printer of the early 1970s. Despite its origin in this rather ephemeral source, it has become quite ubiquitous as a meme for ASCII and binary encoding of data since its use as an illustration to the English Wikipedia article "ASCII" where it is stated as: "copied from the material delivered with TermiNet 300 impact type printer with Keyboard, February 1972, General Electric Data Communication Product Dept., Waynesboro, Virginia." (Wikimedia)

ASCII Code Chart

b7 b6 b5 →				Column → / Row ↓	0 0 0	0 0 1	0 1 0	0 1 1	1 0 0	1 0 1	1 1 0	1 1 1
Bits b4	b3	b2	b1		0	1	2	3	4	5	6	7
0	0	0	0	0	NUL	DLE	SP	0	@	P	`	p
0	0	0	1	1	SOH	DC1	!	1	A	Q	a	q
0	0	1	0	2	STX	DC2	"	2	B	R	b	r
0	0	1	1	3	ETX	DC3	#	3	C	S	c	s
0	1	0	0	4	EOT	DC4	$	4	D	T	d	t
0	1	0	1	5	ENQ	NAK	%	5	E	U	e	u
0	1	1	0	6	ACK	SYN	&	6	F	V	f	v
0	1	1	1	7	BEL	ETB	'	7	G	W	g	w
1	0	0	0	8	BS	CAN	(	8	H	X	h	x
1	0	0	1	9	HT	EM	)	9	I	Y	i	y
1	0	1	0	10	LF	SUB	*	:	J	Z	j	z
1	0	1	1	11	VT	ESC	+	;	K	[	k	{
1	1	0	0	12	FF	FS	,	<	L	\	l	|
1	1	0	1	13	CR	GS	—	=	M	]	m	}
1	1	1	0	14	SO	RS	.	>	N	^	n	~
1	1	1	1	15	SI	US	/	?	O	_	o	DEL

Computational Linguistics: Text Mining and Knowledge Representation

"Text repräsentiert **Wissen** und stellt insofern eine wesentliche Grundlage der Wissensverarbeitung dar. Ein Text besteht aus **Wortformen**, die ihrerseits aus den **Buchstaben** eines Alphabets bestehen. Die **Wortformen und Sätze** eines Textes stellen informationstheoretisch gesehen zunächst einfach nur **Daten** dar. Werden diese Daten **interpretiert** (mit Bezug auf ein vorher festgelegtes **Interpretationsschema**), dann werden die Daten zu **Informationen**. Werden Informationen mit anderen Informationen vernetzt und zur Lösung von Problemen eingesetzt, dann werden sie als **Wissen** bezeichnet. Die **intendierte Nutzung** eines Textes lässt sich oft anhand **externer Merkmale** dieses Textes erkennen." (7f) "Um Wissen [...] extrahieren zu können, müssen zunächst **semantische Relationen** zwischen den Zeichenketten erkannt werden. [...] Wesentliche **Verfahren** hierfür sind **sprach-statistische Verfahren, Clustering-Verfahren** (Cluster-Analyse) und **musterbasierte Verfahren.**" (9f) "**Zeichen** [...] lassen sich [...] zu **Zeichenketten** kombinieren. Eine nach vorher festgelegten Regeln zusammengestellte, endliche Folge von Zeichen und Zuständen, die eine **Information** vermittelt, bezeichnet man als Nachricht. Eine **Nachricht** zusammen mit ihrer **Bedeutung** für den Empfänger ist eine **Information.**" (10) "Die [...] ausgetauschten Nachrichten werden als **Daten** bezeichnet. **Daten** sind also nicht interpretierte **Zeichen** bzw. **Zeichenfolgen**, die erst durch die Herstellung eines **Interpretationsbezugs zu Informationen** werden." (10) "Als Nachricht, die für den Empfänger nach einem festgelegten Informationsschlüssel eine **Bedeutung** hat, besteht eine **Information** aus **Daten**, die in einem **Bedeutungskontext** stehen. Damit allerdings diese Information für den Empfänger auch wertvoll ist, [d.h. zum erfolgreichen **Verstehen**, muss eine Vernetzung stattfinden, d]iese [...] wird durch das **Wissen einer Person oder Organisation** geleistet." (11) "Wird dagegen der Inhalt von Informationen nicht ausgewertet, sondern werden die Informationen nur als sinnhaltige **Datenobjekte** behandelt, spricht man von **Content**. [...] Als **Wirtschaftsgut** wird Content meist als **Asset** bezeichnet." (11) "[Text Mining dient dazu], um aus den verfügbaren **Datenquellen** (**Dokumente** [...] usw.) das implizit bzw. explizit repräsentierte **Wissen** [...] abzuleiten [...]." (17)

Heyer, Gerhard, Uwe Quasthoff, and Thomas Wittig. *Text Mining: Wissensrohstoff Text.* Herdecke: W3L, 2006; revised reprint, Herdecke: W3L, 2008.

"Text represents **knowledge** and thus is an essential basis of knowledge processing. A text consists of **word forms**, which itself consist of **characters** of an alphabet. The word forms and **sentences** of a text are (by means of information science) just **data**. When this data is **interpreted** (using a predetermined **interpretation schema**), it becomes **information**. When information is linked to other information and used to solve problems, it is called **knowledge**. The **intended use** of a text can often be recognised by **external properties**. (7f) To be able to extract knowledge, **semantic relations** between strings have to be identified. Essential **procedures** are **statistical analysis, clustering analysis**, and **pattern analysis**. (9f) Characters can be combined with **strings**. A finite **sequence [stream] of characters** and states, composed using predetermined rules, that convey an information, is called a message. A message together with its meaning for a recipient is information. (10) Exchanged messages are called **data**. Thus data is non-interpreted **characters** or **strings** that only become **information** through an **interpretational reference**. As a message that has a **meaning** for a recipient by an established information key, **information** consists of **data** within a **context of meaning**. For information to be of worth for the recipient and thus making sense, creating **understanding**, there has to be interlinkage, which is provided by **personal** or **organisational knowledge**. (11) If [the content of] information is not used but treated as meaningful **data objects**, it is called **content**. Content seen as **economic good** is usually called **asset**. (11) Text Mining is used to derive implicitly or explicitly represented **knowledge** from data sources (**documents** etc.). (17)
[own translation]

Note: Filter relation between documents and the stream of characters is our addition, as well as 'lexemes' or 'stream of token'.

Text Mining as Knowledge Processing

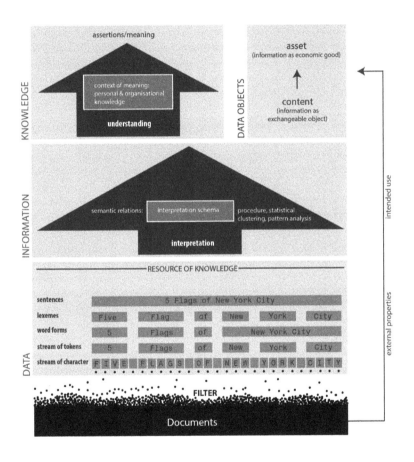

Computational Literary Studies: Burrows's Delta

What is text? When are texts similar? What is the style of a text? Who is the author of a text?

Texts can be described by their *similarity* to each other. Burrows Delta is a measure to quantify the stylistic proximity of texts. To do so, the relative frequency of the most frequent words are - after some normalisation steps - compared across the texts in a corpus, resulting in a score which is Burrows Delta. This operationalization (purposefully) relies on a certain model of text as a set of word occurrences. Word order, phrase, sentence and other textual properties have been neglected here. It is a model of 'style', an operational model that works on the basis of a reductive model of text. The text model from digital literary studies that is applied here is the "bag of words" approach. Style models in traditional literary studies are based on different models of text.

Literature: Burrows, John. '"Delta": A Measure of Stylistic Difference and a Guide to Likely Authorship'. *Literary and Linguistic Computing* 17, no. 3 (2002): 267–287.
Burrows, John. 'Questions of Authorship: Attribution and Beyond: A Lecture Delivered on the Occasion of the Roberto Busa Award ACH-ALLC 2001, New York'. *Computers and the Humanities* 37, no. 1 (2001 2003): 5–32.

Figure: Argamon, Shlomo. 'Interpreting Burrows's Delta: Geometric and Probabilistic Foundations'. *Literary and Linguistic Computing* 23, no. 2 (2008): 131–147 (formula on page 132).

Context: For a discussion of the concepts of 'style' in traditional and digital literary studies, see: Herrmann, J. Berenike, Christof Schöch, and Karina van Dalen-Oskam. 'Revisiting Style, a Key Concept in Literary Studies'. *Journal of Literary Theory* 9 (2015).

Burrows's Delta Formula

$$\Delta(D, D') = \frac{1}{n} \sum_{i=1}^{n} |z(f_i(D)) - z(f_i(D'))|$$

Argamon

Computer Linguistics: An Analytic Stance Towards a Real World Media System

In the room of textuality, authorial intention is expressed through documents, which are understood through reading. Computer linguistics are also interested in studying texts which are found in documents. These are seen as carriers of sequences of characters. In a reductionist approach, other textual features such as layout (indicating textual structures) or modes of written language (like bold, italics etc.) are considered non-essential. Starting from the filtered stream of characters, the authorial expression as words and sentences is detected and from this, the meaning is derived.

The textual model of computer linguistics in its easy computability is very powerful and has led to astonishing results in manifold applications of handling, aggregation, transmission, translation, analysis and use of texts.

Yet, for people focusing on textuality as a somewhat more complex and layered media system, the computational linguistics approach towards text may seem like looking through a keyhole.

The Keyhole Model

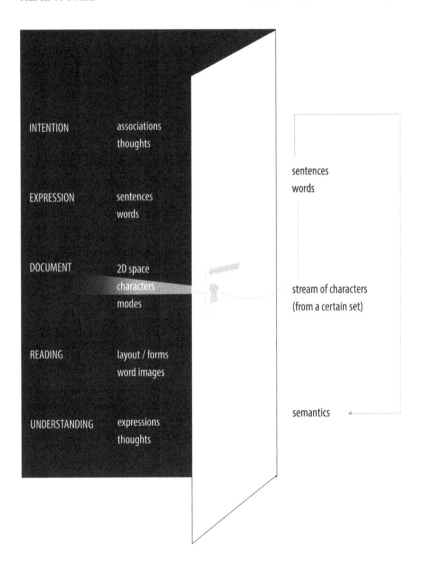

REAL WORLD

COMPUTER LINGUISTICS

INTENTION — associations / thoughts

EXPRESSION — sentences / words

DOCUMENT — 2D space / characters / modes

READING — layout / forms / word images

UNDERSTANDING — expressions / thoughts

sentences
words

stream of characters
(from a certain set)

semantics

PS, JS

Semiotics: The Artistic Text

"But an artistic text is the end product of the exhaustion of different entropy for addressee and addresser, and consequently carries different information for each."

Lotman, Jurij. *The Structure of the Artistic Text*. Translated by Ronald Vroon. University of Michigan, 1977, p. 31.

Information and Entropy of the Artistic Text

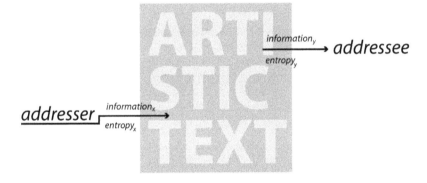

Literary Studies: Text, Textuality and Texture

"The proper business of literary criticism is the description of readings.
Readings consist of the interaction of texts and humans.
Humans are comprised of minds, bodies and shared experiences.
Texts are the objects produced by people drawing on these resources.
Textuality is the outcome of the workings of shared cognitive mechanics,
          evident in texts and readings.
Texture is the experienced quality of textuality."

Stockwell, Peter. 'Text, Textuality and Texture'. In *Texture. A Cognitive Aesthetics of Reading*, pp. 1–16. Edinburgh: Edinburgh University Press, 2009, p. 1.

Circle of Textuality

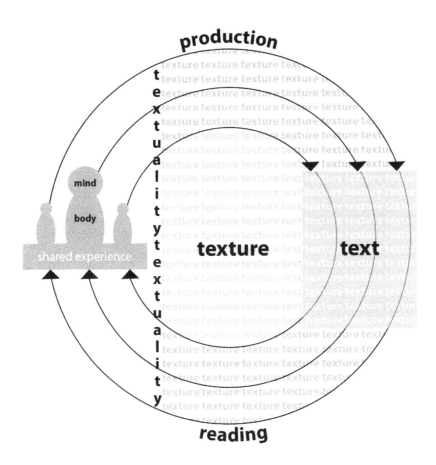

Cultural History: On Spoken and Written Text

"Gesprochene Sprache bindet sich an die Erfahrung unmittelbar gegenwärtiger Personen. Die Stimme löst sich aus dem Körper des Sprechenden wie aus einem tönenden Instrument und findet Resonanz in einem Gegenüber. Rücken Sprecher und Hörer auseinander, werden sie durch Raum und Zeit getrennt [...], so erscheint die Sprache kalt und sichtbar als gefrorene Form, materiell fassbar in ihren Bruchstücken und Fragmenten. Sie hat ihren Aggregatzustand verändert, wird nicht über die ,warme' (luftige, fließende) Stimme *hörbar*, sondern *sichtbar* durch ,kalte' (eisige, erstarrte, tote) Buchstaben. [...] Was wir ,Text' nennen, ist das Ergebnis eines Abzugs aller körpersprachlichen Indizes wie Stimmhöhe, Artikulationstempo, Kontaktsignale, Gestik, Mimik oder Habitus. „Die Bedingung der Möglichkeit für Verfestigung im Medium der Schrift ist die Reduktion."[1] Texte sind charakterisiert durch die Dauer im Wandel, durch ihre erstarrte Gestalt. Derart befördert die Schrift ein Stück gefrorener Gegenwart in eine offene Zukunft [...].

Gesprochene Worte sind unsichtbar. Sie erreichen eine dauerhafte Visualisierung [...] nur unter der Preisgabe ihrer eigentlichen Natur, welche der Ton ist.[2] [... D]ieser Wechsel [geht] gleichzeitig einher mit der Verräumlichung von Zeit. Der Ton, der sich hörbar in der Zeit realisiert, wird zum Buchstaben, der sichtbar im Raum steht. Die ,gefrorene Sprache' wird erst wieder hörbar, aber zugleich auch unsichtbar, wenn die Atmosphäre ,warm' wird, wenn die Buchstaben aufgetaut und als Sprachhandlung wieder verlebendigt werden."

Wenzel, Horst. *Hören Und Sehen, Schrift Und Bild. Kultur Und Gedächtnis Im Mittelalter.* C. H. Beck Kulturwissenschaft. München: Beck, 1995, 244.

1 Assmann, Aleida. 'Fest Und Flüssig: Anmerkungen Zu Einer Denkfigur'. In *Kultur Als Lebenswelt Und Monument*, edited by Aleida Assmann and Dietrich Harth, 181–99. Frankfurt am Main: Fischer, 1991, 189.

2 Kelber, Werner H. *The Oral and the Written Gospel. The Hermeneutics of Speaking and Writing in the Synoptic Tradition, Mark, Paul and Q.* Philadelphia: Fortress Press, 1983, 33.

Spoken language is bound to the experience of immediately present persons. The voice releases itself from the body of the speaker as if from a sounding instrument and finds resonance in a counterpart. When speakers and listeners move apart, they become separated by space and time [...] so the language appears cold and visible as a frozen form, materially tangible in its splinters. It has changed its state of aggregation and does not become audible through the 'warm' (airy, flowing) voice, but visible through 'cold' (icy, frozen, dead) letters. [...] What we call 'text' is the result of a subtraction of all body language indices such as voice pitch, articulation speed, contact signals, gestures, facial expressions or habit. "The condition of the possibility of solidification in the medium of writing is reduction."[1] Texts are characterised by (the) duration in change, by their ossified form. Writing thus conveys a piece of the frozen present into an open future.

Spoken words are invisible. They reach durable visual embodiment [...] only by revealing their actual nature, which is the sound.[2] This change is concurrent with the spatialisation of time. The sound, which is audibly realized in time, manifests itself as letter visible in space. The 'frozen language' only becomes audible again, but at the same time also invisible, when the atmosphere gets 'warm', when the letters are thawed and revived as an act of speech.

[own translation]

See also Wenzel, Horst. 'Poststrukturalismus. Die "fließende" Rede Und Der "gefrorene" Text. Metaphern der Medialität'. In *Herausforderung an die Literaturwissenschaft*, edited by Gerhard Neumann, 481–503. Stuttgart, Weimar: Metzler, 1997. Or Luhmann, Niklas. 'Die Form Der Schrift'. In *Germanistik in Der Mediengesellschaft*, edited by Ludwig Jäger and Bernd Switalla, 405–425. München: Fink, 1994, 422.

Frozen Text

TEXT IS FROZEN LANGUAGE

Cultural History: Text Production and Communication

Text as document as book is always part of a complex communication circuit. In order to understand texts it is necessary to understand the conditions, relations and interactions in the creation, distribution and reception of textual media.

The Communication Circuit

"I am not arguing that book history should be written according to a standard formula, but trying to show how its disparate segments can be brought together within a single conceptual scheme." (75) "[... H]owever [... different book historians] define their subject, they will not draw out its full significance unless they relate it to all the elements that worked together as **a circuit for transmitting texts**." (75)

"At what point did writers [read **authors**] free themselves from the patronage of wealthy noblemen and the state in order to live by their pens? What was the nature of literary career, and how was it pursued? How did writers deal with publishers, printers, booksellers, reviewers, and one another? Until those questions are answered, we will not have a full understanding of the transmission of texts." (75)

"How did **publishers** draw up contracts with authors, build alliances with booksellers, negotiate with political authorities, and handle finances, supplies, shipments, and publicity? The answers to those questions would carry the history of books deep into the territory of social, economic, and political history, to their mutual benefit." (75)

"The printing shop is far better known than the other stages in the production and diffusion of books, because it has been a favorite subject of study in the field of analytical bibliography, whose purpose [...] is 'to elucidate the transmission of texts by explaining the processes of book production.'" (76) "[... B]ibliographers can demonstrate the existence of different editions of a text and of different states of an edition, a necessary skill in diffusion studies. Their techniques also make it possible to decipher the records of **printers** and so have opened up a new, archival phase in the history of printing." (77)

"Little is known about the way books reached bookstores from printing shops. The wagon, the canal barge, the merchant vessel, the post office, and the railroad [, and thus **shippers**] may have influenced the history of literature more than one would suspect." (77)

"[... M]ore work needs to be done on the **bookseller** as a cultural agent, the middleman who mediated between supply and demand at their key point of contact. [...] The book trade, like other businesses during the Renaissance and early modern periods, was largely a confidence game, but we still do not know how it was played. [...] Despite a considerable literature on its psychology, phenomenology, textology, and sociology, reading remains mysterious. How do **readers** make sense of the signs on the printed page? And how has it varied? [...] Reading itself has changed over time. It was often done aloud and in groups, or in secret and with an intensity we may not be able to imagine today." (78) "[... T]exts shape the response of readers, however active they may be. [...]" (79)

"[...B]ooks themselves do not respect limits, either linguistic or national. They have often been written by **authors** who belonged to an international republic of letters, composed by **printers** who did not work in their native tongue, sold by **booksellers** who operated across national boundaries, and read in one language by **readers** who spoke another. Books also refuse to be contained within the confines of a single discipline when treated as objects of study. Neither history nor literature nor economics nor sociology nor bibliography can do justice to all aspects of the life of a book. By its very nature, therefore, the history of books must be international in scale and interdisciplinary in method. But it need not lack conceptual coherence, because books belong to **circuits of communication** that operate in consistent patterns, however complex they may be." (80f)

Darnton, Robert. 'What Is the History of Books?' *Daedalus* 111, no. 3 (1982): 65–83. Figure taken from p. 68, redrawn by Julia Sorouri.

The Communication Circuit

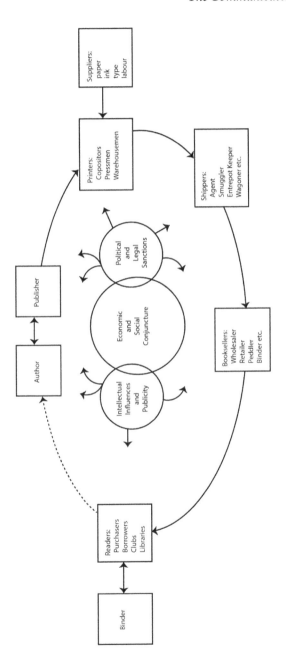

Darnton

Scholarly Editing / Literary Studies: The Document-Work Ecosystem

"[... L]iterary critics have not had a clear enough vision of the problematic nature of physical texts and their assumptions about textual stability [...]. The 'structure of reality of written works' [...] places the writer, the reader, the text, the world, and language in certain relationships and locates the focus of experience of that reality in the reader. This relationship has been mapped by a number of theorists [...] but these maps reveal a gaping hole in our thinking, around which swirls a number of vague and sloppily used terms that only appear to cover the situation. The lack of clear focused thinking on this question is revealed graphically when the **physical materials of literary works of art** are located in a center around which scholarly interests in Works of Art can be visualized. To the West of this physical center is found the scholarship of interest in **creative arts, authorial intentions and production strategies, biography, and history as it impinges on and influences authorial activities**. To the East of the physical center is the scholarship of interest in **reading and understanding, interpretation and appropriation, political and emotive uses of literature**. To the North of the physical center is the scholarship of interest in **language and speech acts, signs and semantics**. All three treat the work of art as mental constructs or meaning units; the physical character of the work is usually considered a vehicular incident , usually transparent. To the South is the scholarship of interest in **physical materials: bibliography, book collecting, and librarianship**. Only in this last area do we detect the appearance of special attention on the Material Text, but, because traditionally scholars in these fields have made a sharp distinction between the Material and the Text[11] and because they have focused their attention on the Material as object, their work has seemed tangential to the interests of the West, North, and East." (57f)

"[11] Note particularly W. W. Greg's often quoted definition: 'What the bibliographer is concerned with is pieces of paper or parchment covered with certain written or printed signs. With these signs he is concerned merely as arbitrary marks; their meaning is no business of his' ('Bibliography—an Apologia,' 247)." (58)

Shillingsburg, Peter L. *Resisting Texts. Authority and Submission in Constructions of Meaning.* 1st ed. Ann Arbor, Michigan: University of Michigan Press, 1997, 57f.

The indirect reference is Greg, Walter Wilson. 'Bibliography—An Apologia'. In *Collected Papers*, edited by J. C. Maxwell, 239–66. Oxford: Clarendon Press, 1966, 247.

The Compass of Material Text

The Language
Speech act theory, Signs, Semantics

The Author   *The Reader*
Time,   Time,
Place,   The Physical Documents   Place,
Intention   for the Work   Interpretation

The Book
Bibliography, Librarianship, Book collecting

Shillingsburg

Sociology and Social Systems Theory on Text: Niklas Luhmann

"The distinction between (self-referential, operatively closed) **systems** and (excluded) **environments** allows us to reformulate the distinction between text and interpretation. The **materiality** of texts [...] always belongs to the environment and can never become a component of the system's operational sequences. But the system's operations determine how **texts** and other objects in the environment are identified, observed, and described. (99=161) That distinction [between medium and form] is meant to replace the distinction substance/accidence, or object/properties (102=165) [... The term **element**] always points to units constructed (distinguished) by an observing system – to units for counting money, for example, or to tones in music. (103=167) [...] The notion of **medium** [...] applies to cases of **'loosely coupled' elements.**" (104f=168) [... Rather, the concept indicates an] open-ended multiplicity of possible connections that are still compatible with the unity of an element – such as the number of meaningful **sentences** that can be built from a single semantically identical **word**. (104=168) [...] **media** can be recognized only by the contingency of the formations that make them possible. (104=168) **Forms** are generated in a medium via a tight coupling of its elements. (104=169) [...] **media** impose limits on what one can do with them. Since they consist of elements, media are nonarbitrary. (105=170) [...] We can further elucidate the medium/form distinction by means of the distinction between redundancy and variety. The elements that form the medium through their **loose coupling** – such as **letters** in a certain kind of **writing** or **words** in a **text** – must be easily recognizable. (105=170) [...] It is worth noting that forms, rather than exhausting the medium, regenerate its possibilities. This [...] can be easily demonstrated with reference to the role of words in the formation of utterances. Forms fulfil this regenerating function, because their duration is typically shorter than the duration of the medium. Forms, one might say, couple and decouple the medium. (105=170) [...] Such elements always also function as forms in another medium. **Words** and **tones**, for example, constitute forms in the **acoustic** medium just as **letters** function as forms in the **optical** medium of the visible. [...] (106=172) Media are generated from elements that are always already formed. (106=172) [...] This situation contains possibilities for an **evolutionary arrangement of medium/form relationships in steps** [...] (106=172) [An] example that illustrates the generality of this **step-wise arrangement**. In the medium of **sound**, **words** are created by constricting the medium into condensable (reiterable) forms that can be employed in the medium of **language** to create **utterances** (for the purpose of communication). The potential for forming **utterances** can again serve as the medium for forms known as **myths** or **narratives**, which, at a later stage, when the entire procedure is duplicated in the **optical** medium of **writing**, also become known as **textual genres** or **theories**. (106=172) [...] The most general medium that makes both psychic and social systems possible and is essential to their functioning can be called **"meaning" [Sinn]**. (107=173) [...] **meaning** is constituted by the distinction between actuality and potentiality (or between the real as momentarily given and as possibility). This implies and confirms that the medium of meaning is itself a form constituted by a specific distinction. (107=173/174) [...] a form can be used as a medium for **further formations.** (108=176) [...] an artwork's **material** participates in the formal play of the work and is thereby acknowledged as form. (109=176)"

Luhmann, Niklas. *Art as a Social System*. Edited by David E. Wellbery. Translated by Eva M. Knodt. Meridian: Crossing Aesthetics. Stanford: Stanford University Press, 2000. "(nnn=nnn)" refers to the pages in the English version and in the German original text (Luhmann, Niklas. *Die Kunst der Gesellschaft*. Frankfurt am Main: Suhrkamp, 1995) - bold type is ours.

Note on the diagram: Black font indicates words used by Luhmann (in the published translation), while words printed in grey indicate our interpretation and/or addition.

The Staircase of Text

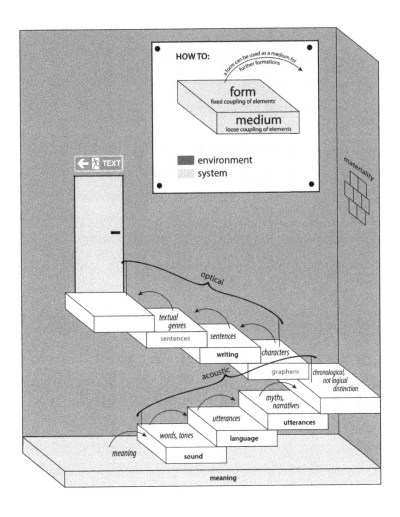

Digital Humanities: How we Read

"[... T]he process of reading a text is not linear, building up one character at a time, but depends on the propagation of hypotheses, and the testing of these regarding all available information concerning a text." (75-77) "It [the encoding scheme] resolves the reading process into a finite set of **'modes of thought'**, or **'states'**, which can be used to track the development of the reasoning process." (49)

"An expert reads [a ...] document by identifying **visual features**, and then incrementally building up knowledge about the document's **characters**, **words**, **grammar**, **phrases**, and **meaning**, continually proposing hypotheses, and checking those against other information, until s/he finds that this process is exhausted. At this point **a representation of the text** is prepared in the standard publication format. At each level, external **resources** may be consulted, or be unconsciously compared to the characteristics of the document." (82) "[E.g.:] Expert C begins by drawing some conclusions about the **meaning of the document (level 8)** before looking at the **physical attributes (level 0)**. He then discusses what could be possible **features of the text (level 1)**, before noting more **physical attributes of the document (level 0)**. He then produces a **word (level 4)**, looks at the **characters within this word (level 2)**, and revises his initial word. Checking of the **features (level 1)** leads to identification of a **character (level 2)**, the noting of a possible **word (level 4)** and a discussion of **meaning of that word (level 6)**. In this manner the expert vacillates between the different levels in reading a document, until a resolution is reached regarding the **sense of the document (level 8)**, or until he has exhausted all possibilities regarding the **text**." (57) "While the lower level processes, such as the **identification of features and characters**, mostly relate to each other, and the upper levels, such as discussion of **word meaning** and **meaning of document**, mostly relate to each other, it is only the **word** level which shows a relationship with all the different types of information discussed." (61) "The subjects which are discussed for the longest length of time per instance are the **physical characteristics of the document**, and the **overall meaning of the text**. The information regarding these levels is much more complex than the **identification of characters and words**, and tends to be discursive." (63)

Terras, Melissa. *Image to Interpretation: An Intelligent System to Aid Historians in Reading the Vindolanda Texts*. Oxford: Oxford University Press, 2006.

Diagram: The Illustration is our merger of Terras, Melissa. *Image to Interpretation*, Table 2.1 and Figure 2.15.

Terras: Levels of Reading

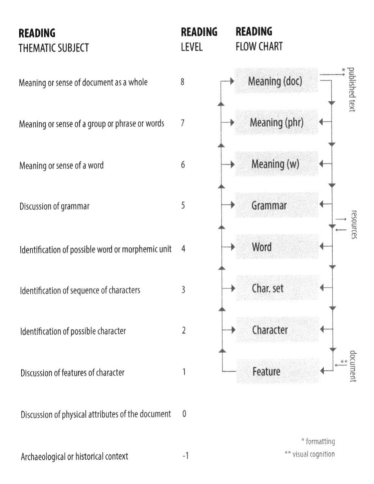

READING THEMATIC SUBJECT	READING LEVEL	READING FLOW CHART
Meaning or sense of document as a whole	8	Meaning (doc)
Meaning or sense of a group or phrase or words	7	Meaning (phr)
Meaning or sense of a word	6	Meaning (w)
Discussion of grammar	5	Grammar
Identification of possible word or morphemic unit	4	Word
Identification of sequence of characters	3	Char. set
Identification of possible character	2	Character
Discussion of features of character	1	Feature
Discussion of physical attributes of the document	0	
Archaeological or historical context	-1	

published text

resources

document

* formatting
** visual cognition

Terras (redrawn PS, JS)

Digital Scholarly Editing: Theories, Models and Methods

"The Text [...] is the meaning(s) that **readers** give to the subset of **dimensions** they derive from a **document** and that they consider interesting for their purpose. As a consequence, texts are immaterial and interpretative." (42)

"**Documents** we take to be physical objects that contain some sort of inscribed information; therefore, a book is a document, a leaf with some writing on it is a document, a stone is a document. More generally, a document is a physical object that has some text on it[...]. [...] All documents (as defined here) contain verbal texts as well as other things: images, graphs, musical notation, arrows blotches, for instance, as well as including the 'bibliographical codes' discussed by McGann." (40)

"Many people can read from the same document and understand slightly or radical different things, depending on their culture, their understanding, their disposition, their circumstances, and so on. There are **facts** in the object (the document), but their meaning is not factual, it is interpretative. For one reader the only interesting dimension could be the **semantic [dimension ...]** (what the text means, the plot, who is the murderer), for another could be the **artistic [dimension ...]**: maybe she/he cannot read the words written in an unfamiliar language, but she/he can still admire and make (some) sense of the iconography and its artistic value." (42f)

"[...] **Documents** have infinite **Facts (F1-F∞)** which can be arbitrarily grouped (dotted lines) into **Dimensions** by a **Reader**; the result of which is the **Text**, which is then a function of the document conjured by a reader[. ...]" (43)

"These **dimensions** are only potentially available within a document, [...] the document itself has no particular meaning: it is an inert object with no particular significance." (42)

"As **dimensions** potentially observable in a document are defined by the purpose of one's interest in the document, it is therefore impossible to draw a stable and complete list of such dimensions." (41)

"[... A] selection of dimensions that does not include consideration of the verbal content of a document is not a text, but must be something else. [...] **Text** has been defined as a particular selection of dimensions operated by a reader according to specific **organising principle**; the defining principle of which is the selection of an infinite set of **facts** with a purpose of study." (44)

"The model proposed here [...] only concerns documents for which a verbal-content can be determined, since it is built to explain the editorial work." (40f)

"[...A] **text** is a model that, among the **facts** selected by the **reader**, includes the verbal content of the **document**. We define then **dimensions** that include the verbal content of a **document** as *Verbal Dimensions*. Other selections which do not include the verbal content of the document are non-textual models." (44)

Pierazzo, Elena. *Digital Scholarly Editing: Theories, Models and Methods*. Aldershot: Ashgate, 2015. [Original emphasises removed and terms used in the graphic highlighted in bold for the sake of consistency.]

Diagram: Pierazzo, Elena. *Digital Scholarly Editin*, p. 43, Figure 2.1: "Conceptual model of texts and documents".

Pierazzo: Dimensions of Text

DOCUMENT

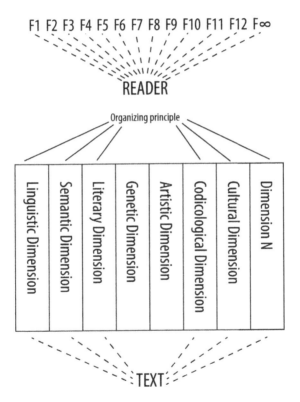

Pierazzo (redrawn JS, AW)

Digital Scholarly Editing: Textual Representation

In scholarly editing, presented texts claim to give a truthful copy, to convey what is essential for a given text or to realize the real text or its author's intention. The various established modes of text representation in editing can be seen as layers, which are not discrete but should rather be seen as points on a continuous scale. Therefore, the scale given here is very much simplified.

Representations are the result of a double process: First, phenomena of a document are either recognized (as being important) or being ignored (filtered out) – secondly, the recognised phenomena are processed according to certain rules to transform them either into textual data or a media expression.

If textual representation is seen as a scale, the end points and directions are sometimes described as being 'close to the document' and 'close to the reader' respectively. To say that there is a gradual progress in 'processing' is another way of describing the scale.

1. Texts are always given as documents. We do not encounter them in another form. Except for situations in which we 'talk *about* a text'.

2. Facsimiles are very close to the text as document. But even mechanical reproductions are means of filtering perception: think of image resolution, lighting, colors and material aspects..

3. An external description (including bibliographic, material, contextual information) is a basic operation in representing a text. It is often done as a first step in creating a proxy for a text. As it can also be described as being highly synthetic, the position of this layer in the scale is disputable.

4. The diplomatic transcription is as true to the document as possible. It does not change anything. However, there are many different levels of "truth" defined by what (which aspect of textuality) is to be observed and what can be neglected.

5. The linguistic codes focus on text as a stream of alphabet characters (including punctuation and other elements of the target writing system).

6. 'Normalised' is just an arbitrary label here. Replace it by 'modernised', 'regularised' or any other label that points at rule-based processes that intervene in and change text.

7. In scholarly editing, to create the 'best text' or to reconstruct 'author's intention' texts are sometimes constructed from several sources or are 'emended' against what can actually be found in the documents.

8. A translation represents the same text, only in a different language.

9. Texts are meant to convey information. This information can be extracted and represented as a set of assertions (like in RDF triples) or values (like in key-value pairs in an entity relationship model).

Cf. e.g. Sahle, Patrick. *Digitale Editionsformen*, vol. 3: *Textbegriffe und Recodierung*. Norderstedt: BoD 2013 [chapter: Dokument und Transkription], 251-340.

Sahle: Text as a Scale

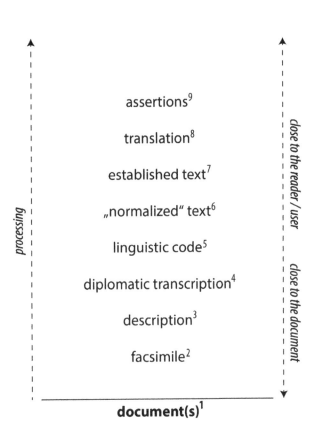

Digital Humanities: Understanding Historical Script

Texts are made of characters? Things are not that simple when you take a closer look ...

"A **grapheme** is associated with one or more **characters** (for 'Character' see below). A **character** is made up of any number of **components**. A **component** in turn can be found in any number of **characters** and can have one or more **features** or indeed any number of further components.

A **character** can also be manifested in one or more **allographs**, and a set of **allographs** makes up a **script**. **Allographs** themselves can have **components** which have **features**, but **allographs** also have **general features** which are the aspects of 'style' [...]. A set of **allographs** together makes up a **script**.

Each **allograph** can be manifested in any number of **idiographs** (which in turn have **components** and **general features**). A set of **idiographs** makes up the practice of a **scribe**.

Each **idiograph** can appear on the **page** as a **graph**; **graphs** have the usual set of **general features** and **components**, as well as a set of coordinates. The set of **graphs** makes up a **scribal hand**.

Scribal hands are written by exactly one **scribe** (but a **scribe** can write many **scribal hands**); a **scribal hand** may also be written in one or more **scripts** and may use one or more **alphabets**."

Stokes, Peter A. 'Describing Handwriting, Part IV: Recapitulation and Formal Model'. *DigiPal* (blog), 14 October 2011. http://www.digipal.eu/blog/describing-handwriting-part-iv-recapitulation-and-formal-model [Original emphases altered from uppercase into bold for the sake of consistency.]

See also Stokes, Peter A. 'Modeling Medieval Handwriting: A New Approach to Digital Palaeography'. In *Digital Humanities 2012*, 382–85. Hamburg, 2012. http://www.dh2012.uni-hamburg.de/conference/programme/abstracts/modeling-medieval-handwriting-a-new-approach-to-digital-palaeography.1.html

Diagram: Stokes, Peter A. 'Describing Handwriting, Part IV: Recapitulation and Formal Model'. *DigiPal* (blog), 14 October 2011, UML Diagram of the conceptual model. http://www.digipal.eu/blog/describing-handwriting-part-iv-recapitulation-and-formal-model. Redrawn by Julia Sorouri.

Stokes: Text as Script

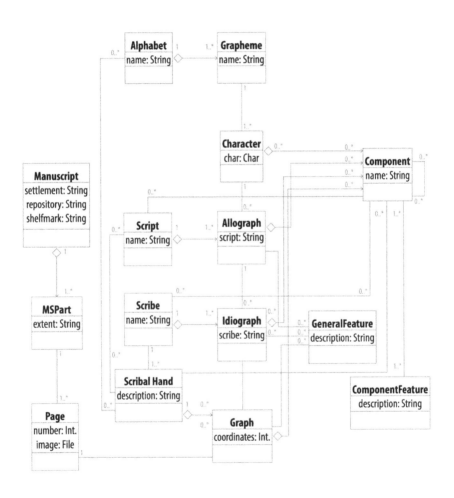

Information Science meets Electronic Texts: Renear and the Content Objects

"The essential parts of any document form what we call **'content objects'**, and are of many types, such as paragraphs, quotations, emphatic phrases, and attributions. (3) [...] Most **content objects are contained in larger content objects**, such as subsections, sections, and chapters. (4) [...] Smaller content objects that occur within a larger one, such as the sections in a chapter, or the paragraphs, block quotes, and other objects within a section, occur in a certain order. **This ordering is essential information, and must be part of any model of text structure.** Combining these essential elements, we can describe a **text as an 'ordered hierarchy of content objects'**, or 'OHCO'. (4)"

> DeRose, Steven J., David G. Durand, Elli Mylonas, and Allen H. Renear. 'What Is Text, Really?' Edited by Terry R. Girill. *Journal of Computer Documentation* 21, no. 3 (1997): 1–24. [First published in 1990 as 'What is Text, Really?' *Journal of Computing in Higher Education* 1, no. 2 (December 1990): 3–26.]

"**OHCO-1**: Text is an ordered hierarchy of content objects."

"Book: **front matter, back matter, body, chapter, section, paragraph** [...]"

> Renear, Allen H., Elli Mylonas, and David Durand. 'Refining Our Notion of What Text Really Is: The Problem of Overlapping Hierarchies', 1993. http://cds.library.brown.edu/resources/stg/monographs/ohco.html. [First presented at the annual joint meeting of the Association for Computers and the Humanities and the Association for Literary and Linguistic Computing, Christ Church, Oxford University, April 1992. Later published as 'Refining Our Notion of What Text Really Is'. In *Research in Humanities Computing*, edited by Nancy Ide and Susan Hockey, Vol. 4. Oxford: Oxford University Press, 1996.]

The OHCO approach is a strange case: As a model it uses a property of a certain text technology (here: text markup) to explain what text is: text is an ordered hierarchy of content objects, *because* markup (with its double principles of (textual) order and (element) hierarchy) seems so suitable to represent text. The argument here is: "the truth is in the practicality" or "if the model works, it must be right – also in its structural characteristics".

> "[... T]he reason this model of text is so functional and effective is that it **reflects what text really is**."

> Renear, Allen H. 'Representing Text on the Computer: Lessons for and from Philosophy'. *Bulletin of the John Rylands Library* 74, no. 4 (1992): 221–48, 221.

"The comparative efficiency and functionality of treating texts *as if* they were OHCOs is best explained, according to this argument, by the hypothesis that **texts *are* OHCOs**." (#5.1.6)

> Renear, Allen H. 'Theory and Metatheory in the Development of Text Encoding', 1995. https://web.archive.org/web/19970401032906/www.rpi.edu/~brings/renear.target

"[... T]ext is an "Ordered Hierarchy of Content Objects" (OHCO), and **descriptive markup** works as well as it does because it **identifies that hierarchy** and **makes it explicit** and available for systematic processing."

> Renear, Allen H. 'Text Encoding'. In *A Companion to Digital Humanities*, edited by Susan Schreibman, Raymond George Siemens, and John Unsworth, 218–239. Oxford: Blackwell Publishing, 2004, 224f.

The OHCO Model

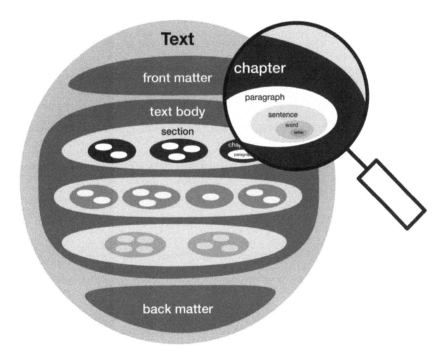

Philosophy and Technology: On Markup

"It is precisely this kind of diacritical ambiguity possessed by markup that can be exploited to devise a dynamic model of the text. Such a model can be expounded through a diagram, a kind of multidimensional matrix, whose elements are connected by a series of operations. The resulting process is a kind of loop. [...]

The structural elements of the expression of the text, represented by embedded or internal markup, are here arranged in the first column of the table. In the second column we find structural elements of the content of the text, as described by data modelling or semantic description languages, that can also be regarded as a form of markup, albeit external. Now, one and the same internal markup construct can be seen either as belonging to the object language of the text, in as much as it is a structural element of its expression, or else as a representation of that very element, separate from the text and belonging to a metalanguage. These two aspects of a markup construct can be severed, and the operation that converts the one into the other is a logical move, that rests on the assumption that the 'meaning of the markup' is 'the set of inferences about the document that are licensed by the markup.'[45] Accordingly, this move posits a markup construct as an inference-licence. If so, we can place it in the lower part of the first column and regard it, to recall Gilbert Ryle's famous description, as an 'inference-ticket,' or a rule-statement 'to move from asserting factual statements to asserting other factual statements'[46] – in our case, to infer from a statement about an observed textual property, to a statement about a property of its content. That content property, in its turn, expressed in a semantic annotation language, can be placed in the upper compartment of the second column as the value of the operation prompted by the instruction found in the lower compartment of the first column. All this means that markup can have both 'descriptive' and 'performative' force,[47] and what has just been said about markup constructs, or the structural elements of the expression of the text, applies also to semantic annotation constructs, or the stuctural elements of its content. We can therefore posit a semantic description as a rule, place it in the lower part of the second column, and move from it to the value of the operation it commands, ending up again with a property of the expression, in the upper part of the first column. And so the cycle is complete."

45 C. M. Sperberg-McQueen, C. Huitfeldt and A. Renear, 'Meaning and Interpretation of Markup,' in *Markup Languages: Theory & Practice*, 2:3 (2000), 215–234, p. 231.

46 G. Ryle, The Concept of Mind, London, Hutchinson's University Library, 1949 , p. 121.

47 Renear, 'The descriptive/procedural distinction' [in *Markup Languages: Theory & Practice*, 2:4 (2001)] p. 419 (134f).

Text: Buzzetti, Dino. 'Digital Text Representation: Expression and Content'. In Contexts: Proceedings of ANPA 31 (Alternative Natural Philosophy Association, 31st International Meeting, Wesley House, Cambridge, August 2010), edited by A. D. Ford, 124–145. London: ANPA, 2011.

Diagrams: Buzzetti, Dino. 'Digital Editions and Text Processing'. In *Text Editing, Print, and the Digital World*, edited by M. Deegan and K. Sutherland, 45–62. Aldershot: Ashgate, 2009, Figure 3.1

Buzzetti, Dino. 'Digital Text Representation: Expression and Content'. In *Contexts: Proceedings of ANPA 31 (Alternative Natural Philosophy Association, 31st International Meeting, Wesley House, Cambridge, August 2010)*, edited by A. D. Ford, 124–145. London: ANPA, 2011.

Buzzetti, Dino, and Manfred Thaller. *Beyond Embedded Markup*. Hamburg, 2012, Figure 1.

Buzzetti: Text as Expression and Content

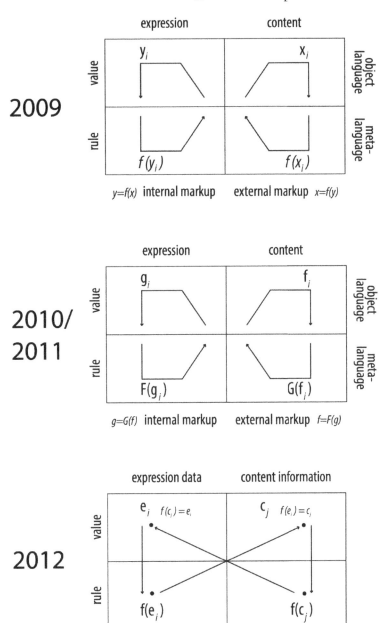

Buzzetti (redrawn JS)

Digital Humanities: Text According to the TEI

The TEI (or more precise: the guidelines of the TEI) are probably the most important standard for the information rich representation of texts in electronic form. With hundreds of elements for the description of textual structures and phenomena it embodies a pluralistic theory of text, developed over three decades by a large number of textual scholars representing various fields of research.

In a formal view which would cover all possibilities of text encoding with TEI and would regard all elements, modules, classes and handbook chapters, the set of TEI tags, attributes and the rules for their usage and nesting would lead to a confusing image of vast options and eventualities.

In a more pragmatic view on basic assumptions and common practices however, it can simply be said that the TEI nowadays has a threefold approach towards text. As a representation of text, a TEI instance always contains (1.) a section (TEIHeader) that describes the text as an object or work and its representation by data. That description in turn is made up of four important areas of information with their own widely ramified structures. The text itself is represented (2.) either following a material or visual paradigm, where a text bearing object becomes a facsimile, further subdivided into surfaces (like pages) and (writing) zones – again containing potentially complex information structures. Or (most often) the text is represented (3.) in accordance to a text logic paradigm that is based on a stream of character with embedded or stand-off annotations that describe further structures and add transcriptive or interpretative information to it. Within the abundance of elements to express textual information, they can roughly be divided into those that describe genre specific structures and phenomena and those that help to encode rather analytic or interpretative knowledge about the text. The set of elements and attributes however is so rich, that a sharp distinction cannot be made and many other divisions and classifications of the TEI vocabulary are likewise possible.

It is noteworthy that the material and the logic view on text are not exclusive but that both can be used at the same time and that they may well refer to each other to capture all aspects of a text and together yield a complete picture of our understanding of that text.

TEI: "[C]ontains a single TEI-conformant document, combining a single TEI header with one or more members of the model.resourceLike class. Multiple TEI elements may be combined to form a teiCorpus element."

teiHeader: "[S]upplies descriptive and declarative metadata associated with a digital resource or set of resources."

facsimile: "[C]ontains a representation of some written source in the form of a set of images rather than as transcribed or encoded text."

text: "[C]ontains a single text of any kind, whether unitary or composite, for example a poem or drama, a collection of essays, a novel, a dictionary, or a corpus sample."

TEI Consortium. 'P5: Guidelines for Electronic Text Encoding and Interchange (Version 3.4.0)', n.d. http://www.tei-c.org/guidelines/p5/.

TEI's Triangle of Text

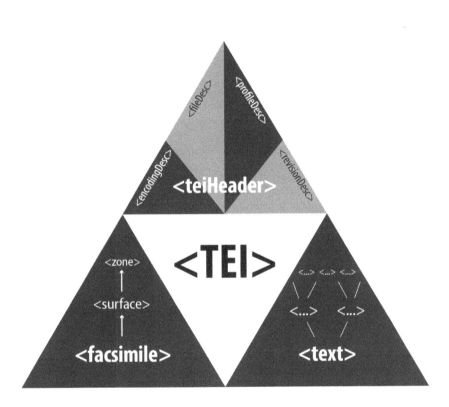

Bibliography, Library and Information Science

FRBR

"The entities in the first group [...] represent the different aspects of user interests in the products of intellectual or artistic endeavour. The entities defined as **work** (a distinct intellectual or artistic creation) and **expression** (the intellectual or artistic realization of a work) reflect intellectual or artistic content. The entities defined as **manifestation** (the physical embodiment of an expression of a work) and **item** (a single exemplar of a manifestation), on the other hand, reflect physical form.

[... A] **work** may be realized through one or more than one **expression** (hence the double arrow on the line that links **work** to **expression**). An **expression**, on the other hand, is the realization of one and only one **work** (hence the single arrow on the reverse direction of that line linking expression to **work**). An **expression** may be embodied in one or more than one **manifestation**; likewise a **manifestation** may embody one or more than one **expression**. A **manifestation**, in turn, may be exemplified by one or more than one **item**; but an **item** may exemplify one and only one **manifestation**." (13f)

"The first entity defined in the model is **work**: a distinct intellectual or artistic creation. A work is an abstract entity; there is no single material object one can point to as the work. (17) [...] The second entity defined in the model is **expression**: the intellectual or artistic realization of a work in the form of alpha-numeric, musical, or choreographic notation, sound, image, object, movement, etc., or any combination of such forms. An expression is the specific intellectual or artistic form that a work takes each time it is 'realized.' (19) [...] The third entity defined in the model is manifestation: the physical embodiment of an expression of a work. The entity defined as **manifestation** encompasses a wide range of materials, including manuscripts, books, periodicals, maps, posters, sound recordings, films, video recordings, CD-ROMs, multimedia kits, etc. As an entity, manifestation represents all the physical objects that bear the same characteristics, in respect to both intellectual content and physical form. (21) [...] The fourth entity defined in the model is **item**: a single exemplar of a manifestation. The entity defined as item is a concrete entity. It is in many instances a single physical object (e.g., a copy of a one-volume monograph, a single audio cassette, etc.). There are instances, however, where the entity defined as item comprises more than one physical object (e.g., a monograph issued as two separately bound volumes, a recording issued on three separate compact discs, etc.). (24)"

IFLA Study Group on the Functional Requirements for Bibliographic Records. *Functional Requirements for Bibliographic Records. Final Report*, 2009. https://archive.ifla.org/VII/s13/frbr/frbr_2008.pdf

Diagram: IFLA Study Group on the Functional Requirements for Bibliographic Records. *Functional Requirements for Bibliographic Records. Final Report*, 2009, Figure 3.1, 14. Redrawn by Julia Sorouri. [Added cardinalities to arrows.]

FRBR Group One: Hierarchy of Textual Entities

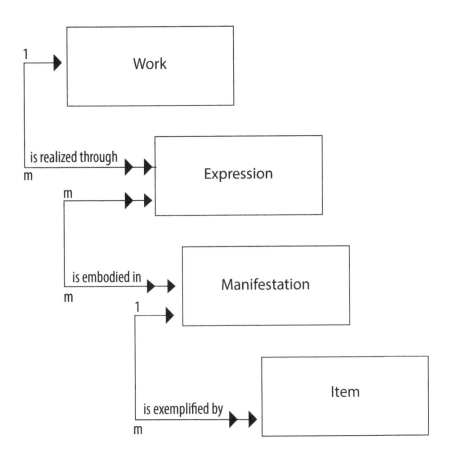

Library and Information Science in the Digital Humanities

FRBRoo

F1 Work

"This class comprises distinct concepts or combinations of concepts identified in artistic and intellectual expressions, such as poems, stories or musical compositions. Such concepts may appear in the course of the coherent evolution of an original idea into one or more expressions that are dominated by the original idea. A Work may be elaborated by one or more Actors simultaneously or over time. The substance of Work is ideas. A Work may have members that are works in their own right." (54)

F2 Expression

"This class comprises the intellectual or artistic realisations of works in the form of identifiable immaterial objects, such as texts, poems, jokes, musical or choreographic notations, movement pattern, sound pattern, images, multimedia objects, or any combination of such forms that have objectively recognisable structures. The substance of F2 Expression is signs. Expressions cannot exist without a physical carrier, but do not depend on a specific physical carrier and can exist on one or more carriers simultaneously. Carriers may include human memory." (55f)

F3 Manifestation Product Type

"This class comprises the definitions of publication products. An instance of F3 Manifestation Product Type is the "species", and all copies of a given object are "specimens" of it. An instance of F3 Manifestation Product Type defines all of the features or traits that instances of F5 Item normally display in order that they may be recognised as copies of a particular publication. However, due to production problems or subsequent events, one or more instances of F5 Item may not exhibit all these features or traits; yet such instances still retain their relationship to the same instance of F3 Manifestation Product Type." (56f)

F4 Manifestation Singleton

"This class comprises physical objects that each carry an instance of F2 Expression, and that were produced as unique objects, with no siblings intended in the course of their production. It should be noted that if all but one copy of a given publication are destroyed, then that copy does not become an instance of F4 Manifestation Singleton, because it was produced together with sibling copies, even though it now happens to be unique. Examples of instances of F4 Manifestation Singleton include manuscripts, preparatory sketches and the final clean draft sent by an author or a composer to a publisher." (57)

F5 Item

"This class comprises physical objects (printed books, scores, CDs, DVDs, CDROMS, etc.) that carry a F24 Publication Expression and were produced by an industrial process involving an F3 Manifestation Product Type." (58)

Bekiari, Chryssoula, Martin Doerr, Patrick Le Boeuf, and Pat Riva, eds. *Definition of FRBRoo: A Conceptual Model for Bibliographic Information in Object-Oriented Formalism*, 2015. https://www.ifla.org/files/assets/cataloguing/FRBRoo/frbroo_v_2.4.pdf

(One possible view on) Text in FRBRoo

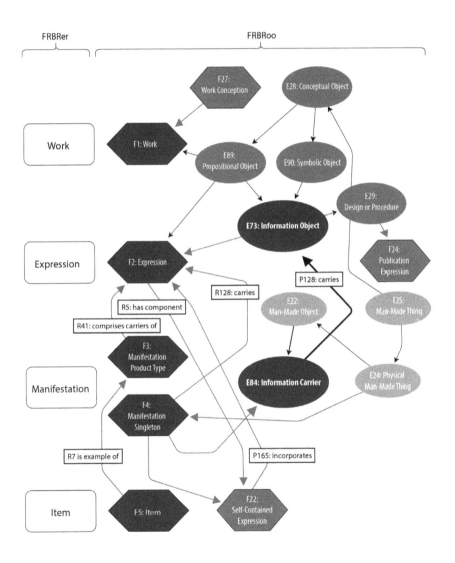

Cultural Heritage Documentation Meets Domain Specific Research

CRMtex

"[...]CRMtex [... is] an extension of CIDOC CRM created to support the study of ancient documents and to identify relevant textual entities involved in their study; furthermore, it [the documentation of CRMtex] proposes the use of CIDOC CRM to encode them and to model the scientific process of investigation related to the study of ancient texts in order to foster integration with other cultural heritage research fields. After identifying the key concepts, assessing the available technologies and analysing the entities provided by CIDOC CRM and by its extensions, the extension introduces new specific classes more responsive to the specific needs of the various disciplines involved (including papyrology, palaeography, codicology and epigraphy)." (4)

> Murano, Francesca, and Achille Felicetti. *'Definition of the CRMtex. An Extension of CIDOC CRM to Model Ancient Textual Entities'*. Edited by CIDOC CRM - SIG, January 2017.

"**TX1 Written Text**. Subclass of E25 Man-Made Feature intended to describe a particular feature (i.e., 'set of glyphs') created (i.e., written) on various kinds of support, having semiotic significance and the declared purpose of conveying a specific message towards a given recipient or group of recipients" (7)

"**TX2 Writing**. Subclass of E12 Production indicating the activity of creating textual entities using various techniques (painting, sculpture, etc.) and by means of specific tools on a given physical carrier in a non-mechanical way" (7)

"**TX3 Writing System**. Subclass of E29 Design or Procedure, refers to a conventional system (e.g., the Greek alphabet) consisting of a set of characters (graphemes, E90) used to codify a natural language. A writing system can be used to notate different natural languages, by means of specific rules in the combination and phonological value assignment of the chosen graphemes. It is used to produce a TX1 Written Text through a TX2 Writing event" (8)

"**TX4 Writing Field**. Subclass of E25 Man-Made Feature, usually understood as the surface or portion of the physical carrier reserved, delimited and arranged for the purpose of accommodating a writ- ten text, to highlight and isolate it from the other parts of the object to which it belongs, to enhance and guarantee its readability" (10)

"**TX6 Transcription**. Subclass of E7 Activity, referring to the activity of re-writing the text conducted by an editor. This operation, in some cases, involves a writing system (TX3) different from that of the original text (e.g., Latin characters to render a Coptic text); this results in a re-encoding of the text itself and, from a linguistic point of view, it is indicated more properly as a 'transliteration', because it implies a 1 : 1 relation between the signs of the two writing systems" (12)

"**TX7 Written Text Segment**. Subclass of TX1 Written Text, can be used to highlight specific portions of text on which the study focuses, specific phenomena appear or from which it is possible to derive special meanings." (15)

> 'CRMtex Updates'. presented at the 40th CIDOC CRM and 33rd FRBR CRM, Cologne, 2018. http://www.cidoc-crm.org/crmtex/sites/default/files/CRMtex_Koeln.ppt.

> Diagram: Arch of Constantine: CRMtex Representation, taken from 'CRMtex Updates'. Presented at the 40th CIDOC CRM and 33rd FRBR CRM, Cologne, 2018. http://www.cidoc-crm.org/crmtex/sites/default/files/CRMtex_Koeln.ppt. Redrawn by Julia Sorouri.

CRMTex

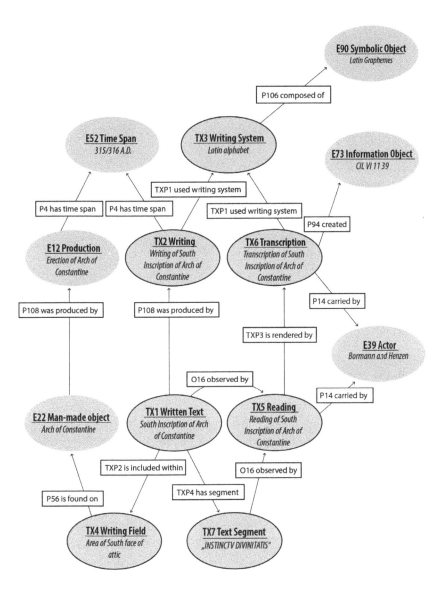

Literary Studies: A Meta Model

"What is text? I am not so naive as to imagine that question could ever be finally settled. Asking such a question is like asking 'How long is the coast of England?'"

> McGann, Jerome. 'Dialogue and Interpretation at the Interface of Man and Machine. Reflections on Textuality and a Proposal for an Experiment in Machine Reading'. *Computers and the Humanities* 36, no. 1 (2002): 95–107 [quote on p. 96].

What text is depends on the stance you take towards it. It depends on the tools you use to measure its "length" or shape. Looking closer, measuring more exactly, the length will increase. Taking different measures, using different tools – in textual research that is: using different perspectives or theoretical assumptions – yield a different coastline. Text can be seen through different lenses. It can have different dimensions.

Furthermore, text is not an object in nature. It is constructed through models of text and it is perceived through models of understanding. The shoreline is not the shelf is not the water line at low water is not the water line at high water.

"Texts are not independent from all kinds of tradition. They do not come innocent or naked. They are always already modelled and 'marked' by codes in various ontological dimensions. [...] Texts are cultural objects. They are produced and read under specific cultural conditions. The coast of England is not the coast of Japan."

Texts are spacetime objects. The yesterday coast of England is not the tomorrow coast of England.

Patrick Sahle interpreting Jerome McGann, with some snippets from an e-mail dialogue between the two. 2017.

"When we read, we decipher the instructions embedded in what digital scholars call Marked Text. All texts are marked texts, i.e., algorithms—coded sets of reading instructions. This important fact about textuality comes to dramatic focus when we pay attention to a document's graphical and bibliographical features. Unlike a text's linguistic elements, bibliographical codes lay bare their devices: they announce that they are executing a 'non-natural' language system. Consequently, their instructional or 'performative' character is apparent for those who have a will to see: tables of contents or indices; type font, trim size, and book design; chapters and all the many protocols for divisioning (pagination, paragraphing, and punctuation)."

> McGann, Jerome. *A New Republic of Letters. Memory and Scholarship in the Age of Digital Reproduction.* Cambridge (MA): Harvard University Press, 2014, 169.

Text is Like the Coast of England

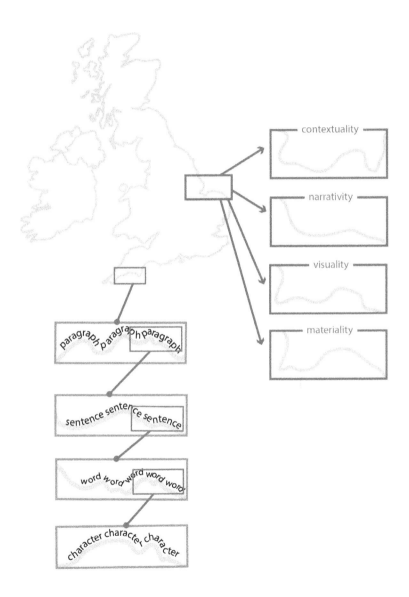

Digital Humanities: A Pluralistic Approach

A powerful ontological lever: you know a thing when you know its identity conditions. When are an abstract (allographic) thing (like text) and its representation (like with a document) "the same thing"? This depends upon the perspective one takes. And in turn, the perspective creates the identity conditions for "the thing". Tell me your perspective on text and I will derive the set of identity conditions from that.

To define what text is we may ask what has to be retained in a representation of that text (as being a document) and what may be ignored, neglected or changed. What is essential to call two objects one text, that is: the same text? A pluralistic theory of text acknowledges that the answer to this question may differ from respondent to respondent. Only in respect to the respective notion of text, to the respective underlying theory, to the view on text one takes, can it be determined which aspects of a given text (and texts are always given as media expression) are essential and which are arbitrary.

Within such a pluralistic view, we can describe how texts are seen by people, theories or technologies: If you consider certain textual features as being important, then you take a certain perspective, you use certain glasses, you apply a certain filter, you stand on the ground of a certain theory.

A pluralistic theory of text helps us to map, to localise, to position, and to relate people, theories and technologies. "You are here! You are close to that approach. This technology covers this spectrum of views. That approach towards text focuses on …"

The pluralistic model of text claims that first of all text is the result of a three-step-process and that text thus is three things: There is (1) an intended meaning, (that becomes) a (2) linguistic expression, (that becomes) a (3) media and material document. Between these positions there are further notions and perspectives. Text as a work has a structure that is less specific than the linguistic expression but more specific than the general intention. On the document, the verbal expression takes a specific (e.g. orthographical) version and shape. The document itself is always given visually and the visual form itself is a reading instruction and conveys parts of the intended meaning. Since the document (the text) as a complex visual sign is part of the intended (and/or perceived) message, the model has to take the form of a circle instead of a scale or set of layers.

The different perspectives are criteria for identity. Things that are identical under one perspective are different under another. Text as a work may have different verbal expressions (like with translations) but it is still the same work. But as a linguistic expression the English and German versions are two different texts. Orthographic versions may be seen as the same verbal expression but they are different texts when it comes to editing the "right" or the "best" text. Manuscript A is not manuscript B of a work. And the original of a medieval charter (due to its visual features) in some situations might not have the same effect, and is not the same thing as its copy.

Freely paraphrased after Sahle, Patrick. *Digitale Editionsformen, Teil 3: Textbegriffe und Recodierung*. Vol. 9. Schriften des Instituts für Dokumentologie und Editorik. Norderstedt: Books on Demand, 2013.

Sahle: The Text Wheel

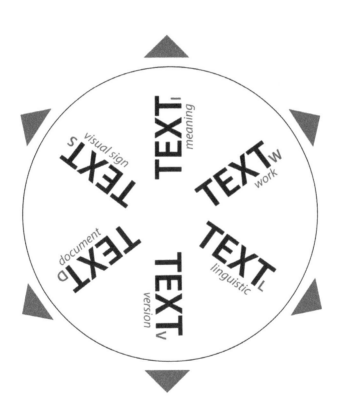

Digital Humanities: Witmore on Text

"For a text to be a **text**, it must be **addressable** at an indefinite number of levels of **abstraction** or **scales**."

> Michael Witmore, 'Latour, the Digital Humanities, and the Divided Kingdom of Knowledge'. *New Literary History* 47, no. 2 & 3 (2016). https://muse.jhu.edu/article/631303.

"[...] what makes a text a text is its ability to serve as an **open-ended destination of address**."

> Witmore, Michael. Re: 'Text: A Massively Addressable Object'. Blog comment. *Wine Dark Sea - Literary and Cultural History at the Level of the Sentence* (blog), 2010; commented 2011, May 11. http://winedarksea.org/?p=926#comment-784.

"**Addressable** here means that one can query a position within the text at a certain level of abstraction. [...] What makes a text a text – its susceptibility to varying levels of address – is a feature of book culture and the flexibility of the textual imagination. We address ourselves to this level, in this work, and think about its relation to some other. [...] A physical text or **manifestation** is a provisional unity. There exists a **potentially infinite array of such unities**, some of which are already lost to us in history: what was a relevant level of address for a thirteenth century monk reading a manuscript? Other provisional unities can be operationalized now, as we are doing in our experiment at Wisconsin, gathering 1000 texts and then counting them in different ways. Grammar, as we understand it now, affords us a level of abstraction at which texts can be stabilized: we lemmatize texts algorithmically before modernizing them, and this lemmatization implies provisional unities in the form of grammatical objects of address. [...] The ontological status of the individual text is the same as that of the **population of texts**: both are massively addressable, and when they are stored electronically, we are able to act on this flexibility in more immediate ways through iterative searches and comparisons. [...] Physical texts were already massively addressable before they were ever digitized, and this variation in address was and is registered at the level of the **page**, **chapter**, the binding of **quires**, and the like. When we encounter an index or marginal note in a printed text — for example, a marginal inscription linking a given passage of a text to some other in a different text — we are seeing **an act of address**. Indeed, the very existence of such notes and indexes implies just this **flexibility of address**. [...] Here's the twist. We have physical manifestations of ideal objects (the ideal 1 Henry VI, for example), but these manifestations [in the sense of OCLC's FRBR hierarchy] are only provisional realizations of that ideal. [...] The **book** or physical instance, then, is one of many levels of address. Backing out into a larger population, we might take a **genre** of works to be the relevant level of address. Or we could talk about individual **lines** of print; all the **nouns** in every line; every third **character** in every third line. All of this variation implies massive flexibility in levels of address. And more provocatively: when we create a digitized population of texts, our modes of address become more and more abstract: all concrete nouns in all the items in the **collection**, for example, or every item identified as a '**History**' by Heminges and Condell in the First Folio. Every level is a provisional unity: stable for the purposes of address, but also: stable because it is the object of address. **Books** are such provisional unities. So are all the proper **names** in the phone book."

> Witmore, Michael. 'Text: A Massively Addressable Object'. *Wine Dark Sea – Literary and Cultural History at the Level of the Sentence* (blog), 2010. http://winedarksea.org/?p=926.

> Image: https://commons.wikimedia.org/wiki/File:Ezra_Cornell%27s_first_book.jpg

Text as Massively Addressable Object

Digital Humanities: Witmore on Text

"[...] I argued that a text might be thought of as **a vector through a meta-table of all possible words**. Why is it possible to think of a text in this fashion? Because a text can be queried at the level of single words and then related to other texts at the same level of abstraction: the table of all possible words could be defined as the aggregate of points of address at a given level of abstraction (the word, as in Google's new n-gram corpus). Now, we are discussing ideal objects here: addressability implies different levels of abstraction (**character**, **word**, **phrase**, **line**, etc) which are stipulative or nominal: such levels are not material properties of texts or Pythagorean ideals; they are, rather, conventions."

Witmore, Michael. 'Text: A Massively Addressable Object'. *Wine Dark Sea – Literary and Cultural History at the Level of the Sentence* (blog), 2010. http://winedarksea.org/?p=926. We refer to the version as it appears on December 2017 (cf. https://web.archive.org/web/20180214133057/http://winedarksea.org/?p=926).

Diagram: Witmore, Michael. 'Texts as Objects II: Object Oriented Philosophy. And Criticism?' *Wine Dark Sea – Literary and Cultural History at the Level of the Sentence* (blog), 2009. http://winedarksea.org/?p=381.

Witmore: Text as a Vector

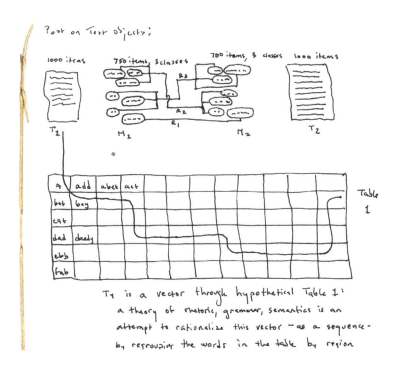

Post on Text objects:

T_1 is a vector through hypothetical Table 1:
a theory of rhetoric, grammar, semantics is an
attempt to rationalize this vector — as a sequence —
by regrouping the words in the table by region

Salmons Combining Meta Models

"How far can we take Witmore's idea of **"text as massively addressable object"**? In particular, how do we identify and focus on the "trajectories" of the multitude of vectors through meta-tables, not just of all possible words, but through the multi-matrices of atomic model elements of all possible conceptual models that can be brought to the examination of text. [...] **Sahle's model** provides an insightful basis vector along which we can enumerate and organize the multitude of modeling abstractions that cover the many ways we humans (and increasingly, our agent-based soft machines) access and understand Text. [...] Let's "unwind" Sahle's model to **lay it along a Z-axis** in relation to Witmore's "T1-T2" example. This will help us to visualize and organize those "massively addressable" levels of abstraction at the many levels of scale that open up as cultural heritage texts are increasingly available as digital computational objects. [...] In the figure at the top of this section, I accentuated Witmore's "stitching thread" metaphor by shading the "pierce points" of the "vector through all possible words" being the plane of the metaphorical quilt. From a graph theoretic perspective, the "thread" between these shaded cells maps relationship vectors/edges between the word nodes in a graph that complements this visualization. [...] any particular Text as Object (of study) will have a **unique "fingerprint"/signature** when expressed/abstracted through the lens of any specific conceptual reference or metamodel. [...] As the "devil is in the detail," virtually any metamodel with sufficient descriptive and/or explanatory power is going to be a multi-dimensional hypergraph that stretches our visual metaphors helping to frame this discussion. [...] I'll wrap this piece up with an example describing the intersection of the two seemingly disparate domains of Witmore's T(sub L) computational or statistical literary linguistic studies with FactMiners' T(sub S) focus on semantics, meaning, and content depiction. The proposed integration of these two "emerging levels of massive addressability" of Text is just one example of potential contributions by the Digital Humanities to the multi-disciplinary Computer Science domain of Cognitive Computing."

Salmons, Jim. 'FactMiners' Fact Cloud & Witmore's Text as Massively Addressable Object'. *CODE | WORDS: Technology and Theory in the Museum An Experiment in Online Publishing and Discourse* (blog), 9 April 2015. https://medium.com/code-words-technology-and-theory-in-the-museum/factminers-fact-cloud-witmore-s-text-as-massively-addressable-object-13c7be3dbd37.

Diagram: Salmons, Jim. 'FactMiners' Fact Cloud & Witmore's Text as Massively Addressable Object'. *CODE | WORDS: Technology and Theory in the Museum An Experiment in Online Publishing and Discourse* (blog), 9 April 2015. https://medium.com/code-words-technology-and-theory-in-the-museum/factminers-fact-cloud-witmore-s-text-as-massively-addressable-object-13c7be3dbd37.

Salmons: The Vector Wheel Flipper Machine

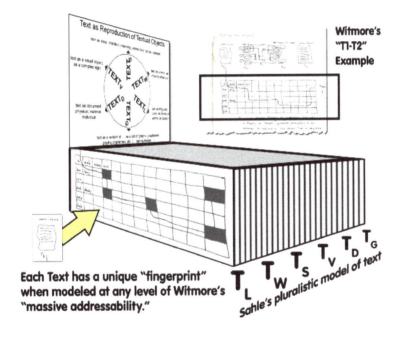

Each Text has a unique "fingerprint" when modeled at any level of Witmore's "massive addressability."

A Comprehensive Meta Model

In the creation of text, we do not have a simple expression pipeline from idea through verbalisation to media expression. The various layers of information with their specific affordances condition each other. The same holds true for seeing, using and reading.

The text is an operator object that connects a sender to receivers on many levels. Usually, we will agree on its material form. But in decoding the other information layers, in reading what has been written and in understanding what was meant, there is a possible gap of disagreement that widens in the course of ever more abstract (re)constructions.

Text as Kintsugi

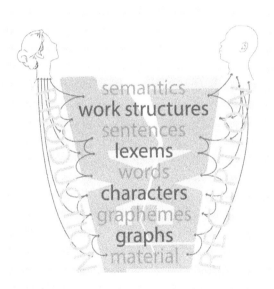

PS, NG, JS

Bibliography

Abbagnano, Nicola, *Dizionario di filosofia* (Turin: Utet, 1998).

Abelson, H. and Sussman, G.J., *Structure and Interpretation of Computer Programs* (Cambridge, MA: MIT Press, 1996).

Acker, Wouter, and Pieter Uyttenhove, 'Information and Space: Analogies and Metaphors', *Library Trends*, 61.2, Special Issue (2012), pp. 271-285.

van den akker, Chiel, Susan Legêne, Marieke Erp, Lora Aroyo, Roxane Segers, Lourens Meij, and others, 'Digital Hermeneutics: Agora and the Online Understanding of Cultural Heritage', *Journal of Automated Reasoning - JAR* (2011), https://doi.org/10.1145/2527031.2527039

Alessio Giovanni and Battisti, Carlo, *Dizionario Etimologico Italiano* (Firenze: Barbera Università degli studi, 1965)

Allan, Keith, and Kasia M. Jaszczolt, eds., *The Cambridge Handbook of Pragmatics*, Cambridge Handbooks in Language and Linguistics (Cambridge: Cambridge University Press, 2012), https://doi.org/10.1017/CBO9781139022453

'An Intermediate Greek-English Lexicon—Hardcover—H. G. Liddell; Robert Scott—Oxford University Press', global.oup.com/ushe/product/an-intermediate-greek-english-lexicon-9780199102068

Armaselu, Florentina, PhD thesis, *Le livre sous la loupe: Nouvelles formes d'écriture électronique*, Papyrus, University of Montreal Institutional Repository (2010), https://papyrus.bib.umontreal.ca/xmlui/handle/1866/3964

Armaselu, Florentina, and Charles van den Heuvel, 'Metaphors in Digital Hermeneutics: Zooming through Literary, Didactic and Historical Representations of Imaginary and Existing Cities', *Digital Humanities Quarterly*, 011.3 (2017), http://www.digitalhumanities.org/dhq/vol/11/3/000337/000337.html.

Austen, Gillian, 'Self-Portraits and Self-Presentation in the Work of George Gascoigne', *Early Modern Literary Studies*, 14.1, Special Issue 18 (2008), http://purl.oclc.org/emls/14-1/article1.htm

Averbukh, Vladimir, 'Global Visualization Metaphors', *2nd Conference and Exhibition on Semiotics & Visual Communication. 2-4 October 2015. Lemesos. Cyprus* (2015), https://www.researchgate.net/publication/282655107

Averbukh, Vladimir L., 'Sources of Computer Metaphors for Visualization and Human-Computer Interaction', *IntechOpen* (2019), https://doi.org/10.5772/intechopen.89973

Baigrie, Brian S., *Picturing Knowledge: Historical and Philosophical Problems Concerning the Use of Art in Science*, Toronto Studies in Philosophy (Toronto: University of Toronto Press, 1996), https://www.jstor.org/stable/10.3138/9781442678477

Bailer-Jones, Daniela M., 'Scientific Models as Metaphors', in *Metaphor and Analogy in the Sciences*, ed. by Fernand Hallyn, Origins (Dordrecht: Springer Netherlands, 2000), pp. 181–198, https://doi.org/10.1007/978-94-015-9442-4_11

Bakhtin, Mikhail M., 'Forms of Time and the Chronotope in the Novel. Notes toward a Historical Poetics', in *The Dialogic Imagination: Four Essays*, ed. by Michael Holquist (Austin: University of Texas Press, 1981), pp. 84–258.

Barth, Fredrik, *Principles of Social Organization in Southern Kurdistan* (Oslo: Universitetets etnografiske museum, 1953).

—, *Models of Social Organization*, Royal anthropological institute of Great Britain and Ireland, Occasional Paper, 23 (Glasgow: Glasgow University Press, 1966).

—, 'Overview: Sixty Years of Anthropology', *Annual Review of Anthropology* 36, pp. 1–16 (2007), https://doi.org/10.1146/annurev.anthro.36.081406.094407

Bertin, Jacques, and Marc Barbut, *Sémiologie graphique. Les diagrammes, les réseaux, les cartes* (Paris, La Haye: Mouton; Gauthier-Villars, 1967).

Betti, Arianna, and Hein van den Berg, 'Modelling the History of Ideas', *British Journal for the History of Philosophy*, 22 (2014), pp. 812–835, https://doi.org/10.1080/09608788.2014.949217

Black, Max, *Models and Metaphors Studies in Language and Philosophy* (Ithaca, N.Y.: Cornell University Press 1962).

d'Alembert, Jean-Baptiste le Rond, 'Preliminary Discourse', *Encyclopedia of Diderot & d'Alembert—Collaborative Translation Project* (2009), http://hdl.handle.net/2027/spo.did2222.0001.083

Bod, Rens, *A New History of the Humanities: The Search for Principles and Patterns from Antiquity to the Present* (Oxford: Oxford University Press, 2013).

—, 'Modelling in the Humanities: Linking Patterns to Principles', *Historical Social Research, Supplement*, 31 (2018), pp. 78–95, https://doi.org/10.12759/hsr.suppl.31.2018.78-95

Bode, Katherine, 'Why You Can't Model Away Bias', *Modern Language Quarterly*, 81.1 (2020), pp. 95–124, https://doi.org/10.1215/00267929-7933102

Bonderup Dohn, Nina, 'Modelling, Metaphors and Metaphorical Thinking – From an Educational Philosophical View', in *Models and Modelling between Digital and Humanities - A Multidisciplinary Perspective*, ed. by Arianna Ciula, Øyvind Eide, Cristina Marras, and Patrick Sahle, *Historical Social Research/ Historische Sozialforschung. Supplement*, 31 (2018), pp. 46-58, https://doi. org/10.12759/HSR.SUPPL.31.2018.46-58

Borgman, Christine L., 'Personal digital libraries: creating individual spaces for innovation'. Presented at NSF Workshop on Post-Digital Libraries Initiative Directions. Chatham, MA 4 June 2003 (2003), http://www.sis.pitt. edu/~dlwkshop/paper_borgman.pdf

Boroditsky, Lera, and Paul H. Thibodeau, 'Natural Language Metaphors Covertly Influence Reasoning', *PLOS ONE* January 2013 (2013), https://doi. org/10.1371/journal.pone.0052961

Bradley, John, and Harold Short, 'Texts into Databases: The Evolving Field of New-style Prosopography', *Literary and linguistic computing*, 20 (2005), pp. 3–24.

Bradley, John, et al., *Factoid Prosopography*, London: King's College London, Department of Digital Humanities (2020), https://www.kcl.ac.uk/ factoid-prosopography

Bühler, Karl, *Sprachtheorie: Die Darstellungsfunktion der Sprache* (Jena: Gustav Fischer, 1934), http://hdl.handle.net/11858/00-001M-0000-002A-F889-C

Burkhardt, Armin, and Brigitte Nerlich, *Tropical Truth(s)* (Berlin: De Gruyter, 2010), https://doi.org/10.1515/9783110230215

Buzzetti, Dino, 'Digital Representation and the Text Model', *New Literary History*, 33.1 (2002), pp. 61–88, https://doi.org/10.1353/nlh. 2002.0003

Camillo, Giulio, *Dve trattati dell'eccellentissimo M. Ivlio Camillo : l'vno delle materie, che possono uenir sotto lo stile dell'eloquente, l'altro della imitatione* (Venice: Nella stamparia de Farri, 1544), http://archive.org/details/dvetrattatidelle00cami

Capurro, Rafael, 'Digital Hermeneutics: An Outline', *AI & Society*, 25(1), pp. 35–42 (2010), http://www.capurro.de/digitalhermeneutics.html; https:// doi.org/10.1007/s00146-009-0255-9

Careri, Giorgio, "Intervento", in *Il ruolo del modello nella scienza e nel sapere*, contributi del Centro Linceo Interdisciplinare 'Beniamino Segre', 100, Accademia Nazionale dei Lincei, Rome, pp. 185-186 (1999).

Carnap, Rudolf, *Introduction to Semantics* (Chicago: Chicago University Press, 1942).

Cellucci, Carlo, *Le ragioni della logica* (Rome: Laterza, 1998).

Ciula, Arianna, 'Digital Palaeography: Using the Digital Representation of Medieval Script to Support Palaeographic Analysis', *Digital Medievalist*, 1, Spring (2005) https://journal.digitalmedievalist.org/article/id/6957/

—, 'The Palaeographical Method under the Light of a Digital Approach', in *Kodikologie Und Paläographie Im Digitalen Zeitalter - Codicology and Palaeography in the Digital Age*, ed. by Malte Rehbein, Torsten Schaßan, and Patrick Sahle, Schriften Des Instituts Für Dokumentologie Und Editorik, 2 (Norderstedt: Books on Demand (BoD), 2009), pp. 219–235, http://kups.ub.uni-koeln.de/2971/

—, 'Modelling Textuality: A Material Culture Framework', Keynote at 'Convention 2 – Programme', (slides) *DiXiT* (2016), https://dixit.uni-koeln.de/convention-2-abstracts/

Ciula, Arianna, and Øyvind Eide, 'Reflections on Cultural Heritage and Digital Humanities: Modelling in Practice and Theory', in *Proceedings of the First International Conference on Digital Access to Textual Cultural Heritage*, DATeCH'14 (New York: Association for Computing Machinery, 2014), pp. 35–41, https://doi.org/10.1145/2595188.2595207

—, 'Modelling in Digital Humanities: Signs in Context', *Digital Scholarship in the Humanities* (2017), https://doi.org/10.1093/llc/fqw045

Ciula, Arianna, Øyvind Eide, Cristina Marras, and Patrick Sahle, 'Models and Modelling between Digital and Humanities: Remarks from a Multidisciplinary Perspective', *Historical Social Research*, 43.4 (2018), pp. 343–361, https://doi.org/10.12759/hsr.43.2018.4.343-361

Ciula, Arianna, and Cristina Marras, 'Circling around Texts and Language: Towards "Pragmatic Modelling"', *Digital Humanities Quarterly*, 10.3 (2016), http://www.digitalhumanities.org/dhq/vol/10/3/000258/000258.html

—, 'Exploring a Semiotic Conceptualisation of Modelling in Digital Humanities Practices', in *Meanings & Co: The Interdisciplinarity of Communication, Semiotics and Multimodality*, ed. by Alin Olteanu, Andrew Stables, and Dimitru Borţun, Numanities - Arts and Humanities in Progress (Springer International Publishing, 2019), vi, pp. 33–52, https://www.springer.com/us/book/9783319919850

Ciula, Arianna, Geoffroy Noël, Paul Caton, Ginestra Ferraro, Tiffany Ong, James Smithies, and Miguel Vieira, 'The Place of Models and Modelling in Digital Humanities: Some Reflections from a Research Software Engineering Perspective', in *Vielfalt und Integration —diversitá ed integrazione—diversité et intégration: Sprache(n) in sozialen und digitalen Räumen Eine Festschrift für Elisabeth Burr*, ed. by Marie Annisius, Elena Arestau, Julia Burkhardt, Nastasia Herold, and Rebecca Sierig (Leipzig: Universitätsbibliothek, 2023), pp. 261–281, urn:nbn:de:bsz:15-qucosa2-852367

Colburn, Timothy, and Gary Shute, 'Metaphor in Computer Science', *Journal of Applied Logic*, 6 (2008), pp. 526–533, https://doi.org/10.1016/j.jal.2008.09.005

Condit, Celeste M., Benjamin R. Bates, Ryan Galloway, Sonja Brown Givens, Caroline K. Haynie, John W. Jordan, and others, 'Recipes or Blueprints for Our Genes? How Contexts Selectively Activate the Multiple Meanings of Metaphors', *Quarterly Journal of Speech*, 88.3 (2002), pp. 303–325, https://doi.org/10.1080/00335630209384379

Cooper, Alan, Robert Reimann, and Dave Cronin, *About Face 3: The Essentials of Interaction Design*, [3rd ed.], Completely rev. and updated (Indianapolis, IN: Wiley, 2007).

Cornell Way, E., *Knowledge Representation and Metaphor*, 7 (New York: Springer Verlag, 1991), https://www.springer.com/de/book/9780792310051

Culkin, John M, 'A Schoolman's Guide to Marshall McLuhan', *Saturday Review*, 6 (1967), pp. 51-53.

Daston, Lorraine, ed., *Biographies of Scientific Objects* (Chicago, IL: University of Chicago Press, 2000).

Eide, Øyvind, 'Co-Reference: A New Method to Solve Old Problems', *Book of Abstracts* (presented at the Digital Humanities June 22-25 2009) (Maryland: Maryland Institute of Technology in the Humanities, University of Maryland, 2009), pp. 101–103.

—, 'The Area Told as a Story', An inquiry into the relationship between verbal and map-based expressions of geographical information, PhD thesis, King's College London (2012), https://www.oeide.no/dg/

—, 'Ontologies, Data Modelling, and TEI', *Journal of the Text Encoding Initiative*, 8 (2014-2015), ttps://doi.org/10.4000/jtei.1191

—, 'Sequence, Tree and Graph at the Tip of Your Java Classes', *Proceedings from 9th Digital Humanities July 8-12 2014* (Lausanne, Switzerland: EPFL—UNIL, 2014), pp. 151–152, https://dblp.org/rec/conf/dihu/Eide14

—, *Media Boundaries and Conceptual Modelling: Between Texts and Maps* (Houndmills, Basingstoke: Palgrave Macmillan, 2015).

—, 'Visual Representations as Models of the Past', *Информационные Технологии в Гуманитарных Науках. Сборник Докладов Международной Научно-Практической Конференции. Красноярск, 18–22 Сентября 2017* (Krasnoyarsk: SFU, 2018), pp. 15–26.

Eide, Øyvind, and Zoe Schubert, 'Seeing the Landscape Through Textual and Graphical Media Products', in *Beyond Media Borders*, ed. by Lars Elleström, vol. 2 (London: Palgrave Macmillan, Cham 2021), pp. 175–209, https://doi.org/10.1007/978-3-030-49683-8_7

Elkins James and Erna Fiorentini, *Visual Worlds: Looking, Images, Visual Disciplines* (Oxford: Oxford University Press, 2021).

Elleström, Lars, 'The Modalities of Media: A Model for Understanding Intermedial Relations', in *Media Borders, Multimodality and Intermediality*, ed. by Lars Elleström (London: Palgrave Macmillan UK, 2010), pp. 11–48, https://doi.org/10.1057/9780230275201_2

—, 'Spatiotemporal Aspects of Iconicity', in *Iconic Investigations*, ed. by Lars Elleström, Olga Fischer, and Christina Ljungberg, pp. 95–117 (Amsterdam: John Benjamins Publishing Company, 2013).

—, *Media Transformation: The Transfer of Media Characteristics Among Media* (London: Palgrave Macmillan, 2014).

—, 'A Medium-centered Model of Communication', *Semiotica*, 2018.224 (2018), pp. 269-293, https://doi.org/10.1515/sem-2016-0024

—, 'Modelling Human Communication: Mediality and Semiotics', in *Meanings & Co.: The Interdisciplinarity of Communication, Semiotics and Multimodality*, ed. by Alin Olteanu, Andrew Stables, Dumitru Borțun (Cham: Springer, 2018), p. 7-32 (Springer, 2019a).

—, *Transmedial Narration: Narratives and Stories in Different Media* (Cham: Springer International Publishing, 2019b), https://doi.org/10.1007/978-3-030-01294-6

Fanjoy, Lillian P., A. Luke MacNeill, and Lisa A. Best, 'The Use of Diagrams in Science', in *Diagrammatic Representation and Inference*, ed. by Philip Cox, Beryl Plimmer, and Peter Rodgers, Lecture Notes in Computer Science (Berlin, Heidelberg: Springer, 2012), pp. 303–5, https://doi.org/10.1007/978-3-642-31223-6_33

Fauconnier, Gilles and Mark Turner, 'Conceptual integration networks', *Cognitive Science*, 22 (1998), pp. 133-187.

Fazi, M. Beatrice, 'Beyond Human: Deep Learning, Explainability and Representation', *Theory, Culture & Society*, 38 (7-8), pp. 55-77 (2021), https://doi.org/10.1177/0263276420966386

Findlen, Paula, ed., *Early Modern Things: Objects and Their Histories, 1500-1800* (London: Routledge, 2012).

Fischer, Franz, 'All texts are equal, but... Textual Plurality and the Critical Text in Digital Scholarly Editions', ed. by Wim Van Mierlo, *Variants*, 10 (2012), https://kups.ub.uni-koeln.de/5056/

Flanders, Julia, 'Modeling Scholarship', in *Knowledge Organization and Data Modeling in the Humanities: An Ongoing Conversation, Theoretical Perspectives II (March 15)* (Brown: Brown University, RI, 2012), https://datasymposium.wordpress.com/flanders/

Flanders, Julia, and Fotis Jannidis, *Knowledge Organization and Data Modeling in the Humanities*, 2015, http://www.wwp.northeastern.edu/outreach/conference/kodm2012/flanders_jannidis_datamodeling.pdf

—, eds, *The Shape of Data in Digital Humanities: Modeling Texts and Text-Based Resources*, Digital Research in the Arts and Humanities (London: Routledge, Taylor & Francis Group, 2018).

Floridi, Luciano, 'Harmonising Physis and Techne: The Mediating Role of Philosophy', *Philosophy & Technology*, 24 (2011), pp. 1–3, https://doi.org/10.1007/s13347-010-0012-5

Floridi, Luciano, and John W. Sanders, 'On the Morality of Artificial Agents', *Minds and Machines*, 14 (2004), pp. 349–379, https://doi.org/10.1023/B:MIND.0000035461.63578.9d

Frigg, Roman, 'Scientific Representation and the Semantic View of Theories', *THEORIA*, 21.1 (2006), pp. 49–65, https://doi.org/10.1387/theoria.553

Gal, Ofer, and Raz Chen-Morris, *Baroque Science* (London: The University of Chicago Press, 2014).

Gardiner, Alan H, *The Theory of Speech and Language* (Oxford: The Clarendon Press, 1932).

Geertz, Clifford, *The Interpretation of Cultures* (New York: Basic Books Publishers, 1973).

Geißler, Nils, and Michela Tardella, 'Observational Drawing: From Words to Diagrams', in *Models and Modelling between Digital & Humanities - A Multidisciplinary Perspective*, ed. by Arianna Ciula, Øyvind Eide, Cristina Marras, and Patrick Sahle, *Historical Social Research, Supplement*, 31 (2018), pp. 209–225, https://doi.org/10.12759/hsr.suppl.31.2018.209-225

Gelfert, Axel, *How to Do Science with Models: A Philosophical Primer* (Cham: Springer, 2016), https://doi.org/10.1007/978-3-319-27954-1

Génova, Gonzalo, María Cruz Valiente, and Mónica Marrero, 'On the Difference between Analysis and Design, and Why It Is Relevant for the Interpretation of Models in Model Driven Engineering', *The Journal of Object Technology*, 8.1 (2009), pp. 107–127, https://doi.org/10.5381/jot.2009.8.1.c7

Gensini, Stefano, 'Vedere il simile? In margine ad Aristotele (Poetica 21-22)', in *Metafore del vivente*, ed. by Elena Gagliasso and Giulia Frezza (Milan: Franco Angeli, 2010).

Gentner, Dedre, 'Are Scientific Analogies Metaphors ?', in *Metaphor: Problems and Perspectives* (Harvester Press, 1982), pp. 106-132, https://groups.psych.northwestern.edu/gentner/papers/Gentner82a.pdf

—, 'Structure-Mapping: A Theoretical Framework for Analogy', *Cognitive Science* (1983), pp. 155–170, https://doi.org/10.1016/S0364-0213(83)80009-3

Gentner, Dedre, and Donald R. Gentner, 'Flowing Waters or Teeming Crowds: Mental Models of Electricity', in *Mental models*, ed. by Dedre Gentner & Albert L. Stevens (Hillsdale, NJ: Lawrence Erlbaum Associates 1983), pp. 99-129.

Gentner, Dedre, and Albert L. Stevens, *Mental Models* (Hillsdale, NJ: Lawrence Erlbaum Associates, 1983).

Gentner, Dedre, and Wolff, Phillip, 'Metaphor and knowledge change', in *Cognitive dynamics: Conceptual and representational change in humans and machines*, ed. by Eric Dietrich and Albert B. Markman (Hillsdale, NJ: Lawrence Erlbaum Associates Publishers, 2000), pp. 295–342.

Giardino, Valeria, and Gabriel Greenberg, 'Introduction: Varieties of Iconicity', *Review of Philosophy and Psychology*, 6.1 (2015), pp. 1–25, https://doi.org/10.1007/s13164-014-0210-7

Gillis Steven, Walter Daelemans, Koenraad DeSmedt, 'Artificial Intelligence', in *Cognition and Pragmatics*, ed. by Dominiek Sandra, Jan-Ola Östman, Jef Verschueren (Amsterdam, Philadelphia: John Benjamins Publishing Company, 2009), pp. 16-40, https://doi.org/10.1075/hoph.3.02gil

Godfrey-Smith, Peter, 'Models and Fictions in Science', *Philosophical Studies*, 143.1 (2009), pp. 101–116.

Gooding, David, 'Varying the Cognitive Span: Experimentation, Visualization, And Computation', in *The Philosophy of Scientific Experimentation*, ed. by Hans Radder (Pittsburgh, PA: University of Pittsburgh Press, 2003), pp. 255–284.

Goswami, Bijoya, *The Metaphor, a Semantic Analysis* (Calcutta: Sanskrit Pustak Bhandar, 1992).

Grady, Joseph E., Todd Oakley, and Seana Coulson, 'Blending and Metaphor', in *Metaphor in Cognitive Linguistics*, ed. by Gerard Steen and Raimond Gibbs (Philadelphia: John Benjamins, 1999), http://cogweb.ucla.edu/CogSci/Grady_99.html

Graves-Brown, Paul M., 'Introduction', in *Matter, Materiality and Modern Culture*, ed. by Paul M. Graves-Brown (London: Routledge, 2000), pp. 1–9.

Grice, Paul, 'Meaning', *The Philosophical Review*, 66 (1957), pp. 377–388.

Guarino, Nicola, Giancarlo Guizzardi, and John Mylopoulos, 'On the Philosophical Foundations of Conceptual Models', 29th International Conference on Information Modelling and Knowledge Bases, EJC (2019).

Haken Hermann, Bunz, Herbert, Scott Kelso, 'A Theoretical Model of Phase Transitions in Human Hand Movements', *Biological Cybernetics*, 51(5) (1985), pp. 347-356.

Haken, Hermann, Anders Karlqvist, and Uno Svedin, eds, *The Machine as Metaphor and Tool* (Berlin, Heidelberg: Springer-Verlag, 1993), https://doi.org/10.1007/978-3-642-77711-0

Haley, Michael C., *The Semeiosis of Poetic Metaphor* (Bloomington: Indiana University Press, 1988).

Hamrick, Stephen, ''Set in Portraiture': George Gascoigne, Queen Elizabeth, and Adapting the Royal Image', *Early Modern Literary Studies*, 11.1 (2005), pp. 1–30.

Harré, Rom, 'Metaphor, Model and Mechanism', *Proceedings of the Aristotelian Society*, 60 (1960), pp. 101–122.

—, *The Principles of Scientific Thinking* (London: Macmillian, 1970).

Heilmann, Till A, and Jens Schröter, *Medien verstehen: Marshall McLuhans Understanding Media* (Lüneburg: Meson Press, 2017).

Hesse, Mary, 'Models and Analogies in Science', *British Journal for the Philosophy of Science*, 16.62 (1965), pp. 161–163.

Hesse, Mary B., 'Models and Analogies in Science', *Philosophy and Rhetoric*, 3.3 (1966), pp. 190-191.

Heusinger, Klaus von, Claudia Maienborn, and Paul Portner, *Semantics: An International Handbook of Natural Language Meaning* (Berlin: De Gruyter Mouton, 2011).

Heyligh, Francis, Cliff Joslyn, and Valentin F. Turchin, 'Model in Metasystem Transition Theory', Principia Cybernetica Web (1993), http://pespmc1.vub. ac.be/MODEL.html

Hirst, Graeme, 'Context as a Spurious Concept', *Proceedings of the AAAI Fall Symposium on Context in Knowledge Representation and Natural Language*, Cambridge Massachusetts, 8 November 1997 (1997), pp. 1-19.

Hørte, Torfinn, Odd Sund, Knut Ronold, and Harald Rove, *Strength Analysis of the Oseberg Ship* (Oslo: Det Norske Veritas, 2006).

Jacob, Pierre, 'Meaning, intentionality and communication', in *Semantics: An International Handbook of Natural Language Meaning*, ed. by Claudia Maienborn and Klaus von Heusinger Paul Portner (Berlin: De Gruyter Mouton, 2011), pp. 11-25.

Johnson, Mark, 'Introduction: Why metaphor matters to philosophy', *Metaphor and symbolic activity*, 10 (3) (1981), pp. 157-162.

Klein, Julie Thompson, 'The Metaphorics of Mapping Interdisciplinary Knowledge', in *The Future of Knowledge. Mapping Interfaces*, Interdisciplinary Workshop Report (Strasbourg: IREG, European Science Foundation (2009), pp. 18–24, https://www.alexandria.unisg.ch/71170/

Knuuttilla, Tarja, 'Not Just Underlying Structures: Towards a Semiotic Approach to Scientific Representation and Modeling', in *Ideas in Action*. Proceedings of the Applying Peirce Conference, ed. by Ahti-Veikko Pietarinen, Mats Bergman, Sami Paavola and Henrik Rydenfelt (Helsinki: Nordic Studies on Pragmatism 1, 2010), pp. 163–172, https://www.nordprag.org/nsp/1/Knuuttila.pdf

Knuuttilla, Tarja, and Andrea Loettgers, 'Modeling/Experimentation: The Synthetic Strategy in the Study of Genetic Circuits', ed. by Isabelle F. Peschard and Bas C. van Fraassen, *The Experimental Side of Modeling* (Minneapolis: Minneapolis: University of Minnesota Press, 2018), pp. 118–147, https://doi.org/10.5749/j.ctv5cg8vk

Korta, Kepa, and John Perry, 'Pragmatics', Stanford Encyclopedia of Philosophy Archive   2006,   https://plato.stanford.edu/archives/spr2020/entries/pragmatics/

Kövecses, Zoltán, 'Conceptual Metaphor Theory: Some Criticisms and Alternative Proposals', *Annual Review of Cognitive Linguistics*, 6.1 (2008), pp. 168–184, https://doi.org/10.1075/arcl.6.08kov

Kralemann, Björn, and Claas Lattmann, 'Models as Icons: Modeling Models in the Semiotic Framework of Peirce's Theory of Signs', *Synthese*, 190.16 (2013), pp. 3397–3420, https://doi.org/10.1007/s11229-012-0176-x

Kulstad, Mark A., 'Leibniz's Conception of Expression', *Studia Leibnitiana*, 9.1 (1977), pp. 55–76.

Lakoff, Georg, and Mark, Johnson, *Philosophy in the Flesh: The Embodied Mind and Its Challenge to Western Thought* (New York: Basic Books, 1999).

—, *Metaphors We Live By* (Chicago and London: The University of Chicago Press, 1980).

Lamarra, Antonio, 'Il concetto di rappresentazione in Leibniz. Dall'algebra alla metafisica', *Bollettino del Centro di studi Vichiani*, 21 (1991), pp. 41–60.

Lancioni, Tarcisio, 'Il "doppio ritratto" di Jan Van Eyck. Uno sguardo impertinente', *Rivista dell'associazione Italiana di Studi Semiotici* (AISS), (2012), http://www.ec-aiss.it/index_d.php?recordID=625

Latour, Bruno, *Petite réflexion sur le culte moderne des dieux faitiches. Bruno Latour (1996)* | *Médialab Sciences Po* (1996), https://medialab.sciencespo.fr/en/productions

Lattmann, Claas, 'Iconizing the Digital Humanities: Models and Modeling from a Semiotic Perspective', in *Models and Modelling between Digital and Humanities—A Multidisciplinary Perspective*, ed. by Ciula, Arianna, Øyvind Eide, Cristina Marras, and Patrick Sahle, *Historical Social Research, Supplement*, 31 (2018), pp. 124–146, https://doi.org/10.12759/hsr.suppl.31.2018.124-146

Leary, David E., *Metaphors in the History of Psychology* (Cambridge University Press, 1990).

Leibniz, Gottfried Wilhelm, *Die philosophischen Schriften*, ed. by Carl Immanuel Gerhardt (Hildesheim; New York: Olms, 1978).

—, *Quid sit idea* (1678), in *Sämtliche Schriften und Briefe*, Hrsg Leibniz-Forschungsstelle Münster (Berlin: Deutschen Akademie der Wissenschaften, ab 1999), VI, 4B, pp. 1369-1371.

Levinson, Stephen C., 'Space in Language and Cognition: Explorations in Cognitive Diversity' (Cambridge: Cambridge University Press, 2003), https://doi.org/10.1017/CBO9780511613609

Lister, Martin, 'A Sack in the Sand', *Convergence: The International Journal of Research into New Media Technologies* (2007), pp. 251–274, https://doi.org/10.1177/1354856507079176

Liddell, Henry George, and Robert Scott, *A Greek-English Lexicon A Greek-English Lexicon*, (Oxford: Clarendon Press, 1940).

Ljungberg, Christina, 'Iconicity in Cognition and Communication', *Models and Modelling between Digital and Humanities - A Multidisciplinary Perspective*, ed. by Ciula, Arianna, Øyvind Eide, Cristina Marras, and Patrick Sahle, *Historical Social Research, Supplement*, 31 (2018), pp. 66–77, https://doi.org/10.12759/hsr.suppl.31.2018.66-77

Locke, John, *An Essay Concerning Human Understanding* (1690), https://www.earlymoderntexts.com/assets/pdfs/locke1690book3.pdf

Loemker, Leroy E. ed., *Gottfried Wilhelm Leibniz: Philosophical Papers and Letters* (Dordrecht: Kluwer Academic Publishers, second edition, 1989).

MacEachren, Alan M., *How Maps Work: Representation, Visualization, and Design* (New York: Guilford Press, 2004).

Mahr, Bernd, 'Information Science and the Logic of Models', *Software & Systems Modeling*, 8.3 (2009), pp. 365–383.

Malazita, James W., Ezra J. Teboul, and Hined Rafeh, 'Digital Humanities as Epistemic Cultures: How DH Labs Make Knowledge, Objects, and Subjects', *Digital Humanities Quarterly*, 014.3 (2020), http://www.digitalhumanities.org/dhq/vol/14/3/000465/000465.html

Malinowski, Bronislaw, 'The Problem of Meaning in Primitive Languages', in *The Meaning of Meaning. A Study of the Influence of Language upon Thought and of the Science of Symbolism*, Charles K. Ogden, Ivor Armstrong Richards (New York, London: Harcourt, 1923), pp. 296–336.

Marras, Cristina, 'Scientific Metaphors' entry for the *Enciclopedia Filosofica Italiana*, ed. by Virginio Melchiorre (Milan: Bompiani, 2006), pp. 7364-7366.

—, 'Structuring Multidisciplinary Knowledge: Aquatic and Terrestrial Metaphors', in *Knowledge Organization*, 40.6 (2013), pp. 392–399.

—, 'Metafore acquatiche e organizzazione della conoscenza: *ars inveniendi e ars judicandi*', in *Metafore del Vivente*, a cura di Elena Gagliasso e Giulia Frezza (Milan: Franco Angeli, 2010) pp. 283-294.

—, *Les métaphores dans la philosophie de Leibniz* (Paris-Limoges: Lambert–Lucas, 2017).

Marras, Cristina, and Silvestro Caligiuri, *I linguaggi della ricerca. Parole e immagini: navigare la ricerca*. Scientific report (2018), in ILIESI-CNR: https://www.iliesi.cnr.it/materiali/presentazioni/Marras-Caligiuri_rapporto_scientifico_linguaggi_ricerca.pdf

Maso, Stefano, *L.Ph.G. lingua philosophica Graeca*, Milan: Mimesis, 2010

Mayr, Heinrich C., and Bernhard Thalheim, 'The Triptych of Conceptual Modeling', *Software and Systems Modeling*, 20.1 (2021), pp. 7–24, https://doi.org/10.1007/s10270-020-00836-z

Mazzocchi, Fulvio and G. Carlo. Fedeli, Introduction to the Special Issue: 'Paradigms of Knowledge and its Organization', *Knowledge Organization*, 40.6 (2013), pp. 363-365.

McCarthy, Willard, 'The analogy of computing'. Paper for the Workshop, Analogy in Literature, Churchill College Cambridge, 3 September (2015).

—, *Humanities Computing* (Basingstoke, UK, and New York: Palgrave Macmillan, 2005).

—, 'Modeling: A Study in Words and Meanings', in *A Companion to Digital Humanities*, 2004, https://companions.digitalhumanities.org/DH/content/9781405103213_chapter_19.html

—, 'Exploring the archipelago of disciplines', a seminar for the Interdisciplinary Leadership Seminar Series at King's (2009).

—, 'Telescope for the Mind?', Chapter 8 in *Debates in the Digital Humanities*, ed. by Matthew K. Gold (Minneapolis: The University of Minnesota Press, 2012) https://dhdebates.gc.cuny.edu/read/40de72d8-f153-43fa-836b-a41d241e949c/section/ec044157-dc2f-4510-8bda-9448d9d6ef16#ch08

—, 'Modelling What There Is: Ontologising in a Multidimensional World, in Models and Modelling between Digital and Humanities – A Multidisciplinary Perspective, ed. by Arianna Ciula, Øyvind Eide, Cristina Marras, and Patrick Sahle, *Historical Social Research, Supplement*, n. 31 (2018), pp. 33–45, https://doi.org/10.12759/hsr.suppl.31.2018.33-45

McGann, Jerome, *A New Republic of Letters. Memory and Scholarship in the Age of Digital Reproduction* (Cambridge, MA: Harvard University Press, 2014).

McLuhan, Marshall, *Understanding Media* (London: Routledge, 2001).

Minsky, Marvin, 'Matter, Mind and Models' (1965), https://dspace.mit.edu/handle/1721.1/6119

Moretti, Franco, 'Operationalizing', *New Left Review*, 84 (2013), pp. 103–119.

Morgan, Mary S., *The World in the Model: How Economists Work and Think* (Cambridge: Cambridge University Press, 2012).

Morgan, Mary S., and Tarja Knuuttila, 'Models and Modelling in Economics', in *Philosophy of Economics*, ed. by Uskali Mäki, Handbook of the Philosophy of Science, 13 (Elsevier Science, 2012), pp. 49–87.

Morris, Charles, *Foundations of the Theory of Signs* (Chicago: University of Chicago Press, 1938).

Nerlich, Brigitte, and David D. Clarke, 'Mind, Meaning and Metaphor: The Philosophy and Psychology of Metaphor in 19th-Century Germany',

History of the Human Sciences, 14.2 (2001), pp. 39–61, https://doi.org/10.1177/09526950122120952

Nersessian, Nancy J., *Creating Scientific Concepts* (Cambridge, MA: A Bradford Book, 2008).

Nicholson, William, *Journal of Natural Philosophy, Chemistry & the Arts* (London 1805), vol. x, pp. 1–354, https://www.biodiversitylibrary.org/item/110972

Norman, Donald A., *The Psychology of Everyday Things* (New York: Basic Books, 1988), pp. xi, 257.

Ochs, Elinor, Sally Jacoby, and Patrick Gonzales, 'Interpretive Journeys: How Physicists Talk and Travel through Graphic Space', *Configurations*, 2.1 (1994), pp. 151-171 (1994), https://doi.org/10.1353/CON.1994.0003

Olteanu, Alin, *Philosophy of Education in the Semiotics of Charles Peirce: A Cosmology of Learning and Loving* (Oxford: Peter Lang, 2015).

Olteanu, Alin, Andrew Stables, and Dumitru Borun, *Meanings & Co.: The Interdisciplinarity of Communication, Semiotics and Multimodality* (Cham: Springer, 2019).

Orlandi, Tito, 'Linguistica, Sistemi, Modelli', in *Il ruolo del modello nella scienza e nel sapere*, Contributi del Centro Linceo Interdisciplinare 'Beniamino Segre' (Rome: Accademia Nazionale dei Lincei, 1999), pp. 73-90.

—, 'Reflections on the Development of Digital Humanities', keynote presented at the Digital Humanities 2019, Utrecht, 9-12 July 2019, https://staticweb.hum.uu.nl/dh2019/dh2019.adho.org/programme/keynotes

Ortony, Andrew, ed., *Metaphor and Thought*, 2nd ed. (Cambridge: Cambridge University Press, 1993) https://doi.org/10.1017/CBO9781139173865

Otlet, Paul, *Traité de documentation* (Brussels: Mundaneum, Palais Mondial, 1934).

Pacherie, Elisabeth, 'Towards a Dynamic Theory of Intentions', in *Does Consciousness Cause Behavior? An Investigation of the Nature of Volition*, ed. by Susan Pockett, William P. Banks, and Shaun Gallagher (Cambridge, MA: MIT Press, 2006), pp. 145–167.

Pak, Chris, 'Models of "Model" a Linguistic Network Graph, blog post, King's Digital Lab' (2018), https://kdl.kcl.ac.uk/blog/models-model-linguistic-network-graph

Palmieri, Fabio, *Consciousness in Interaction. The Role of the Natural and Social Context in Shaping Consciousness* (Amsterdam: John Benjamins Publishing Company, 2012).

Pasin, Michele, and Bradley, John, 'Factoid-based Prosopography and Computer Ontologies: towards an integrated approach', *Literary and Linguistic Computing*, 30.1, April 2013, pp. 86–97 (2013), https://doi.org/10.1093/llc/fqt037

Peirce, Charles S, Charles Hartshorne, Paul Weiss, and Arthur W Burks, *Collected Papers of Charles Sanders Peirce* (Cambridge, MA: The Belknap Press of Harvard University Press, 1931-1958).

Pulaczewska, Hanna, *Aspects of Metaphor in Physics: Examples and Case Studies* (Tübingen: Niemeyer, 1999).

Ramsay, Stephen, 'Algorithmic Criticism', in *A Companion to Digital Literary Studies*, Chapter 26, eds by Ray Siemens, Susan Schreibman (Oxford: Wiley 2013), pp. 477–91, https://doi.org/10.1002/9781405177504.ch26

Roeder, Torsten, 'Nobody Can Ignore the Sahle Wheel', Twitter at #teiconf2019; https://T.Co/GDAZOLgh6g', *@torstenroeder*, 2019 reply to: @ideinfo @Fabio_Ciotti   @patrick_sahle,   https://twitter.com/torstenroeder/status/1174223317764661249

Romele, Alberto, Marta Severo, and Paolo Furia, 'Digital Hermeneutics: From Interpreting with Machines to Interpretational Machines', *AI & SOCIETY*, 35 (2018), pp. 73-86, https://doi.org/10.1007/s00146-018-0856-2

Rothbart, Daniel, *Philosophical Instruments, Minds and Tools at Work* (Champaign: University of Illinois Press, 2007).

Rothman, Barbara Katz, *The Book of Life: A Personal and Ethical Guide to Race, Normality and the Human Gene Study* (Boston: Beacon Press, 2001).

Sahle, Patrick, *Digitale Editionsformen, Teil 3: Textbegriffe und Recodierung* (Norderstedt: Books on Demand, 2013).

—, 'How to Recognize a Model When You See One. Or: Claudia Schiffer and the Climate Change', in: *Models and Modelling between Digital and Humanities - A Multidisciplinary Perspective*, ed. by Arianna Ciula, Øyvind Eide, Cristina Marras, and Patrick Sahle, *Historical Social Research, Supplement*, 31 (2018), pp. 183-192, https://doi.org/10.12759/hsr.suppl.31.2018.183-192

Sandra, Dominiek, Jan-Ola Östman, and Jef Verschueren, eds, *Cognition and Pragmatics, Handbook of Pragmatics Highlights*, vol. 3 (Amsterdam and Philadelphia: John Benjamins Pub. Co, 2009).

Schreibman, Susan, Ray Siemens, and John Unsworth, *Companion to Digital Humanities* (Oxford: Blackwell Publishing Professional, 2004), http://www.digitalhumanities.org/companion/

Shiffrin, Richard M., and Katy Börner, 'Mapping Knowledge Domains', *Proceedings of the National Academy of Sciences, PNAS*, 101, suppl. 1 (2004), pp. 5183-5185, https://doi.org/10.1073/pnas.0307852100

Shin, Sun-Joo, Oliver Lemon, and John Mumma, 'Diagrams', *Stanford Encyclopedia of Philosophy Archive*, 2001, https://plato.stanford.edu/archives/win2018/entries/diagrams/

Skouen, Tina, and Ryan Stark, eds, *Rhetoric and the Early Royal Society* (Leiden: Brill, 2014).

Small, Helen, *The Value of the Humanities* (Oxford: Oxford University Press, 2013).

Smithies, James, *The Digital Humanities and the Digital Modern*, 1st edn (London: Palgrave Macmillan, 2017).

Smithies, James, and Arianna Ciula, 'Humans in the Loop: Epistemology & Method in King's Digital Lab', in *Routledge International Handbook of Research Methods in Digital Humanities*, ed. by Kristen Schuster and Stuart Dunn (London: Routledge, 2020), pp. 155–172.

Smithies, James, Patrick ffrench, and Arianna Ciula, 'Droit de Cité: Towards a Socialized Model for Technology Development in the Arts & Humanities', in *Digital Humanities and Laboratories: Perspectives on Knowledge, Infrastructure and Culture*, ed. by Urszula Pawlicka-Deger and Chris Thomson (London: Routledge, 2023), pp.52-66, https://doi.org/10.4324/9781003185932

Sperber, Dan, and Deirdre Wilson, *Relevance: Communication and Cognition* (Harvard: Harvard University Press, 1986).

Stachowiak, Herbert, *Allgemeine Modelltheorie* (Wien and New York: Springer, 1986).

Stewart, Dugald, *Elements of the Philosophy of the Human Mind - Digital Collections - National Library of Medicine*, 2 vols (Boston: Wells and Lilly, 1818), https://collections.nlm.nih.gov/catalog/nlm:nlmuid-2573020R-bk

Stone, Rachel, 'Building a Charter Database 1: The Factoid Model and Its Discontents | The Making of Charlemagne's Europe' (2014), https://charlemagneseurope.ac.uk/blog/building-a-charter-database-1-the-factoid-model-and-its-discontents/

Suárez, Mauricio, *Fictions in Science: Philosophical Essays on Modelling and Idealization* (London: Routledge, 2008).

Svensson, Patrik, 'The Landscape of Digital Humanities', *Digital Humanities Quarterly*, 2010, 4.1 (2010), http://digitalhumanities.org/dhq/vol/4/1/000080/000080.html

Tagliagambe, Silvano, *Epistemologia del confine* (Milan: Il Saggiatore, 1995).

Taylor, Cynthia, and Bryan M. Dewsbury, 'On the Problem and Promise of Metaphor Use in Science and Science Communication', ASM Journals: *Journal of Microbiology & Biology Education*, 19.1, https://doi.org/10.1128/jmbe.v19i1.1538

Thibodeau, Paul H. and Boroditsky Lera, 'Natural Language Metaphors Covertly Influence Reasoning' Influence Reasoning. *PLOS ONE* 8.1: e52961, 2013, https://doi.org/10.1371/journal.pone.0052961

Trim, Richard, *Metaphor and the Historical Evolution of Conceptual Mapping* (London: Palgrave Macmillan UK, 2011), https://doi.org/10.1057/9780230337053

Türkoğlu, Enes, 'Vom Digitalisat Zum Kontextualisat – Einige Gedanken Zu Digitalen Objekten', [Conference] Digital Humanities im deutschsprachigen Raum 2019, Book of Abstracts, https://zenodo.org/record/4622229/files/259_final-T_RKOGLU_Enes_Vom_Digitalisat_zum_Kontextualisat__einige_Ge.pdf

Turnbull, David, 'Maps Narratives and Trails: Performativity, Hodology and Distributed Knowledges in Complex Adaptive Systems – an Approach to Emergent Mapping', *Geographical Research*, 45 (2007), pp. 140–149, https://doi.org/10.1111/j.1745-5871.2007.00447.x

Tversky, Barbara, *Mind in Motion: How Action Shapes Thought*, 1st edn (New York: Basic Books, 2019).

Vaage, Nora S., 'Living Machines: Metaphors We Live By', *NanoEthics*, 14.1 (2020), pp. 57–70, https://doi.org/10.1007/s11569-019-00355-2

Van Den Heuvel, Charles, 'Mapping Knowledge Exchange in Early Modern Europe: Intellectual and Technological Geographies and Network Representations', *International Journal of Humanities and Arts Computing*, 9.1 (2015), pp. 95–114, https://doi.org/10.3366/ijhac.2015.0140

Vasilescu, Florentina, 'Le livre sous la loupe: Nouvelles formes d'écriture électronique', Theiss, 2010, http://hdl.handle.net/1866/3964

Veale, Toni, and Mark T. Keane, 'Conceptual Scaffolding: Using Metaphors to Build Knowledge Structures', *10th European Conference on Artificial Intelligence*, 8.3 (1992), pp. 93–100.

Veale, Tony, Ekaterina Shutova, and Beata Beigman Klebanov, *Metaphor: A Computational* Perspective (San Rafael, California: Morgan & Claypool Publishers, 2016).

Verschueren, Jef, 'The pragmatic perspective', *Handbook of Pragmatics*, 16 (Amsterdam: John Benjamins Publishing Company, 2012, pp. 1-36), https://doi.org/10.1075/hop.16.prag.

Way, Eileen Cornel, *Knowledge Representation and Metaphor, Studies in Cognitive systems* (Dordrecht: Kluwer Academic Publishers, 1991).

Weiner, E. Judith, 'A Knowledge Representation Approach to Understanding Metaphors', *Computational Linguistics*, 10.1 (1984), pp. 1–15.

Wintermeyer, Niklas, 'A novel entropy stable discontinuous Galerkin spectral element method for the shallow water equations on GPUs' (PhD thesis, Universität zu Köln, 2018), https://kups.ub.uni-koeln.de/9234/

Wolynes, Peter G., 'Landscapes, Funnels, Glasses, and Folding: From Metaphor to Software', *Proceedings of the American Philosophical Society*, 145.4 (2001), pp. 555–563.

Wynn, David C., and P. John Clarkson, 'Process Models in Design and Development', *Research in Engineering Design*, 29.2 (2018), pp. 161–202, https://doi.org/10.1007/s00163-017-0262-7

Zimmermann, Rainer E., Sandra Ley, Vladimir G. Budanov and V. E. Voitsekhovitch. 'Models and Metaphors. Part I: From the Boundaries of Formalization to the Visualization of the Non-Formalized', *arXiv: Adaptation and Self-Organizing Systems* (2002), https://www.semanticscholar.org/paper/Models-and-Metaphors.-Part-https://api.semanticscholar.org/CorpusID:250494825

Zoltán, Kövecses, 'Conceptual metaphor theory: Some criticisms and alternative proposals', *Annual Review of Cognitive Linguistics*, 6.1 (2008), pp. 168–184, https://doi.org/10.1075/arcl.6.08kov

Index

About the Team

Alessandra Tosi was the managing editor for this book.

Melissa Purkiss and Evie Rowan performed the editing and proofreading.

Melissa also indexed the volume.

Jeevanjot Kaur Nagpal designed the cover. The cover was produced in InDesign using the Fontin font.

Cameron Craig typeset the book in InDesign. The serif text font is Tex Gyre Pagella and the sans-serif text font is Calibri; the heading font is Californian FB.

Cameron also produced the the paperback, hardback, EPUB, PDF, HTML, and XML editions — the conversion was made with open-source software and other tools freely available on our GitHub page at https://github.com/OpenBookPublishers.

This book has been anonymously peer-reviewed by experts in their field. We thank them for their invaluable help.

This book need not end here...

Share

All our books — including the one you have just read — are free to access online so that students, researchers and members of the public who can't afford a printed edition will have access to the same ideas. This title will be accessed online by hundreds of readers each month across the globe: why not share the link so that someone you know is one of them?

This book and additional content is available at:
https://doi.org/10.11647/OBP.0369

Donate

Open Book Publishers is an award-winning, scholar-led, not-for-profit press making knowledge freely available one book at a time. We don't charge authors to publish with us: instead, our work is supported by our library members and by donations from people who believe that research shouldn't be locked behind paywalls.

Why not join them in freeing knowledge by supporting us:
https://www.openbookpublishers.com/support-us

Follow @OpenBookPublish

Read more at the Open Book Publishers **BLOG**

You may also be interested in:

Digital Technology and the Practices of Humanities Research
Jennifer Edmond

https://doi.org/10.11647/OBP.0192

Digital Humanities Pedagogy: Practices, Principles and Politics
Brett D. Hirsch

https://doi.org/10.11647/OBP.0024

Digital Scholarly Editing: Theories and Practices
Matthew James Driscoll, Elena Pierazzo et al.

https://doi.org/10.11647/OBP.0095

www.ingramcontent.com/pod-product-compliance
Lightning Source LLC
LaVergne TN
LVHW061956050326
832904LV00009B/297